Postcard History Series

The Rockaways

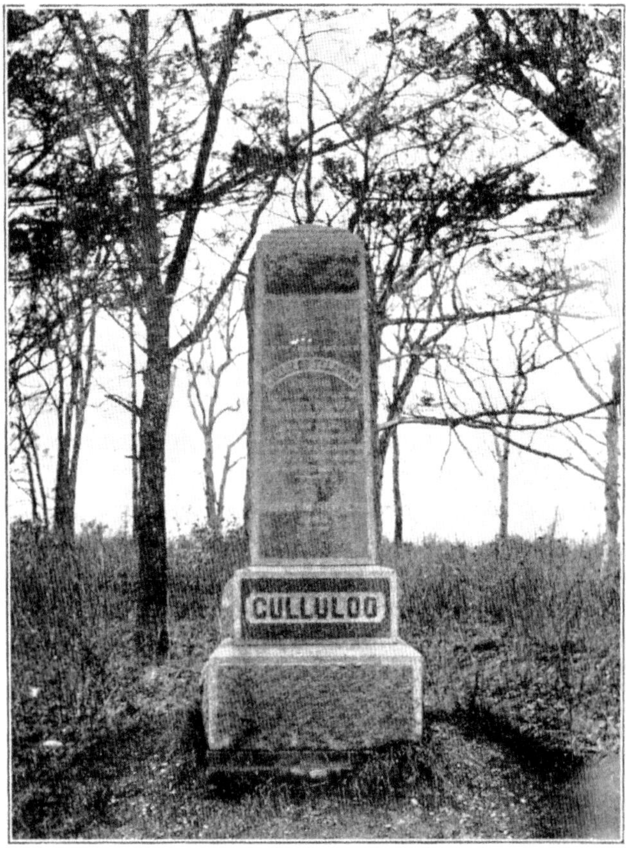

The famous Indian monument of Culluloo Telawana,
Far Rockaway, L. I.

New York City purchased land from the Neponsit Land Company near the point for a seaside park in 1911. The name selected was Culluloo Telawana Park in honor of the last Delaware Indian documented by pioneer Abraham Hewlett in the 1880s. A monument to Telawana is in neighboring Woodsburgh, not in Riis Park.

On the front cover: When first viewed, this seaside photograph taken from the iron pier at Beach 105th Street could not be matched to any known atlas of the area. The postmark date is 1906; however, research proves that it was actually taken in 1887 on Beach 103rd Street and Beach 102nd Street. (Author's collection.)

On the back cover: These charming ladies had their souvenir real-photo postcard shot by an unknown cameraman. The depth of field in this photograph is remarkable for this type of work, and it is not readily noticed in other souvenir real-photo postcards. Perhaps this was taken during a Fourth of July holiday visit. (Author's collection.)

POSTCARD HISTORY SERIES

The Rockaways

Emil R. Lucev Sr.

ARCADIA
PUBLISHING

ISBN 978-0-7385-4990-3

Published by Arcadia Publishing
Charleston, South Carolina

Printed in the United States of America

Library of Congress Catalog Card Number: 2006938814

For all general information contact Arcadia Publishing at:
Telephone 843-853-2070
Fax 843-853-0044
E-mail sales@arcadiapublishing.com
For customer service and orders:
Toll-Free 1-888-313-2665

Visit us on the Internet at www.arcadiapublishing.com

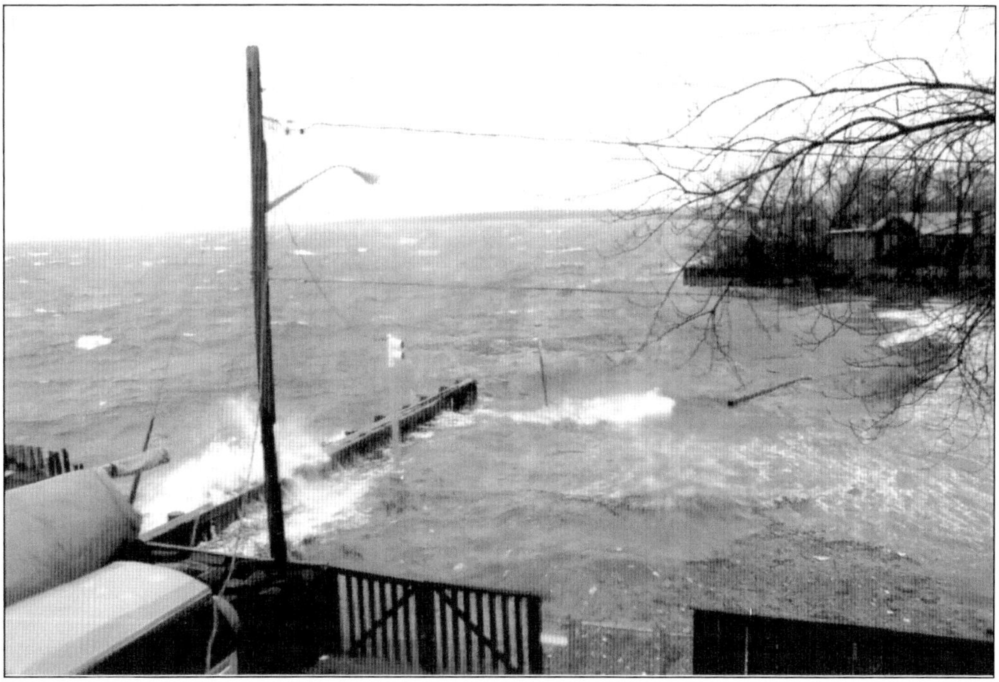

Global warming is a reality. Bigger storms and higher tides are now a threat to the East Coast, as seen here. During the nor'easter of late 1992, waters poured over the bulkhead at Beach 69th Street and Jamaica Bay, the high point of Arverne, for the first time ever. (Courtesy of the Russell family.)

Contents

Acknowledgments

One fine evening long ago, thanks to my wife Aldine's shopping and a Coney Island memorabilia salesman at the King's Plaza Shopping Center in Brooklyn, I made the trade of my life.

While talking to Alex Goldstein at his display tables in the hall of the mall, I mentioned that I had an old antique embossed Coney Island soda bottle. Alex then made me an offer for the glass container. I was presented with a host of vintage items from Coney Island and a set of half a dozen antique postcards with images of Rockaway Beach and Far Rockaway—my hometown. The very next evening Alex had his old Coney Island green glass bottle, which he carefully rolled up in more newspaper than I ever did.

These old postals were shown to a friend of mine, and he told me of a postcard collector's club in Manhattan that meets once a month where people can buy and sell postcards. I went, I saw, I joined, and now I have a large stash of old postals mailed from the Rockaways to points near and far, even overseas.

Thanks to the staff of the Queensborough Public Library, Long Island Division, located in Jamaica, Queens, I was able to find thousands of words needed to tell the stories of postcard images, displaying scenes that no longer exist on the Rockaway Peninsula. While doing this, my quest for further knowledge about my hometown led to an association with the local *Wave* newspaper and its past publisher Leon S. Locke, who held the same passion for local history as yours truly. Through Leon, the newspaper morgue dating back to 1893 was made available to me, and in return, articles and pictures were submitted for publication in the *Wave* editions. These articles have developed into a weekly column called "Historical Views of the Rockaways," and I became the foremost historian of the Rockaways.

The picture postcard has preserved images of historical importance, not just of the Rockaways but of all the surrounding environs north, west, and east. To the south are the beaches of the Rockaways, and the postals show century-old views of the great enemy of all beaches—coastal erosion.

This book is especially dedicated to all postcard dealers and amicable collectors and all Rockawayites past and present, like me, who remark as to still having "sand in my shoes."

Unless otherwise stated, all images are from the author's collection.

—Emil R. Lucev Sr.

INTRODUCTION

The part of the New York City borough of Queens known as the Rockaway Peninsula stretches west–southwest 11 statute miles from the southwest corner of Long Island in Nassau County. At the point of the peninsula, a stone hook jetty placed in 1933 curves to the south, preventing any western extension of littoral drift sands into the navigable ship channels of the New York Bight to the west.

As part of the Long Island Barrier beach system, the Rockaways, which are commonly referred to as Far Rockaway and Rockaway Beach, have pristine beachfronts once described as "the brightest jewel within the diadem of imperial Manhattan." The Rockaway Peninsula also acts as a buffer between the beautiful Jamaica Bay to the north and the Atlantic Ocean to the south. Many times large destructive storms struck New York City and environs with the peninsula bearing the brunt of the ocean's rage while protecting Jamaica Bay and the city mainland areas to the north and west.

The Rockaways consist of 10 distinct sections or communities, some of which have been delegated to the history books by the postal service. Far Rockaway and Rockaway Beach are mainly used by the post office as the official designation, and zip codes suffice for the rest. Older residents still prefer the old names to go with the zip code numbers.

Far Rockaway is the most eastern section, which long ago acted as the coastal headland upon which the Rockaway Peninsula formed itself to the west by the natural accretion of littoral drift sands traveling along the southern Long Island coast acting as a natural conveyor belt, if you will.

Next in line is the Edgemere section, then Arverne, Hammels, Holland, Seaside, Rockaway Park, Belle Harbor, Neponsit, and the point. The latter consists of the Riis Park and Fort Tilden areas of the Gateway National Recreation Area/Rockaway Division and the residential part known as the Breezy Point Cooperative. The point communities of Roxbury, Breezy Point, and Rockaway Point make up the cooperative.

The Rockaway beachfront is the greatest asset on the peninsula of sand. For more than a century, topsoil, asphalt, concrete, and blacktop paving have been used to cover the sand, and structural footings as well as supportive piling have been placed or driven down. The latter provide strong foundations for structures of a single story to high-rises of multiple stories built upon the soft sands of the Rockaway Peninsula.

The Rockaways of today look nothing like the Rockaways of yore. At the present time, all of the empty lots that once had a life in a great beach resort are being filled with condominiums and other forms of multiple dwellings to the point that some residents are shouting, "Stop!" Others are wondering what will happen when that long overdue superstorm strikes the peninsula of sand to further erode thinning beach land.

The Rockaways have taken many hits from all kinds of storms, and they have also experienced an earthquake or two. The latter were minimal-damage events, but the former were catastrophic in losses of buildings, erosion of beaches, and the loss of all facilities built by the old-time proprietors who thought highly of their riparian rights to the beach property(s) they owned and cared for. When Mother Nature and King Neptune dealt them a dirty blow (pun intended), each rebuilt at his or her own expense, bigger and better than the old place.

The resorts and amusement places in the Rockaways and Coney Island were stiff (and sometimes bitter) competitors for the masses of inner-city folks wanting to escape the heat of the inner city during hot summers. Both provided fresh sea air, sunshine, and a cool dip in the ocean, as well as food and refreshments to the heart's content. There were numerous hotels, rooming houses, tent cities, and bungalows that could be rented by the day, week, or season. All were catered to with dignity and respect. Places were set aside for churches and orphan homes to bring their charges down to the beach, and some even relocated their respective establishments to the Rockaways. The sick and infirm young ones were also provided for.

It took some time, but individually built boardwalks with gaps became one continuous ocean promenade, 117 blocks long, from Far Rockaway to the west end of Rockaway Park at Beach 126th Street. That is a total of about six miles, and if the Riis Park walk is added, that makes seven.

The pick of the draw has always been the boardwalk and the pristine beaches, but they are no longer supplemented by public and private baths, hotels, restaurants, food and drink concessions, penny arcades, poolrooms, and the old amusement parks of James S. Remsen and William Wainwright, George C. Tilyou, LaMarcus A. Thompson, and Geist family, to name a few. Amusement parks in the Rockaways once held four large roller coasters known as the Hurricane, the Thunderbolt, the Thriller, and the Jackrabbit, and these fun places competed with each other, as well as Coney Island amusement parks. Luna Park, Dreamland, and famous Steeplechase Park were all gone by 1965, but the Rockaways' Playland survived for two more decades.

Images of the old Rockaways appearing in this book will make you ask what happened and why it happened that not one specimen from the old fun days has survived. There is no proper answer other than progress and change are inevitable.

Western Union transatlantic cables came ashore in Hammels, and the old Commercial Cable Company underocean cables landed in Far Rockaway. Each had a large cable station building constructed for the cables to be connected to their respective receivers of messages to be relayed.

In addition, other historic events have connections with the Rockaways. The first transatlantic flight to England began at the Rockaway Naval Air Station in 1919, eight years before Charles Augustus Lindbergh. The largest hotel in the world (1,000 rooms) was built in 1880 at the western end of the Rockaway Peninsula, but never opened, and it was torn down in 1889 after standing unopened for eight years. A young medical student delivered milk in the summer at Seaside and later was in contention with another about the discovery of the North Pole. The assassination of an American president in 1901 was instrumental in making the Rockaways a great amusement park mecca in later years.

Yours in Rockaway history,
Emil R. Lucev Sr.

One

Far Rockaway
Nassau County Line West to Beach 32nd Street

In the historical records of the year 1685, Far Rockaway (then known as Rockaway Neck) was sold to settler John Palmer by the Rockaway Indian tribe. Two years later, Palmer sold the neck to Richard Cornell, a wealthy ironmaster from Flushing, Queens. The land was used for farming by the Cornell family for many decades.

By the late 1700s, shore residents had begun providing room and board, as well as ocean bathing spots for those wishing to cool off in summer on the ocean shore of western Long Island. During the early 1800s, this practice became commonplace, and local residents were making ends meet a little better by supplementing cash crops with ocean bathing proceeds instead of selling land. Stagecoach lines were organized to transport patrons to the baths at the shore from outlying places. Noting all this, Benjamin Cornell (a descendant of the Richard Cornell who first settled Far Rockaway in 1690) converted the old homestead to the Rockaway Bath on his high ground overlooking the ocean.

Watching Cornell's new business, and the eagerness in which the stagecoach owners extended their lines to the Rockaway Bath, after the bath—using the old English style of bathing—opened in 1816, John Leake Norton of Far Rockaway came up with a grand plan.

This plan, and the operations of Benjamin Cornell, was the beginning of the Rockaways' future as an ocean beach resort. Norton's idea was to build a bigger bath, complete with a hotel, a lavish restaurant, and turnpikes to and from the area.

Himself a wealthy man, Norton gathered together a group of well-to-do friends and ex-political figures, and he formed the Rockaway Association. This group purchased land all around the Rockaway Bath and the bath proper, which was now being managed by the grandson of Benjamin Cornell, Benjamin having died in 1821. His grandson held onto the homestead bath site, and he sold it to the association only after he had received assurance that he would run the bathing operation for the intended Marine Pavilion Hotel and Ocean Resort.

The Marine Pavilion Hotel and Resort opened for the 1833 season and was an instant success. The specially built Rockaway Turnpike to the front door was a log-covered road (the Corduroy Highway) with the roughness smoothed by grass and loam. Immediately thereafter, other smaller hotels appeared as well as some classy residences, a store, a church, a school, and a harness shop for horse-drawn conveyances. The Marine Pavilion burned to the ground in 1864 and was never rebuilt. Lesser hotels and cottages later appeared on the site.

The South Side Railroad came to Far Rockaway from Valley Stream in 1869 to start another building boom, and an offshore outer bar beach developed by 1872. Locals such as William Caffrey and James Mulry quickly filled the outer beach with bathing facilities to make Far Rockaway an ocean bathing mecca once again. By 1880, more hotels were built near the shore.

In between the outer bar beach, dubbed "Hog Island," and the main shore of Far Rockaway was an inlet/outlet waterway to the Atlantic Ocean called Far Rockaway Bay. A man-made canal was then dug up Beach 32nd Street to connect Jamaica Bay and Far Rockaway Bay via Norton Basin.

In September 1893, a direct hit by a hurricane destroyed Hog Island Beach, but the bar slowly came back, much closer than the old one. Bridges replaced the cable ferries to bring patrons out to the new bathhouses. The hurricane of 1903 destroyed the new Hog Island forever.

Far Rockaway's biggest problem was that it ran out of building space. Over the years, about 32 developments were completed, but only a few of the original names have survived, such as Bayswater and Wavecrest.

Five years after the 1903 storm, private beaches were built on the shore at Far Rockaway. Roche's and Ostend and Simmis/Coronada Beaches appeared between Beach 19th Street and Beach 1st Street and lasted for decades until the city boardwalk and concrete promenades were built.

Most bungalow courts built in southwest Far Rockaway, as well as the old hotels throughout the section, have been replaced by high-rise buildings of brick and stone and hundreds of smaller homes and condominiums. The Far Rockaway Electric and Gas Plant has been around since the early 1900s, and these facilities have grown by demand. At present, Far Rockaway is overgrowing, and residents demand downzoning all around.

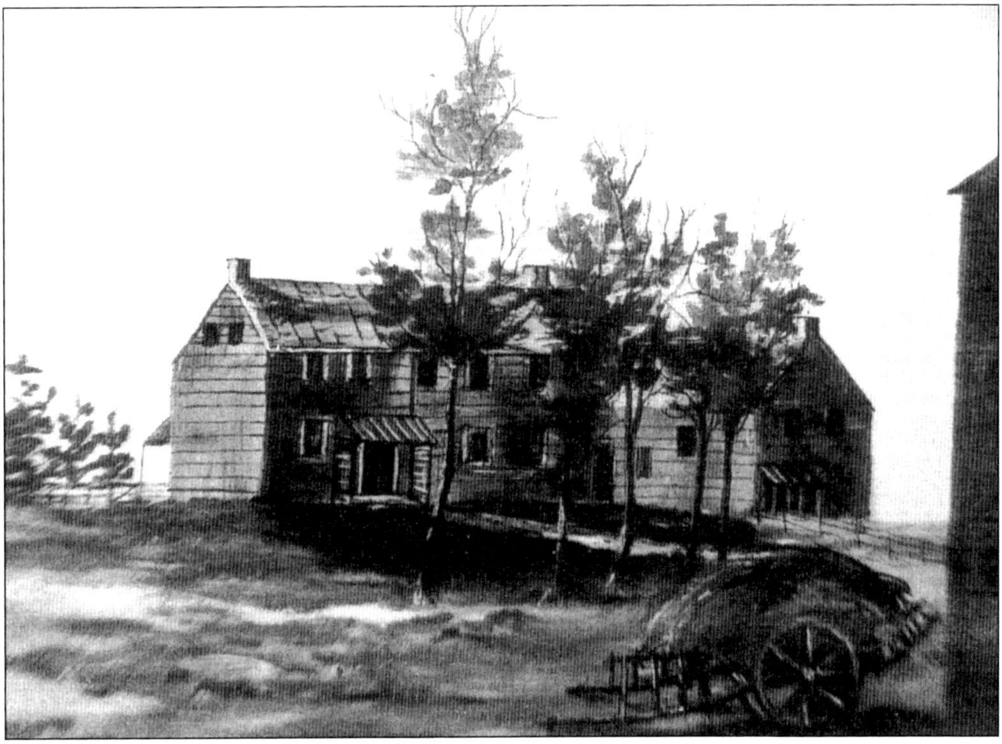

Richard Cornell, a relative of Ezra Cornell, the founder of Cornell University, built the first homestead on a bluff overlooking the Atlantic Ocean at Far Rockaway in 1690. The house was located below the present area of Beach 20th Street and Plainview Avenue in the old Wavecrest section of Far Rockaway. This sketch is from the 1918 *Bellot's History of the Rockaways* by Alfred Bellot.

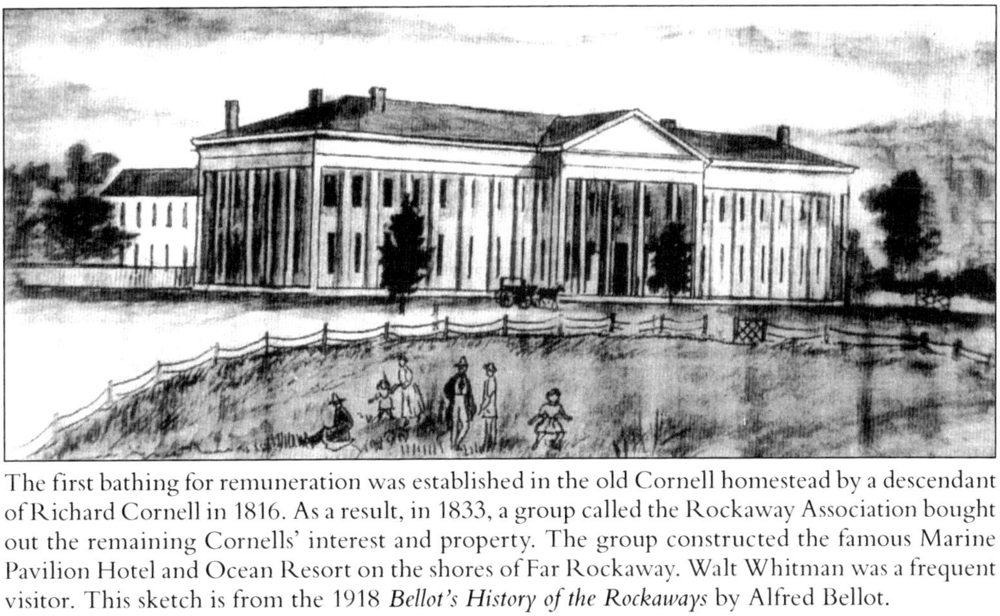

The first bathing for remuneration was established in the old Cornell homestead by a descendant of Richard Cornell in 1816. As a result, in 1833, a group called the Rockaway Association bought out the remaining Cornells' interest and property. The group constructed the famous Marine Pavilion Hotel and Ocean Resort on the shores of Far Rockaway. Walt Whitman was a frequent visitor. This sketch is from the 1918 *Bellot's History of the Rockaways* by Alfred Bellot.

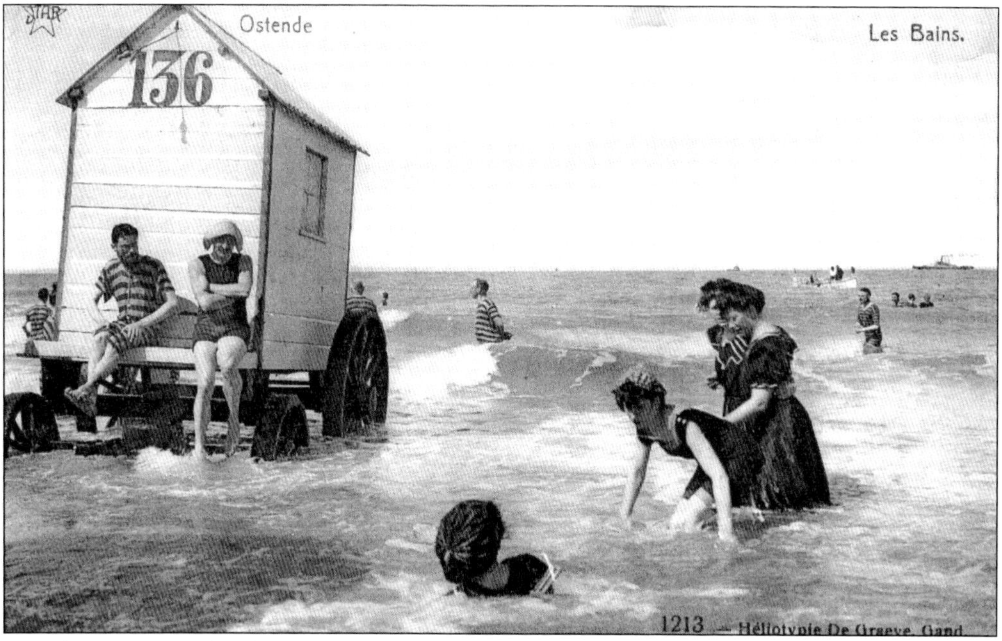

Seen here is a sample of Anglo-European or Old English style of bathing. Horses backed the bathhouse on wheels into the surf for the bathers to change to and from. When the bathing was over, the horses were hitched to pull the house out and back on shore or dry beach. Ostend Beach was in Far Rockaway, but this example is in Belgium.

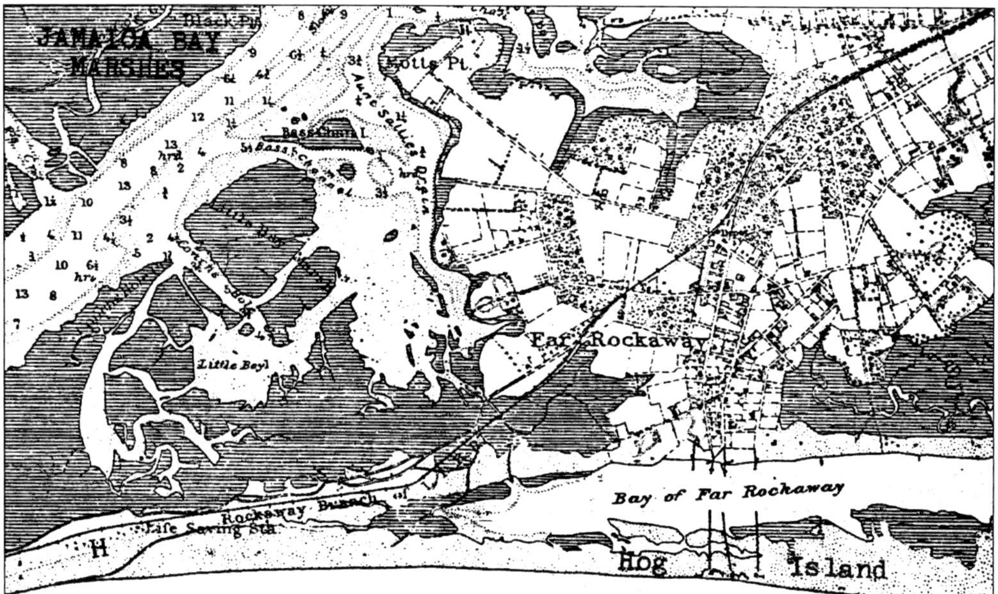

This portion of an old 1879 No. 542 chart of Jamaica Bay shows the Hog Island outer bar beach and docks for ferries to the outer shore via Far Rockaway Bay. A direct hit by a hurricane in September 1893 completely destroyed Hog Island. (Courtesy of the National Archives.)

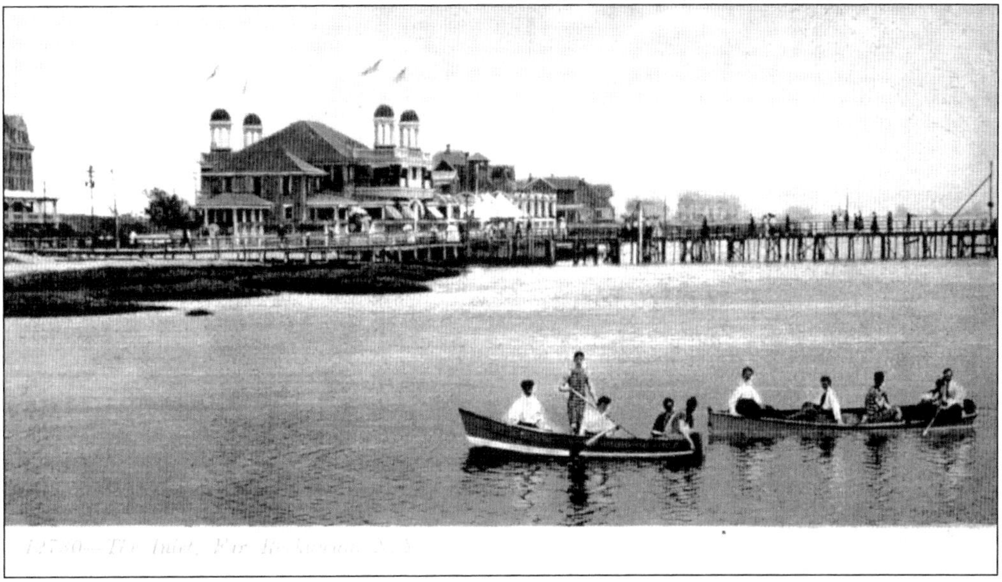

This 1902 view of Far Rockaway Bay or Inlet from the Atlantic Ocean shows a group of boaters who have just shoved off from the bank of Far Rockaway's outer bar beach. A series of footbridges crossed the inner bay to the outer swimming beach. The bay was connected to Jamaica Bay (behind camera) and the ocean in the reverse.

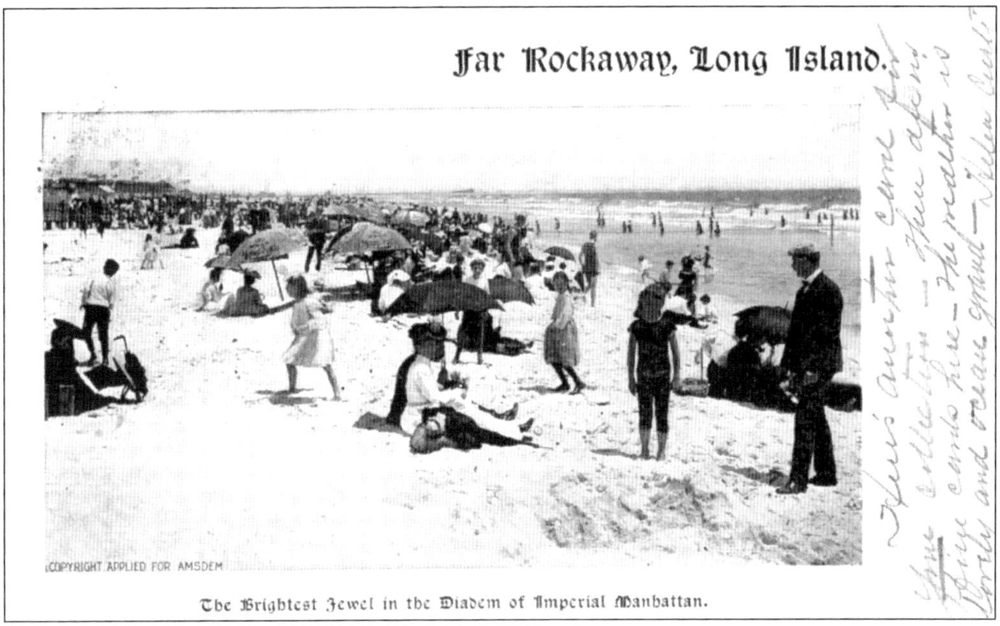

The pristine beach at Far Rockaway, with clean and sparkling sand, was the trademark of individual riparian proprietors who provided bathing facilities for perennial patrons. Each establishment was adequately staffed, catering to the whims of all patrons.

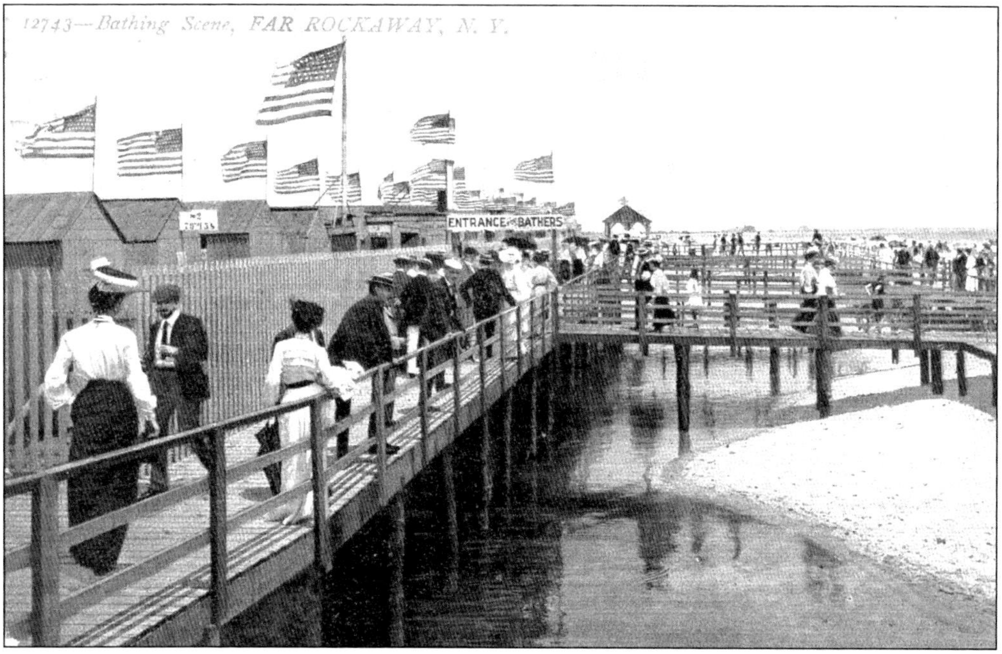

Patrons of the beach at Far Rockaway had the option to bypass the baths and go directly to the outer part of the beach to the boardwalk where the eating and drinking pavilions were located. Chairs and beach umbrellas could also be rented at reasonable prices. At this afternoon time, the tide is high, and the beach is much narrower. Shown is the east end of Caffrey's Bathhouses.

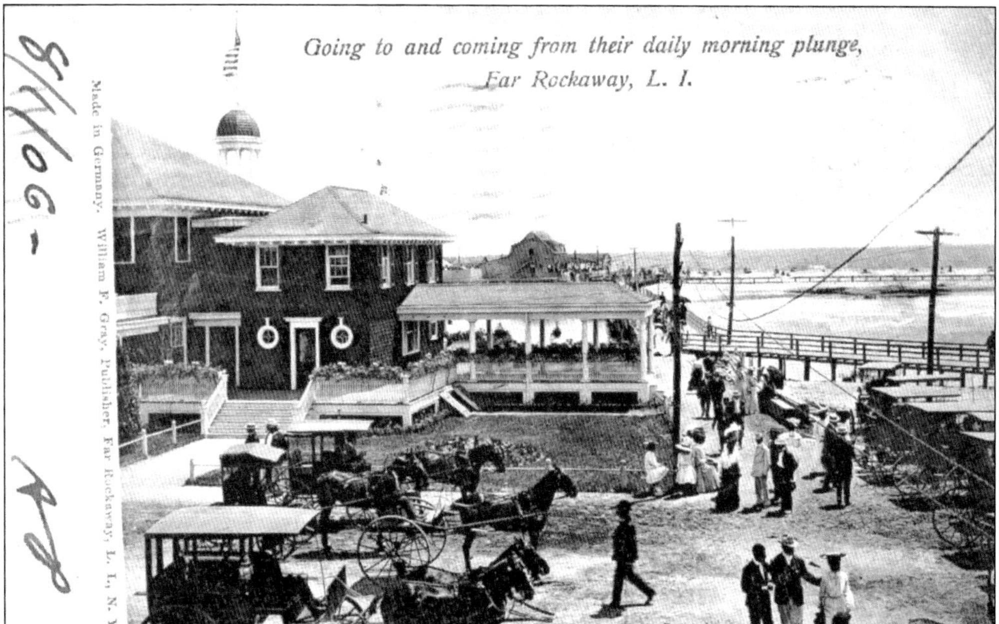

The Caffrey Kuloff Hotel and Casino opened for the season of 1901 on Beach 17th Street just south of South Street (Seagirt Boulevard). The hurricane of 1903, which was a direct hit, carried away Hog Island, all of the bathing facilities, and Far Rockaway's narrow boardwalk, which can be seen at right center. The outer bar beach was never to return off the mainland.

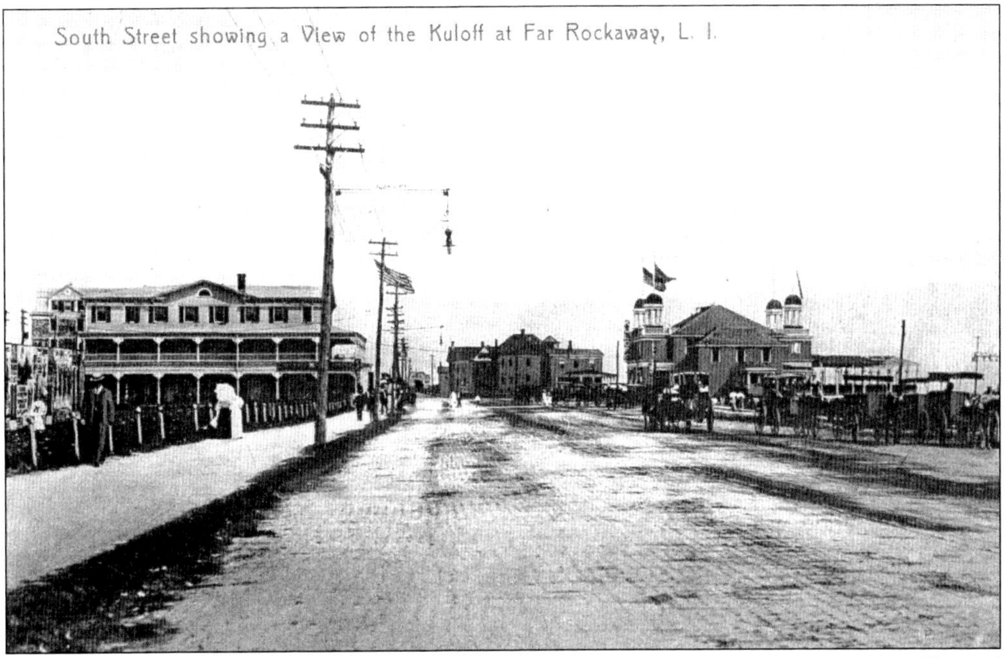

Looking east on South Street from Beach 19th Street to Beach 17th Street, the Kuloff Hotel can be seen on the right, as is the beachfront. The Dolphin Roadhouse, seen on the left, blocks a view of the Tackapousha Hotel, located behind it. The Simmis Beach cottages are seen in the center. South Street is now Seagirt Boulevard and is lined with high-rise buildings.

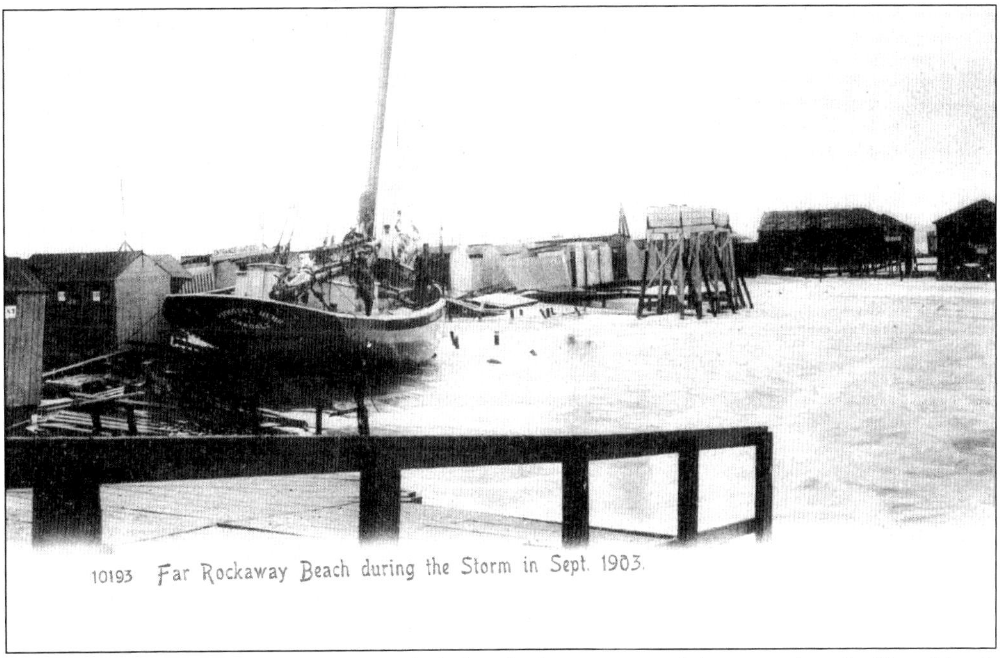

The hurricane of September 1903 ended the glorious career of the outer beach, Hog Island. Horrific damage was inflicted on all baths and facilities, and sand was pushed in and piled on the mainland shore. The inshore pileup of wreckage was cleared, and new owners built onshore baths.

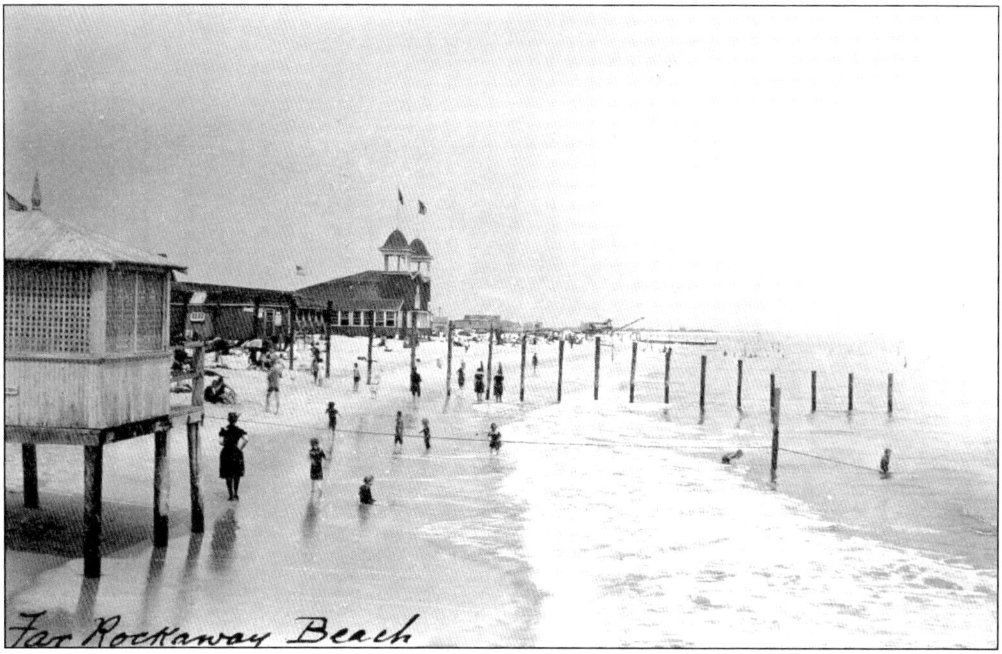

After the storm of 1903, which destroyed the second Hog Island, the Long Beach sandbar to the east of Far Rockaway advanced westward. In doing so, severe beach erosion struck the ocean beach at Far Rockaway. Ostend (rear) and Roche's Beaches (front), divided by the pile row, also suffered. Jetty construction (seen in the background) did not help.

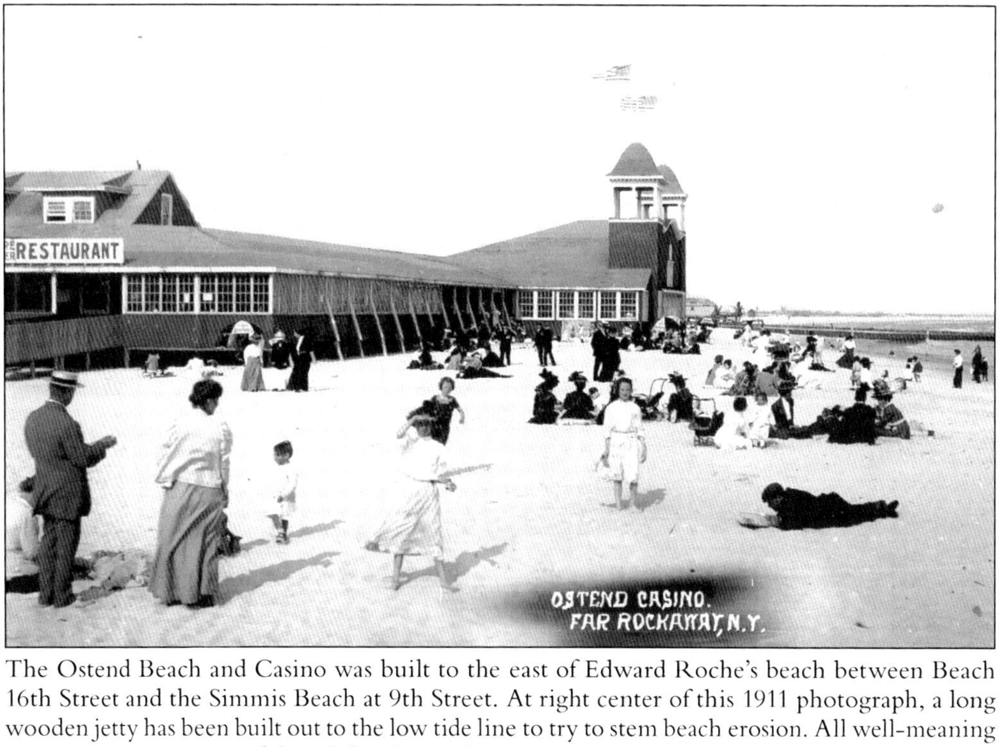

The Ostend Beach and Casino was built to the east of Edward Roche's beach between Beach 16th Street and the Simmis Beach at 9th Street. At right center of this 1911 photograph, a long wooden jetty has been built out to the low tide line to try to stem beach erosion. All well-meaning attempts were unsuccessful, and the city took over.

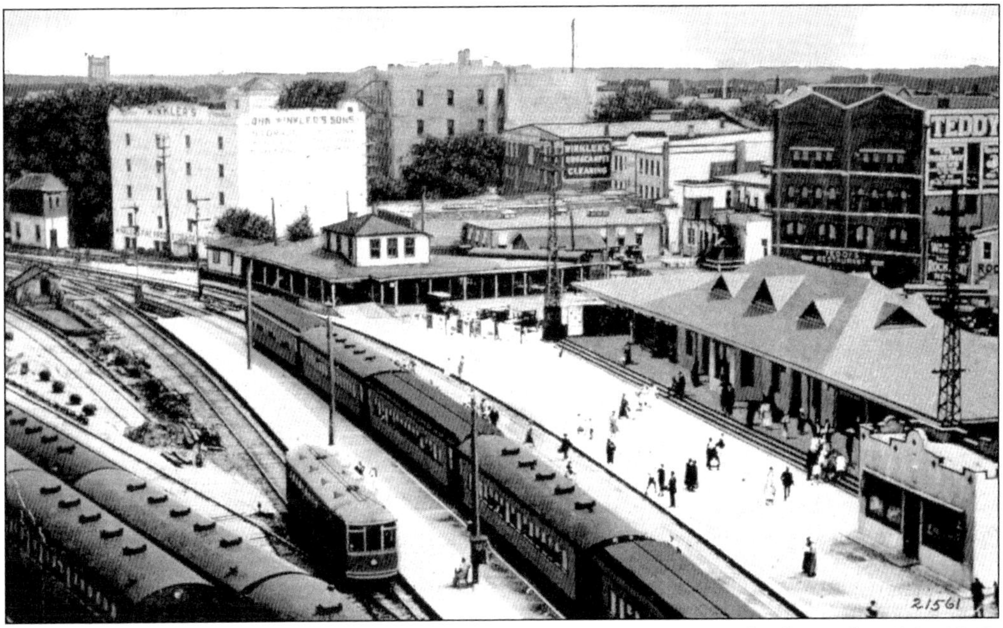

The first railroad station at Far Rockaway was a get-off on the Southside Railroad in 1869. When the Long Island Rail Road came in 1871, its station was on Beach 21st Street in Wavecrest. After the Long Island Rail Road absorbed the old Southside Railroad in 1872, a new station was built where the Southside Railroad ended at Mott and Central Avenues. The station is now a shopping mall.

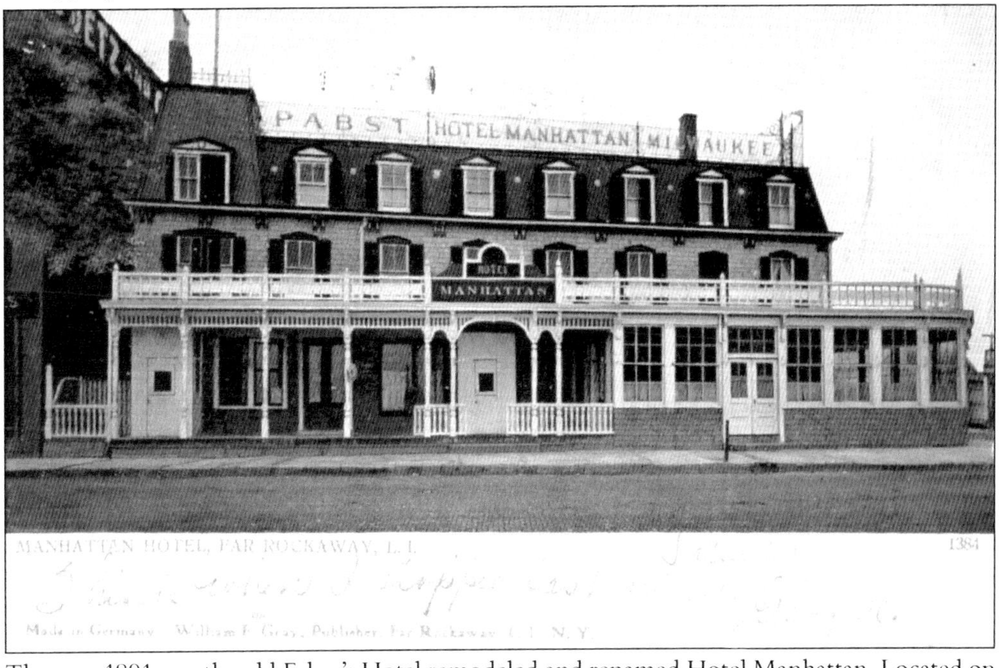

The year 1891 saw the old Faber's Hotel remodeled and renamed Hotel Manhattan. Located on Mott Avenue and White Street (Beach 21st Street), H. C. Gunther, proprietor, offered German sarsaparilla, beefsteak dinners on a Hickory wood fire, and the finest beers and liquors. The White Street fire of 1916 destroyed the hotel.

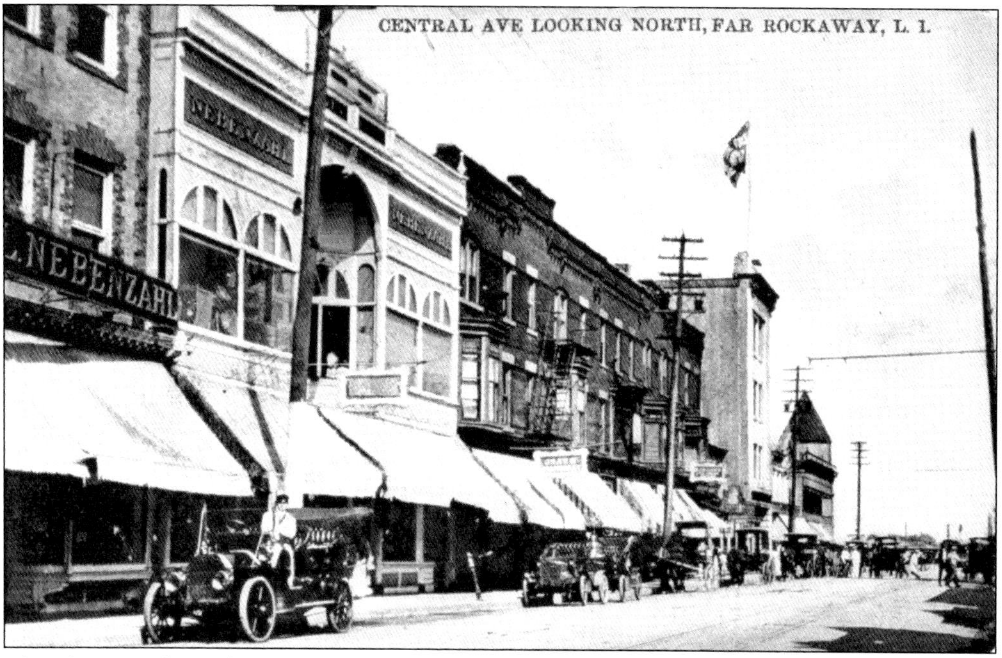

The photographer who snapped this photograph must have had history on his mind, for he captured a trolley power wire pole (right) leaning out over Central Avenue. At times, pictures were retouched to remove a spiderweb of overhead wires to improve the picture clarity. At bottom right is the railroad station where the trolley started and passed Nebenzahl's department store on Central Avenue.

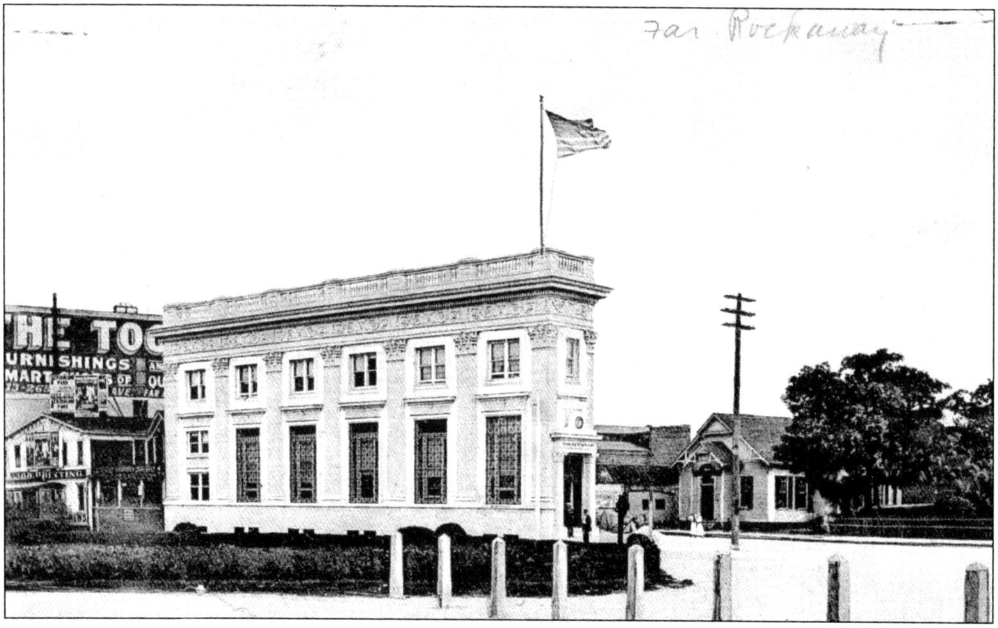

The Far Rockaway National Bank opened in 1912 on the east side of the Far Rockaway station. The former old Katz flat or cast-iron building was removed from the site to construct the bank, which was designed with the same wedge shape and made entirely of granite. The get-off railroad stop in 1869 was on this side of the building. Central Avenue was located on the other side.

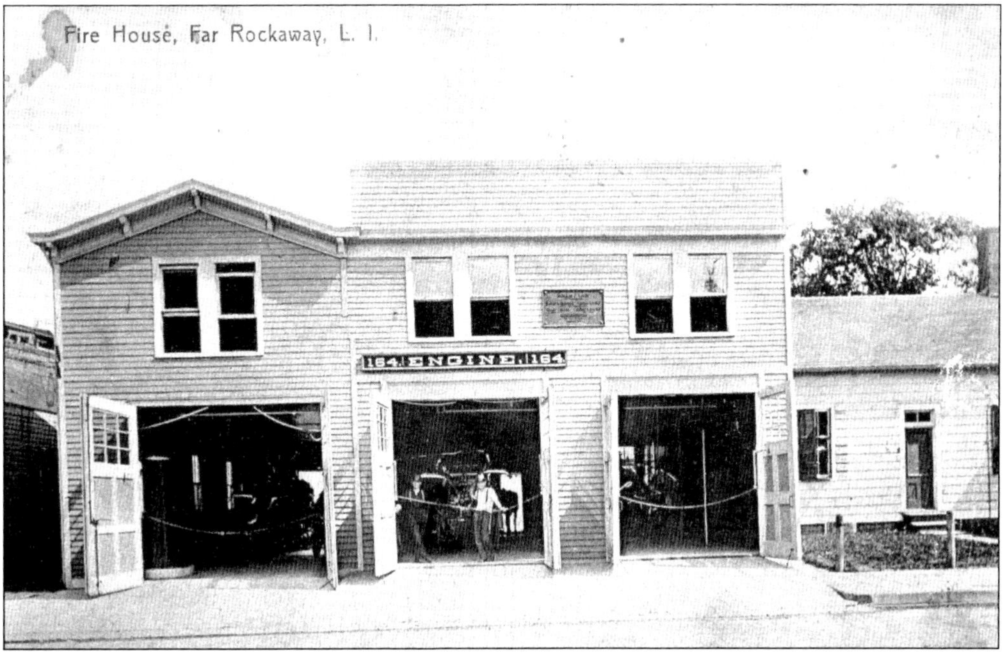

When the Long Island Rail Road built a new station of brick in 1888, the old station building was moved over to the east side of Central Avenue, just north of the courthouse. The new station was fitted up for use by the Far Rockaway Volunteer Fire Department. In 1905, firemen, paid by the city, took over horse-drawn engine No. 164. Trucks came in later years.

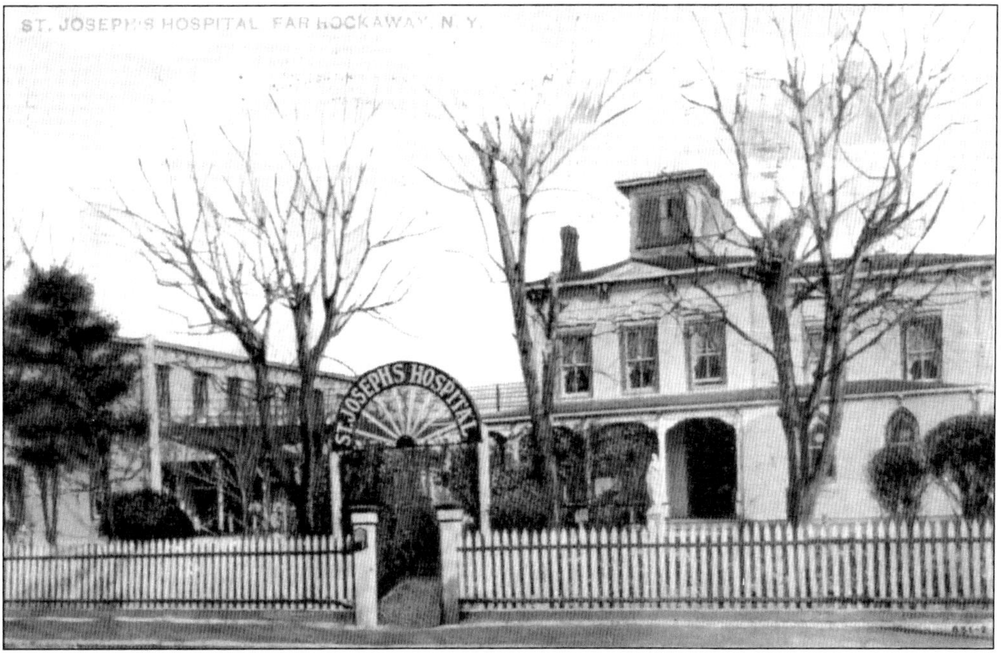

As the population of Far Rockaway and neighboring communities grew, and the nearest hospital was St. John's in Long Island City, the sisters of St. Joseph opened an emergency hospital in one of their buildings on Central Avenue above Plainview Avenue. For the next several years, the need for a larger facility rose.

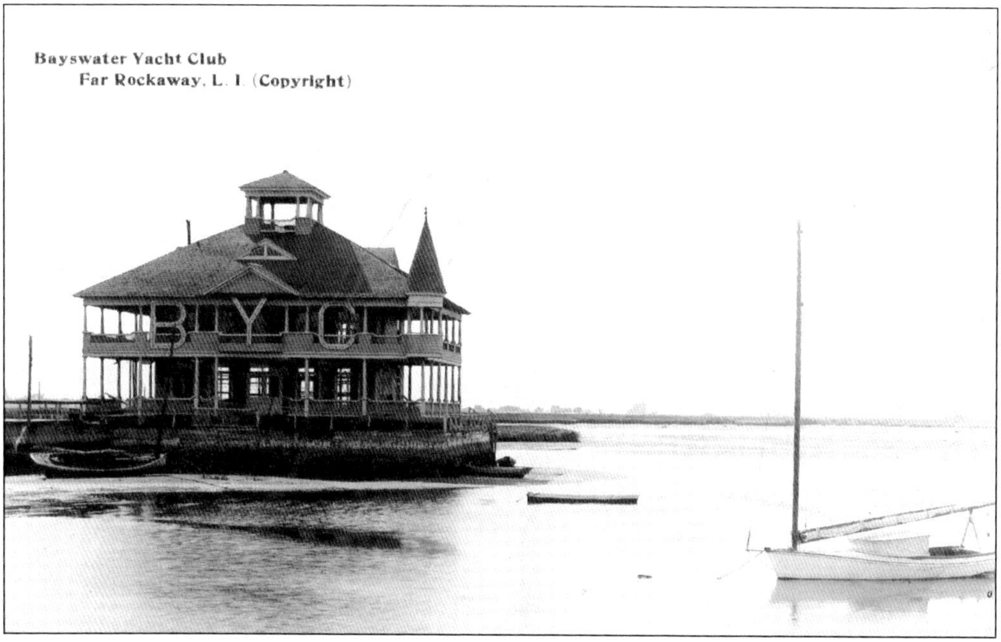

The Bayswater section of Far Rockaway was laid out and developed by William Trist Bailey, an Englishman who named the place after his ancestral home abroad. Opened in 1880, many lots were sold and residences put on them for the next decade. Residents organized and built the Bayswater Yacht Club in 1891 on the east side of Norton Basin near the foot of Healy Avenue.

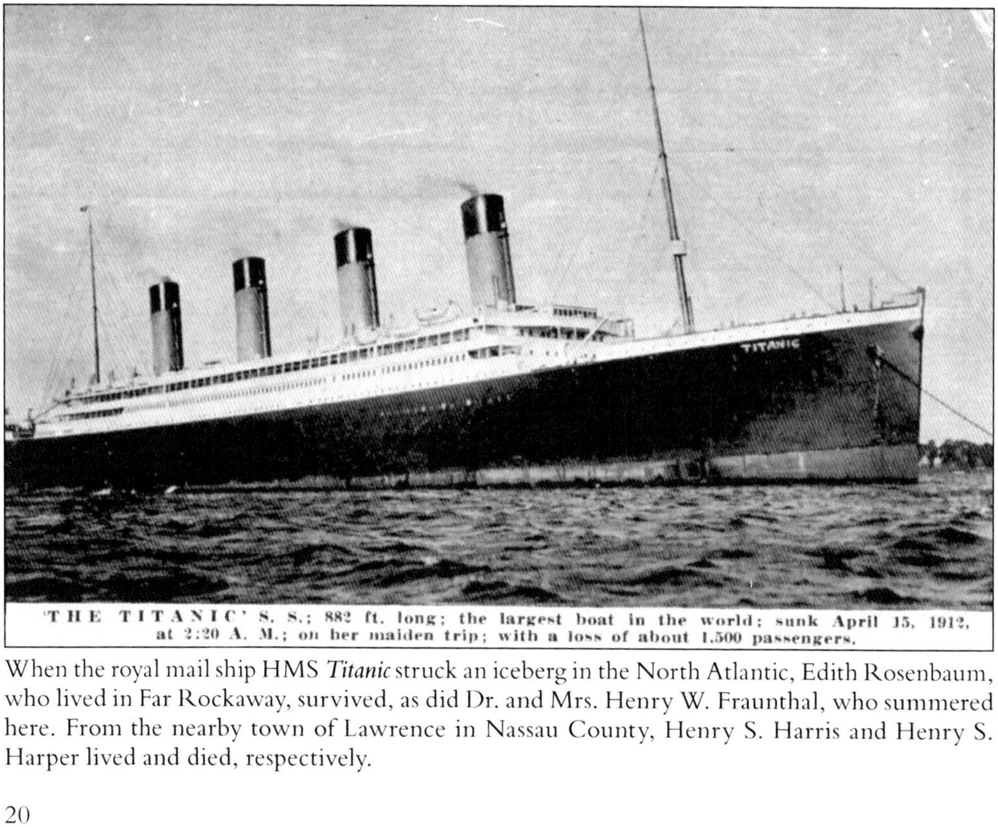

'THE TITANIC' S. S.; 882 ft. long; the largest boat in the world; sunk April 15, 1912, at 2:20 A. M.; on her maiden trip; with a loss of about 1,500 passengers.

When the royal mail ship HMS *Titanic* struck an iceberg in the North Atlantic, Edith Rosenbaum, who lived in Far Rockaway, survived, as did Dr. and Mrs. Henry W. Fraunthal, who summered here. From the nearby town of Lawrence in Nassau County, Henry S. Harris and Henry S. Harper lived and died, respectively.

Two

Edgemere
Beach 32nd Street to Beach 56th Street

During the early 1890s, the New Venice Company planned to develop Edgemere by creating a canal system hooked up to the canal dug out to connect Jamaica Bay and Far Rockaway Bay. New Venice was patterned after the Old World city, complete with gondolas and small craft negotiating the canals. The venture suffered a capital collapse when the contractor, who had underbid the job, absconded with what little money he had left. He was sought after but never found and neither has a plan or blueprint for New Venice.

One year later, the fiasco was compounded by the direct hit of an unnamed hurricane in September 1893. The Lancaster Seabeach Company purchased the site, placed fill in areas that had washed out, and proceeded to construct the giant Edgemere Hotel, the name derived from the former New Venice site.

The massive hotel was built on the west side of Beach 35th Street from the present Sprayview Avenue to the beachfront. At the beachfront, a giant breakwater was put in to protect the building from storm damage after Fred Lancaster had observed firsthand what the raging sea could do at Far Rockaway and Edgemere's beach areas.

When opened for business in 1895, the hotel was serviced by the Long Island Rail Road's station on Beach 35th Street and special stagecoach lines from points north and south.

Over the years, Edgemere had developed into a most desirable summer resort containing the second-largest tent city in the Rockaways, many small frame houses, a few stores, and an assortment of smaller high-class summer hotels and apartment houses. A church and synagogue were built close to the station, and the marshland on the bay side was filled in for homes, bungalows, an airport for light aircraft, marinas, and the now closed Edgemere Landfill. Amstel Boulevard (now Beach Channel Drive) supplemented Rockaway Beach Boulevard and Edgemere Avenue, which straddled the railroad east to west through Edgemere. Bungalow courts and colonies saturated the section, and in the 1960s, urban renewal leveled the beach area north of the boardwalk, which was built in the 1920s. The land remained vacant for about three decades, and it is now being redeveloped. High-rises, one- and two-family homes, and special community planning will see to a rebirth of Edgemere.

The most valuable assets in this area are the beautiful beachfront, the boardwalk, and three Jamaica Bay basins for all sorts of waterfront activities, mainly fishing and boating. A new park site is being developed atop the old Edgemere Landfill.

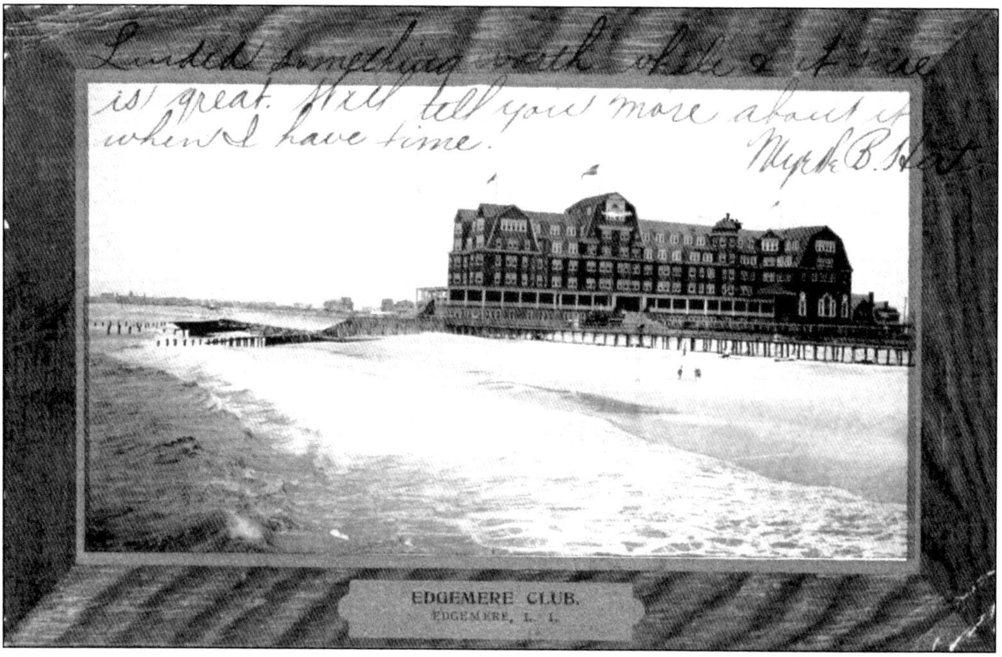

The Edgemere Hotel took up 330 feet of the 610-by-230-foot lot that it stood on. As is seen in this postcard, the big breakwater is broken and needs to be rebuilt at a tremendous cost. The great storms of 1896, 1897, and 1898 cut away the beach shown on the far side to the boulevard and beyond, and they needed to be dredge filled. The walk on the right led to other places.

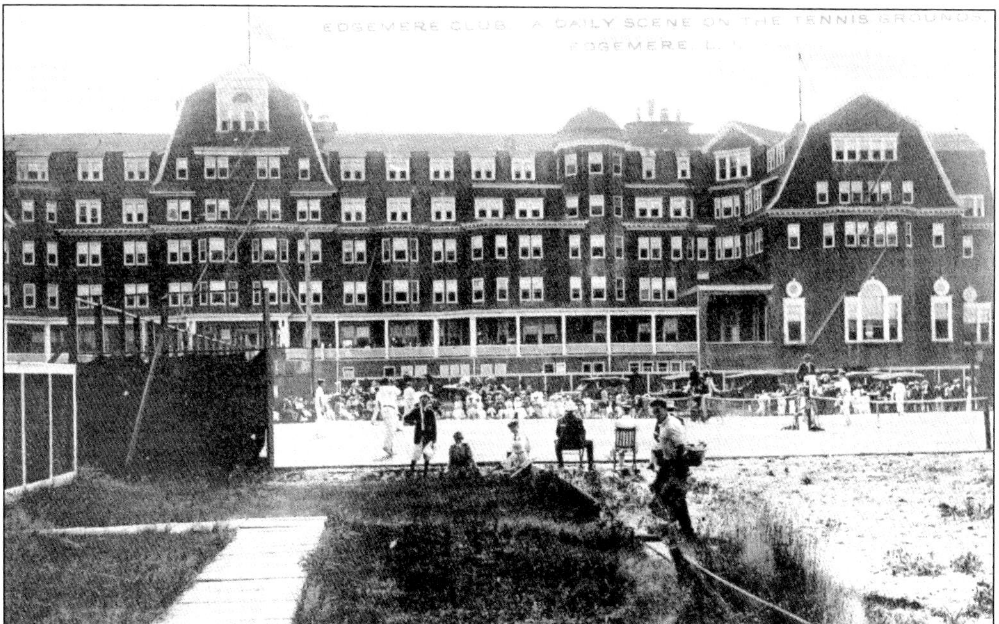

Some of the 400 guests enjoyed the tennis courts on the east side of the hotel, while walkers enjoyed the wooden sidewalks put down on stable ground. For the convenience of the guests, a summer post office was opened at the hotel in 1897, and an ice plant and bakery worked around the clock. When the place was torn down in 1935, the job took a month to complete.

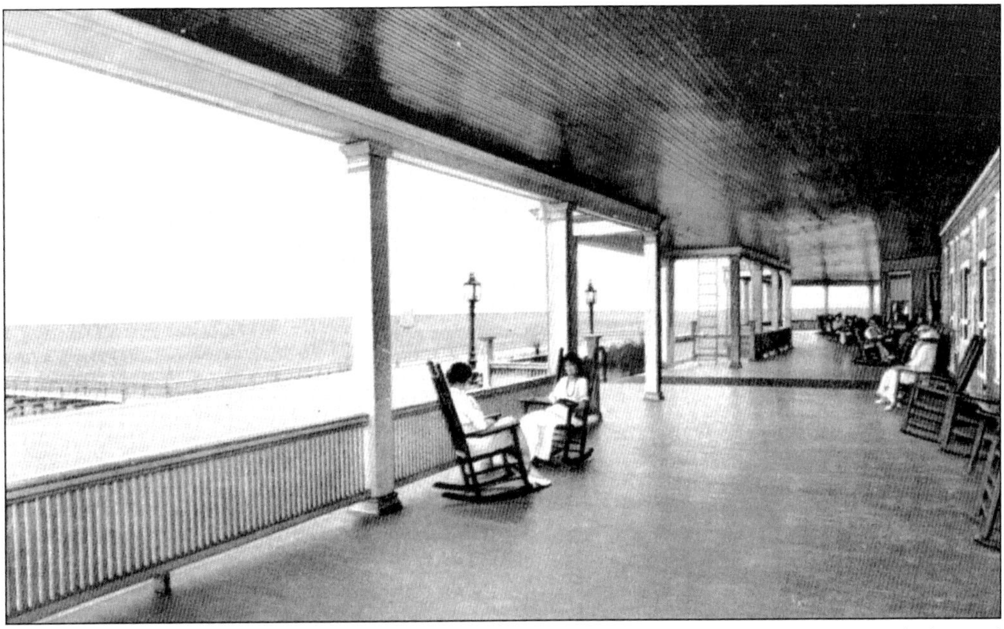

This view from the veranda of the Edgemere Hotel looks toward the breakwater and elevated boardwalks that lead to other hotels, eventually reaching the Long Island Rail Road station. The deck of the hotel is reminiscent of the decks on the ocean liners of the day.

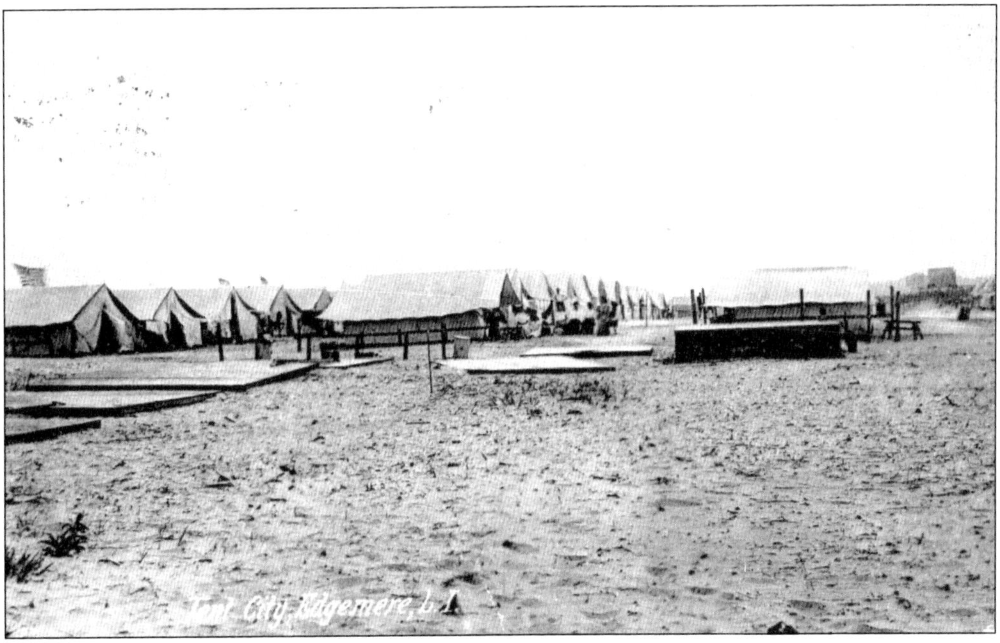

Tilrose Camp was the name given to the Edgemere tent city founded by the Reinhart family of Rockaway Beach. The canvas tents were erected over wooden platforms on the sand. At the end of the season, the tents were folded and put in storage buildings, while the platforms were taken to high ground, stacked, and lashed down for the winter.

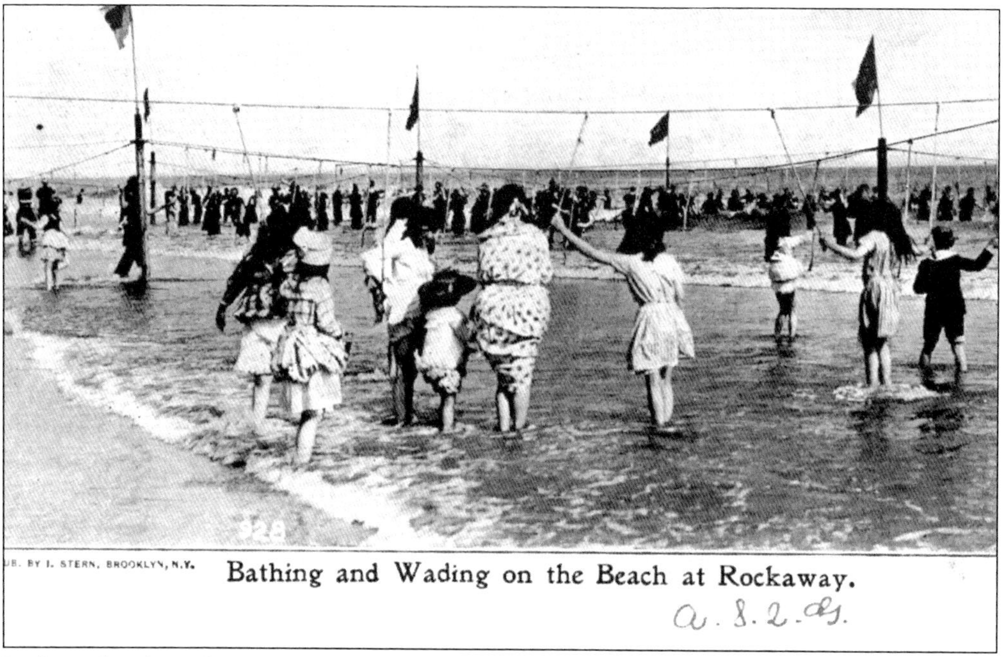

Bather safety lines first appeared on the beaches of the Rockaways in 1876. After installations, the drowning rate dropped considerably from Far Rockaway to the new west end beaches. Heavy ropes were strung from poles to the outer surf line from the high berm area, and short stringers provided stability from rough surf at times.

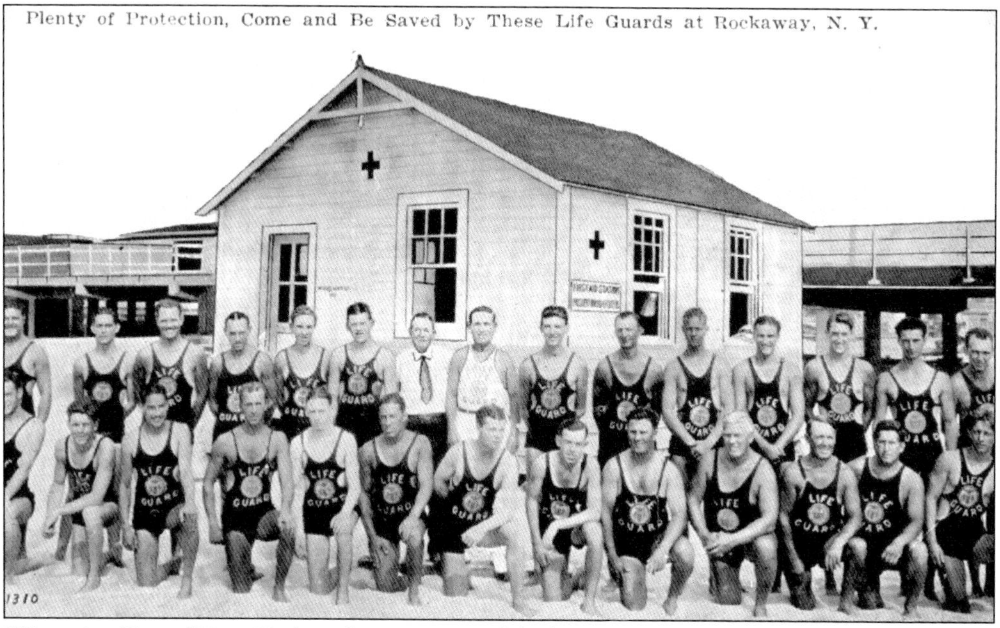

When the City of New York took possession of the beach and shorefront in the Rockaways in the 1920s, the old system of paid professional lifeguards came to an end. The future lifesavers came out of the civil service system, and they were tested. If they passed, they were hired and trained to work on the beaches of the Rockaways. This group poses at the lifeguard shack in Edgemere.

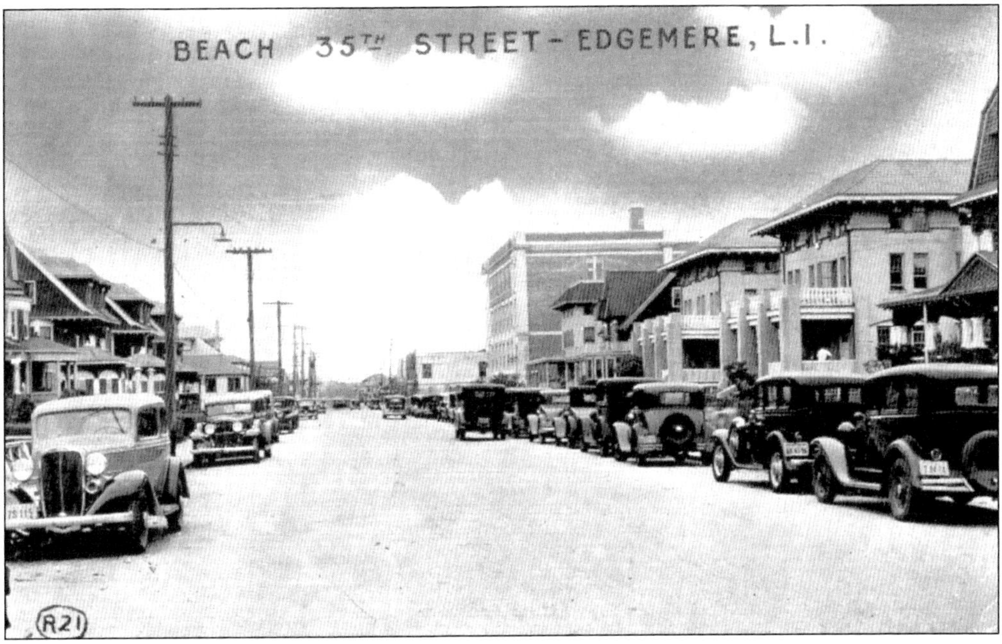

By the late 1930s, Edgemere literally ran out of space to build year-round residences and summer facilities for the throngs of beach lovers coming down to bathe. Public School No. 106 appeared on Beach 35th Street, and the Edgemere Hotel property (on the left) filled with bungalows and rooming houses after the giant hostelry was torn down.

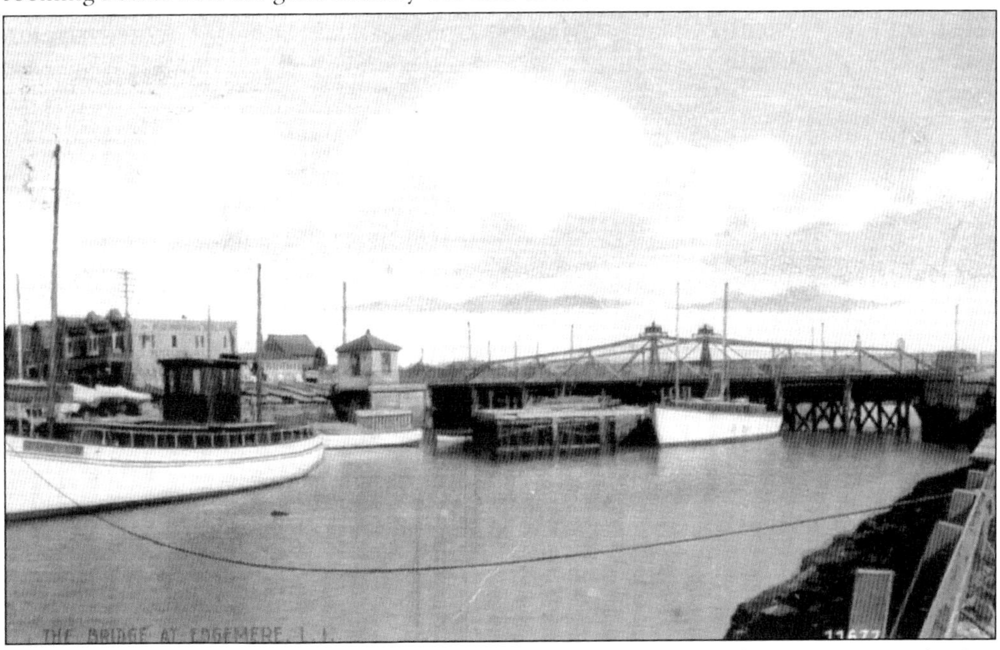

Norton's iron swing bridge, built in 1894, crossed the man-made canal connecting Jamaica Bay and the outlet to the Atlantic Ocean via Far Rockaway Bay. The bridge opened only once for a test, due to the railroad's noncompliance to build an opening bridge–type crossing south of Norton's bridge. These boats used the waters of Norton Basin on Jamaica Bay, which can be seen in the foreground.

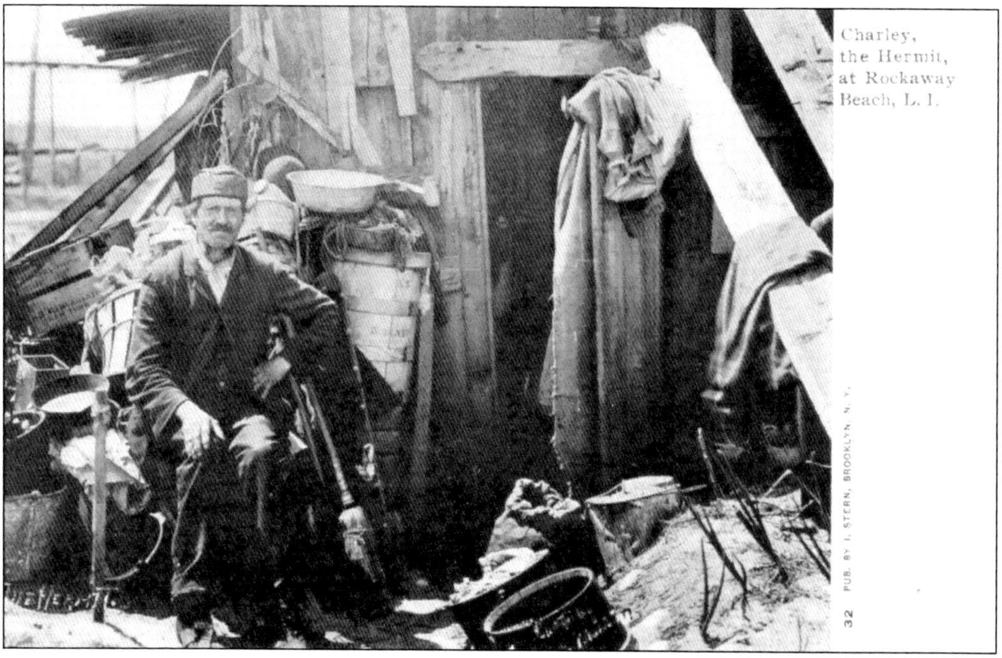

Charley the hermit lived in a self-made shack east of Rockaway Junction between the railroad track and the main boulevard at about 54th Street. After coming to America, Charley's betrothed back home married his brother using the money he had sent her. It has been said that Charley threw away his carpenter tools and never worked another day in his life.

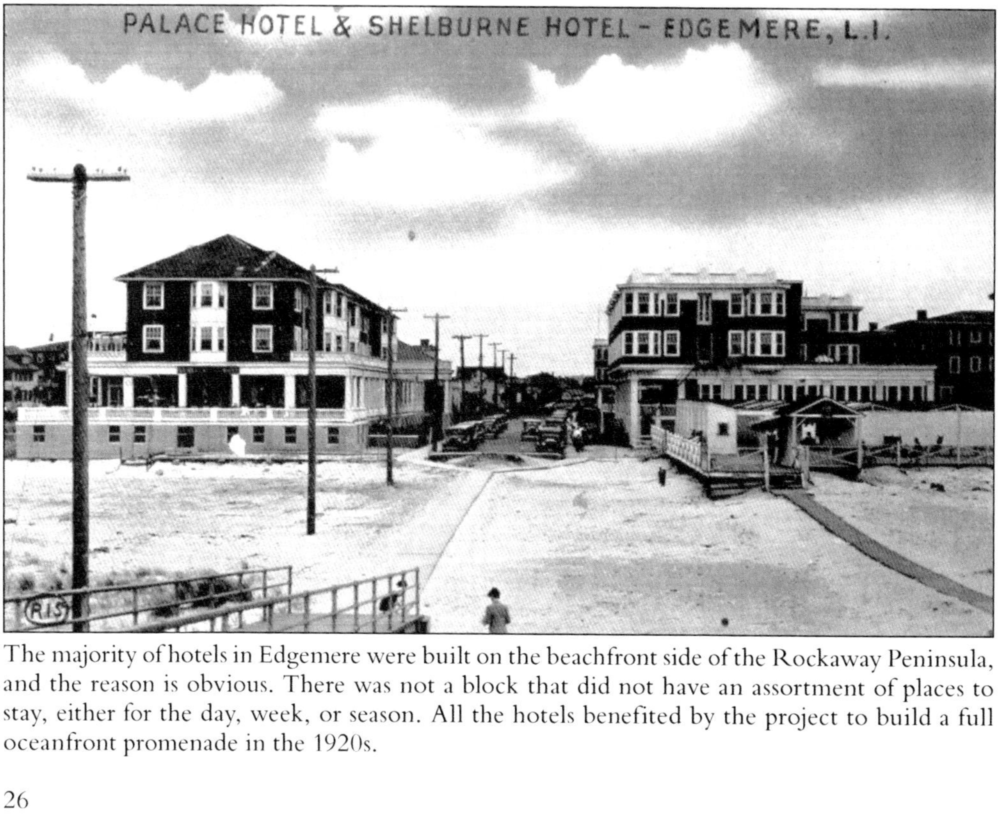

The majority of hotels in Edgemere were built on the beachfront side of the Rockaway Peninsula, and the reason is obvious. There was not a block that did not have an assortment of places to stay, either for the day, week, or season. All the hotels benefited by the project to build a full oceanfront promenade in the 1920s.

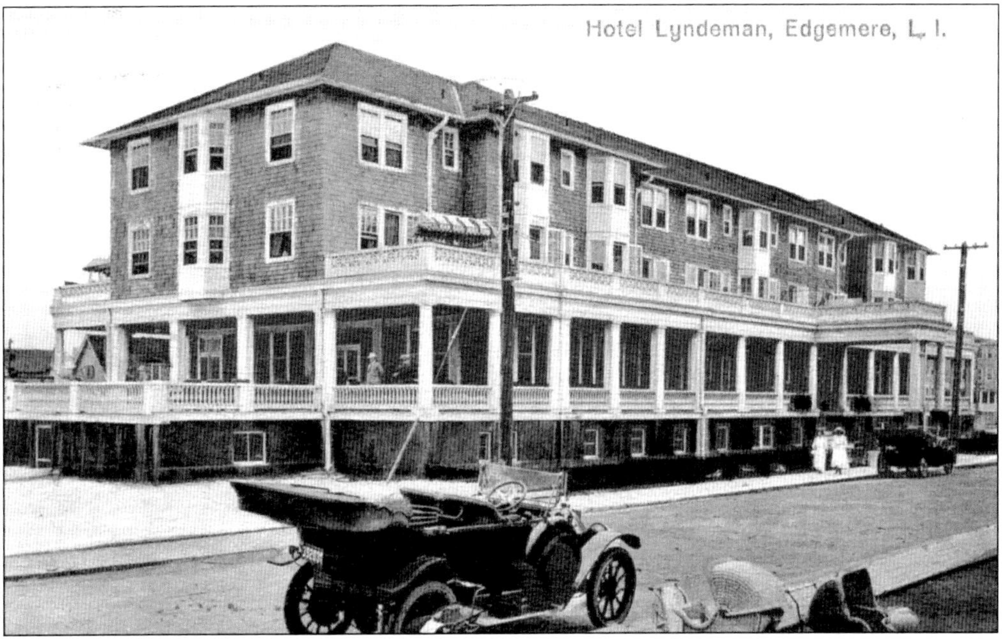

Hotel Lyndeman, sometimes spelled Linderman, was one of the more upscale hotels in Edgemere. Two or three places had the Lindeman name associated with them. Statistics and data on the old hotels as to the number of rooms, entertainments, activities, notable guests, and so on are for all intents and purposes nonexistent and a loss.

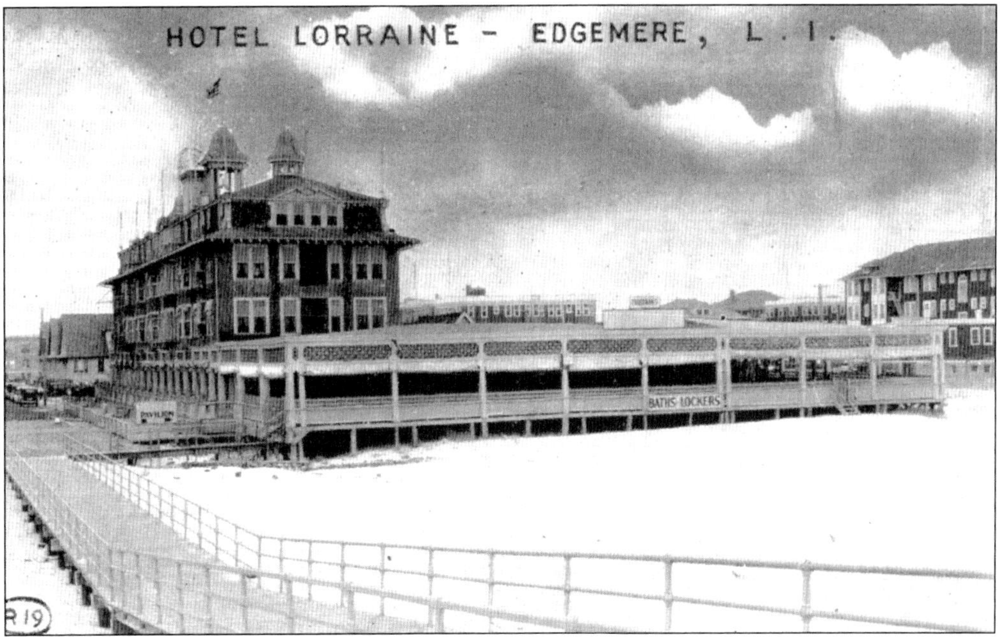

The Hotel Lorraine on Beach 29th Street joined ranks with the Edgemere Hotel in the early 1900s as a first-class hostelry. Alex Hart was the owner and manager. The long ramp leads to the city boardwalk, built for the length of the Rockaways in the late 1920s. With a tax lien on it, and being in poor condition, the Lorraine was torn down to build a parking lot in 1941.

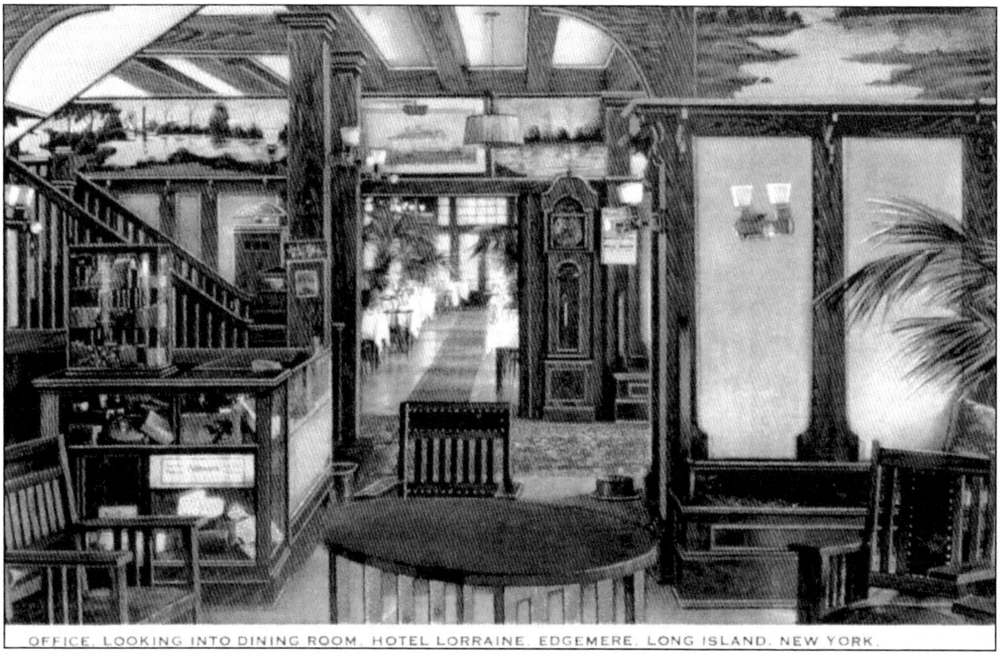

Looking toward the dining room of the Hotel Lorraine from the office, a performance by the singer Belle Baker is posted next to the grandfather clock while Schraft's candy is displayed in the glass case the bottom left. Interior views of the old hotels are very rare.

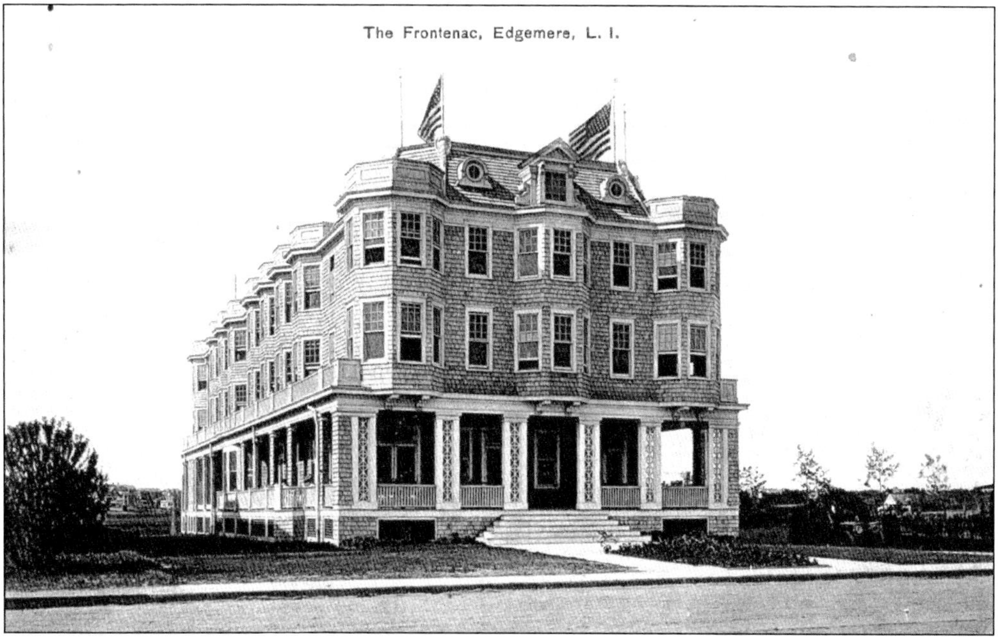

The Hotel Frontenac was the only Edgemere hotel to survive into modern times as an apartment house, a rooming house, and a single-room occupancy house. There was an attempt to restore the building in the late 1990s, but it did not work out. The old hostelry was torn down as the new Public School No. 43 was being built nearby.

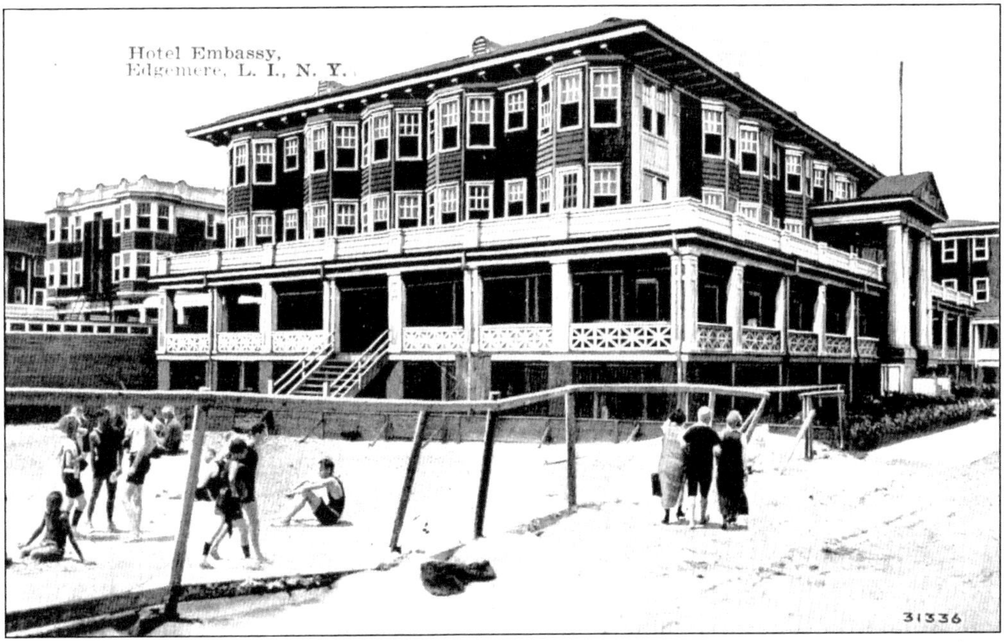

The Grand Embassy Hotel was another survivor in East Edgemere, and after being closed for a time, it burned to the ground in 1967. At the time, there was an urban renewal plan for Edgemere put in place by the New York City Planning Commission. In the old days, all told there were 60-plus hotels in Edgemere.

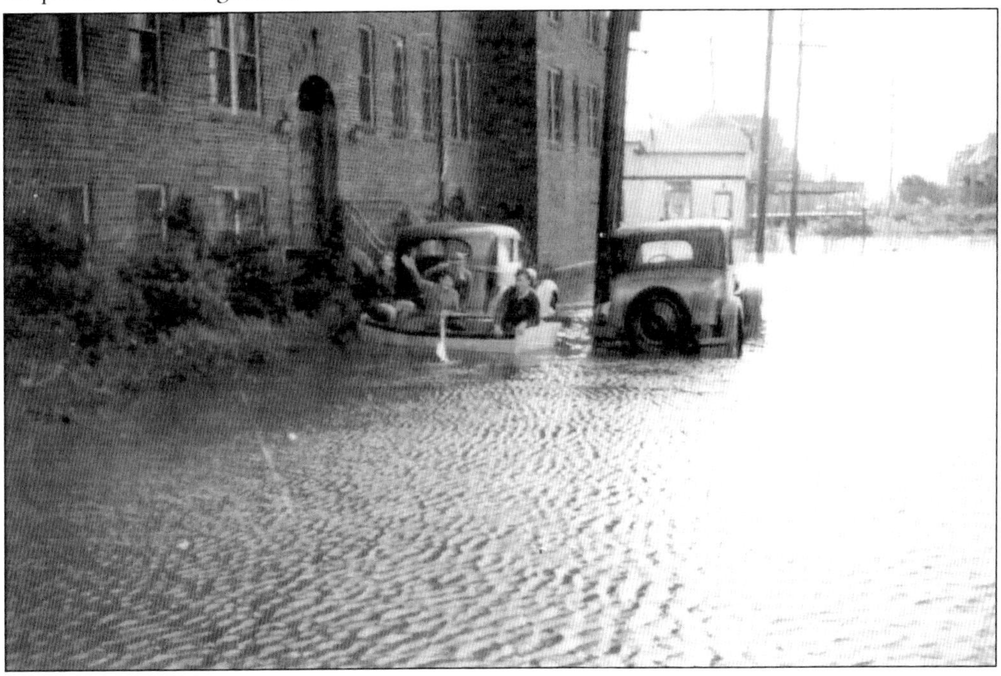

The bay side of Edgemere, north of Rockaway Beach Boulevard, and the railroad station in the background flooded out first and quickly in September 1938, as the bay area was topographically lower than the beachfront. The cars and a boatload of residents are leaving the Beach 36th Street apartments. Amstel Boulevard (Beach Channel Drive) is behind the photographer.

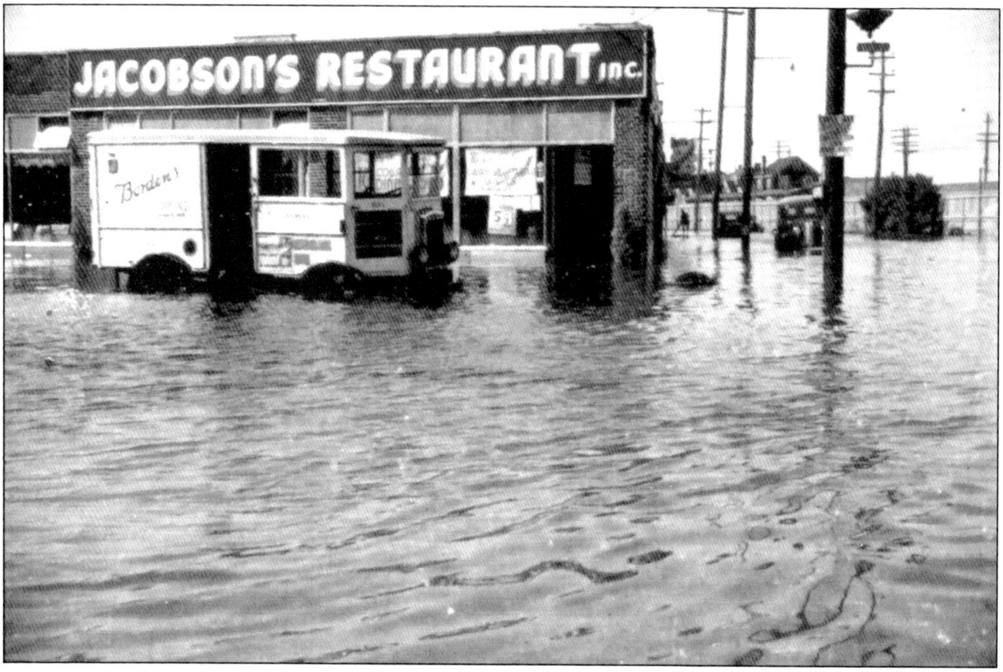

As the low point of the Rockaway Peninsula, the Edgemere section flooded at the mere mention of rain. This photograph of Beach 35th Street and Edgemere Avenue has survived to show how much damage the hurricane of 1938 did to the main business portion of Edgemere. The railroad station in the background was deluged. Low tide brought some relief.

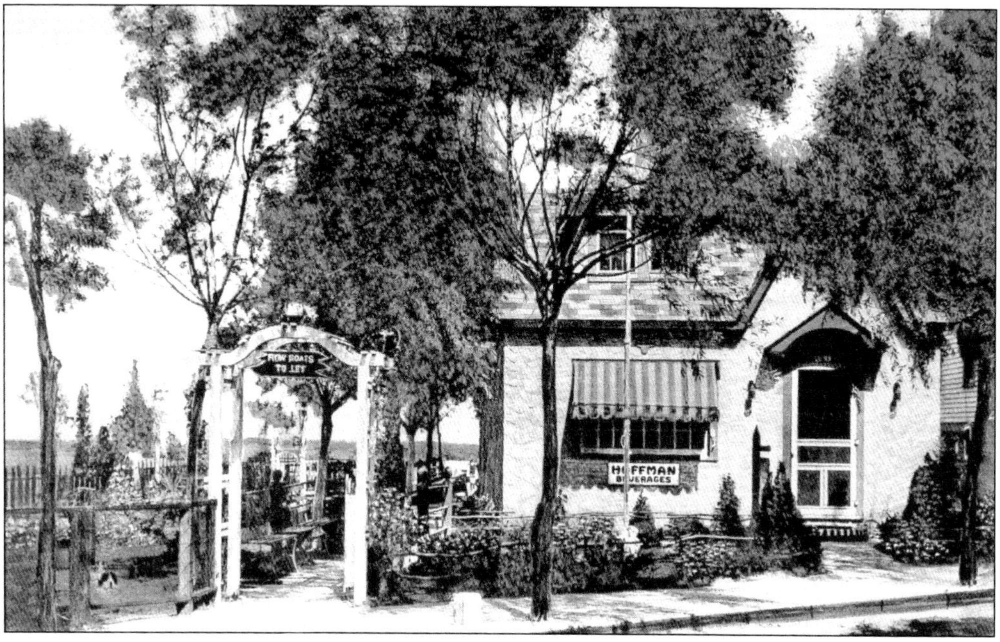

The Cozy Corner, described as Rockaway's nicest place for refreshment, was situated on the shore of Jamaica Bay in Edgemere at the foot of Beach 46th Street. Conch Basin (Little Bay) was nearby, and boating, fishing, and peace and quiet were available. Soft drinks and libations were also on tap. An outdoor terrace provided fresh-air seating for a hearty appetite.

Three

Arverne
Beach 56th Street to Beach 79th Street

The bay front of Arverne was dark and foreboding in the 1850s, and a snakelike and often wash-outed wagon road from Far Rockaway worked its way west to the point of the Rockaway Peninsula. The Long Island Rail Road passed through the wilds of Arverne in 1872 also on its way west from Far Rockaway. A handful of houses existed in the area, and the new Rockaway Beach Boulevard ran to the west alongside the railroad in the early 1880s.

The houses aforementioned were built in 1882, one by Remington Vernam, a New York lawyer, who after taking up residence began to barter, bargain, compromise, and sue to become the owner of considerable beach property, as well as marshes to the north.

In 1888, Vernam built the huge Arverne Hotel near the beach on the west side of Remington Avenue (Beach 69th Street). The building of the hotel and the community around it put Arverne on the map with all other owners of property accepting Arverne as the name of the entire section. A building boom followed with stores appearing on Arverne Boulevard, and the railroad put in two stations, one at Beach 59th Street and the other at Beach 67th Street.

Vernam had big plans for the marshland of North Arverne. To curtail flooding, a concrete viaduct was to wrap around the bay shore, the landfill from the bay bottom was to be dredged up, land was set aside for a hospital, a school site was reserved, and a canal was to be cut north of the railroad to Beach 63rd Street and then up to the bay.

Vernam died in 1907, and plans for the area drastically changed. The hospital was built elsewhere, the city bought land for a school, and city rules and regulations threw a wrench in the rest of the plans. Edward Somerville and William Scheer did bulkhead and fill North Arverne later, and the basins on the east and west were greatly improved in the 1920s. Long before his death, Vernam was instrumental in having the rail line from Far Rockaway hooked up to the bay trestle in 1887.

Arverne flourished with new housing a little at a time, especially on the bay side. Sidewalks and sewers were put in, but the crash of 1929 halted all construction, and nature grew weed-filled lots that were prone to fire. Some new homes went up in the 1960s and more in recent years. The great urban renewal plan of the 1960s leveled all of the 385 acres of Arverne/Edgemere beachfront, with the site remaining empty for decades.

The bay side of Arverne continues to flourish. More high-rise structures have been built here and there, and a part of the road under the elevated railway is now out of service. The Rockaway

Freeway was opened in 1944, while the elevated railway opened in 1943. Much bay front land in the northwest corner has been warehoused for future parks, and a new beach community called Arverne-by-the-Sea is being developed.

Arverne owners built an elevated boardwalk on the beach in 1901, and the city walk was built in 1926–1931 from Far Rockaway to Beach 126th Street. Both walks were lined with food, drink, and fun places along with an open-air movie theater.

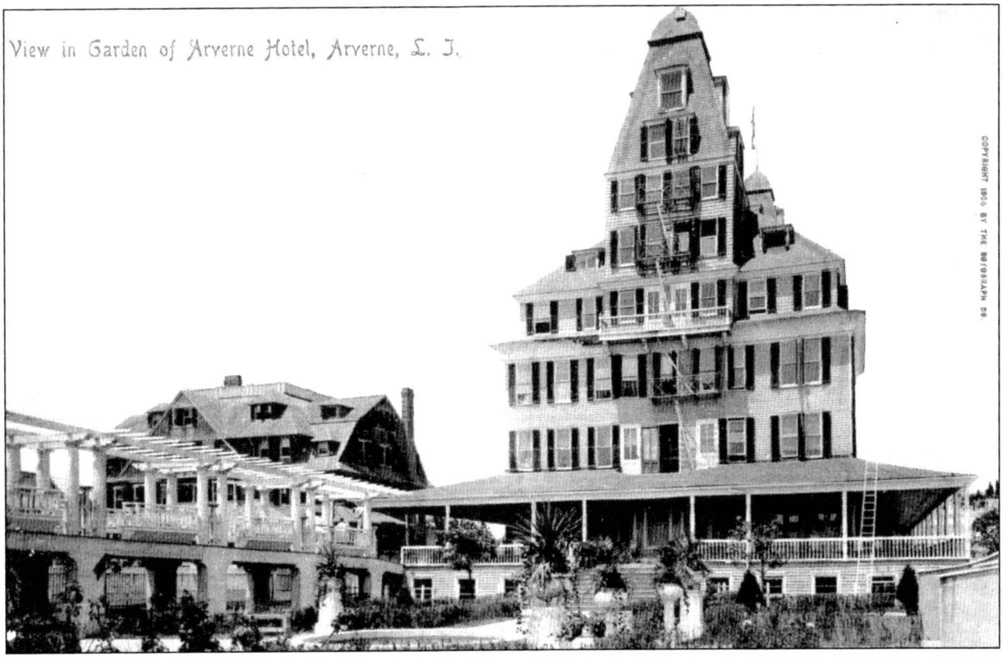

The Italian gardens of the Arverne Hotel were located between the main hotel building and the hotel casino. This half of the garden was close to the hotel, and a trellised elevated walk led to the half close to the casino. Attendants brought out chairs for guests to be seated in the sunny grotto; there were some shaded areas as well.

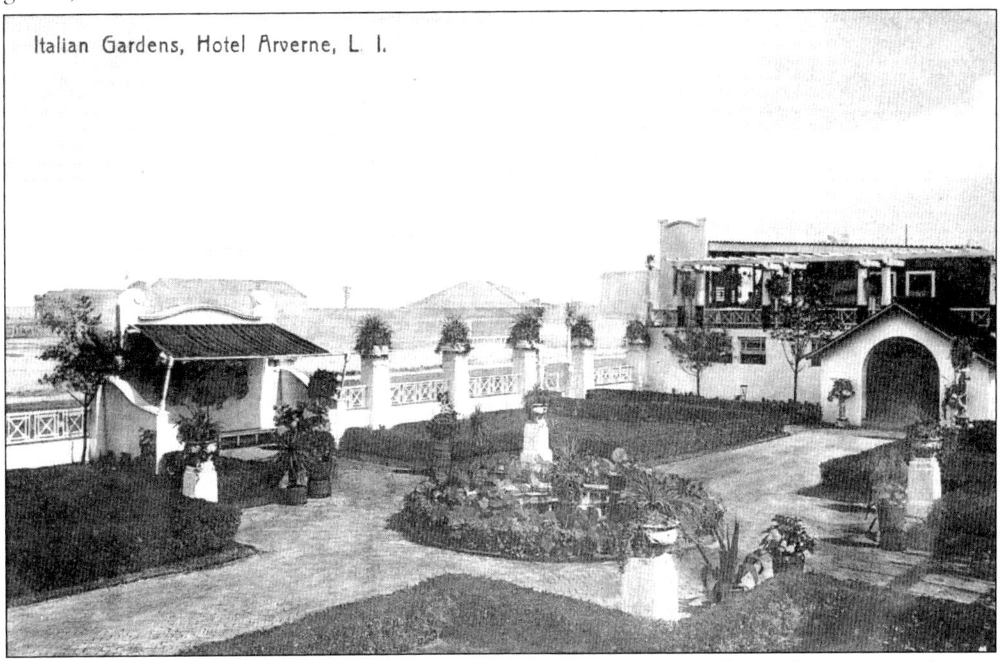

The part of the Arverne Hotel gardens closest to the casino had different landscaping than its counterpart. The elevated walk on the front garden is at the right, as is a separating wall and refreshment rooms with an overhead porch arrangement. There are also some benches under the awning at the left center.

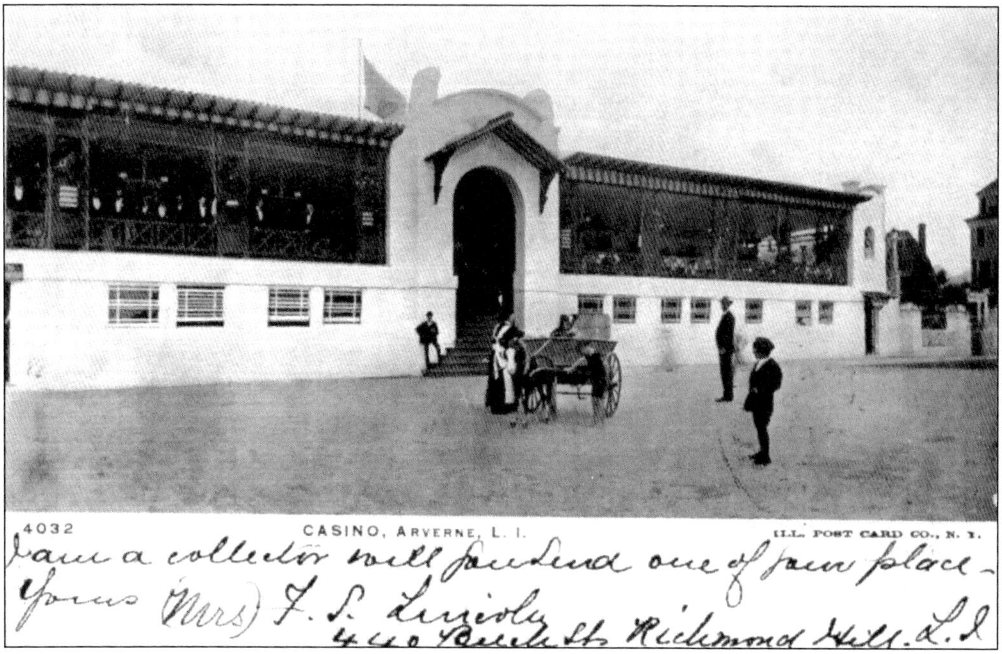

The Arverne Hotel casino was under the management of William A. Rogers and offered bowling, billiards, 100 bathrooms six feet by five feet, and verandas on three sides. Tennis courts were nearby, and massages were also available.

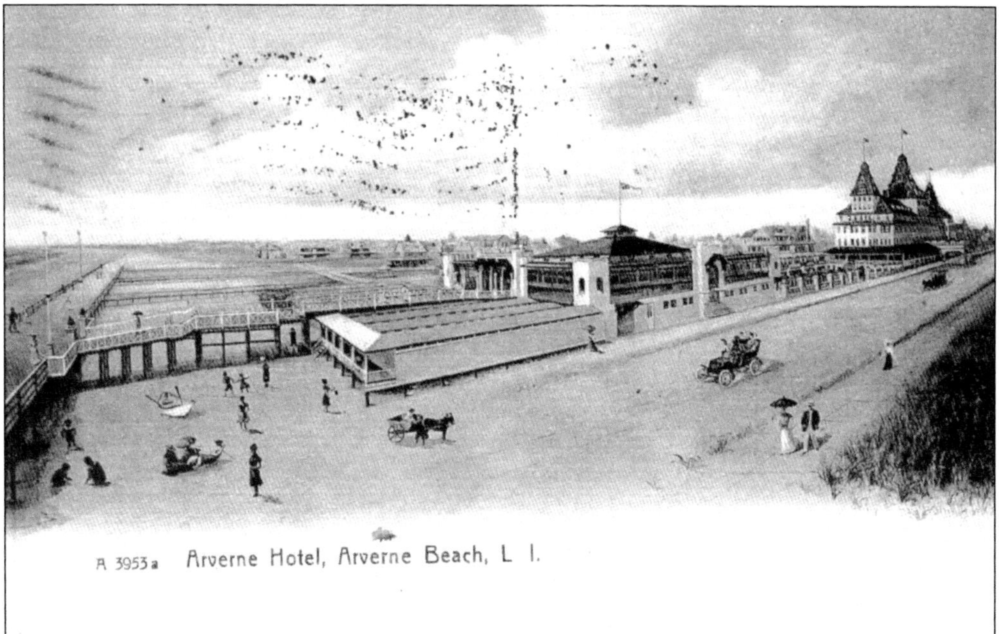

Shown here is one artist's elongated view of the Arverne Hotel and area attractions. An elevated walk leads from the boardwalk and goes past the bather bathhouses to the casino and continues to the hotel proper. Here the west side of the casino can be seen, which has a sign atop noting Roger's Casino, the gardens on the next level, and the cottages for rent on Arverne Boulevard.

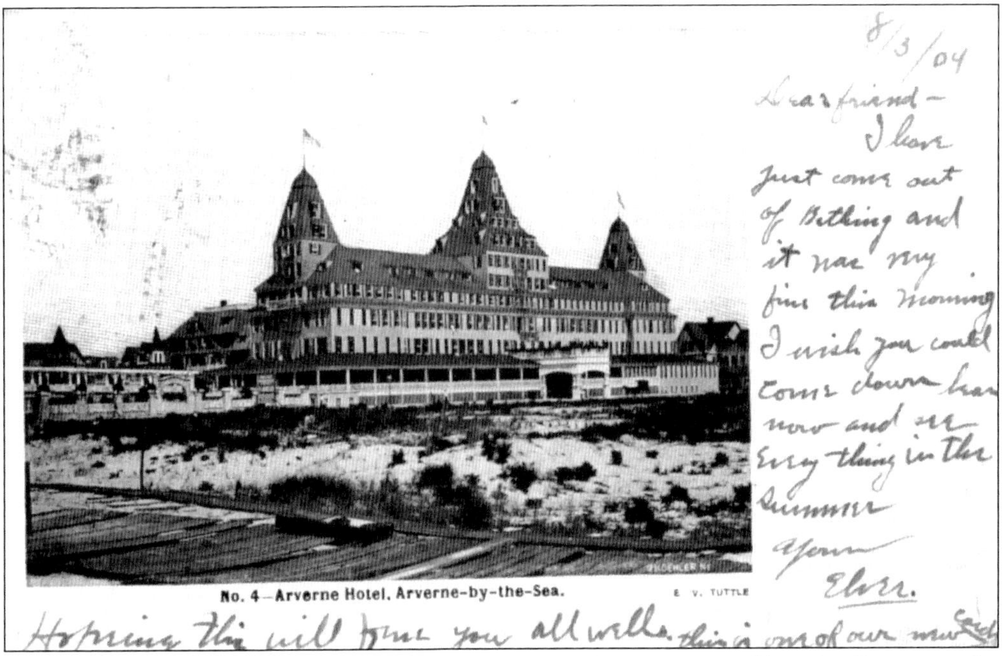

With the Arverne Hotel in the background, one of the old Arverne sand boardwalks crosses the foreground. Most likely this walk was the last built before the elevated oceanfront promenade went up in 1901.

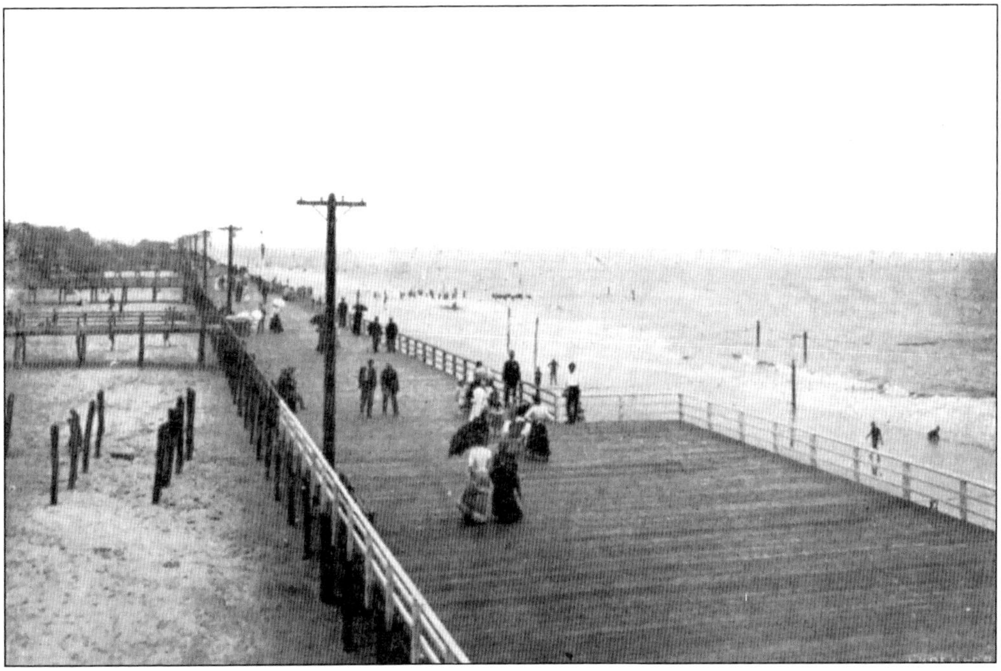

The new elevated oceanfront promenade was bare on completion in 1901. Shown is the east end of the wide portion near Remington Avenue. Soon many stores appeared on the land side at the left. The piling is what is left of a storm's past visit before the new walk was built. The year 1903 saw another.

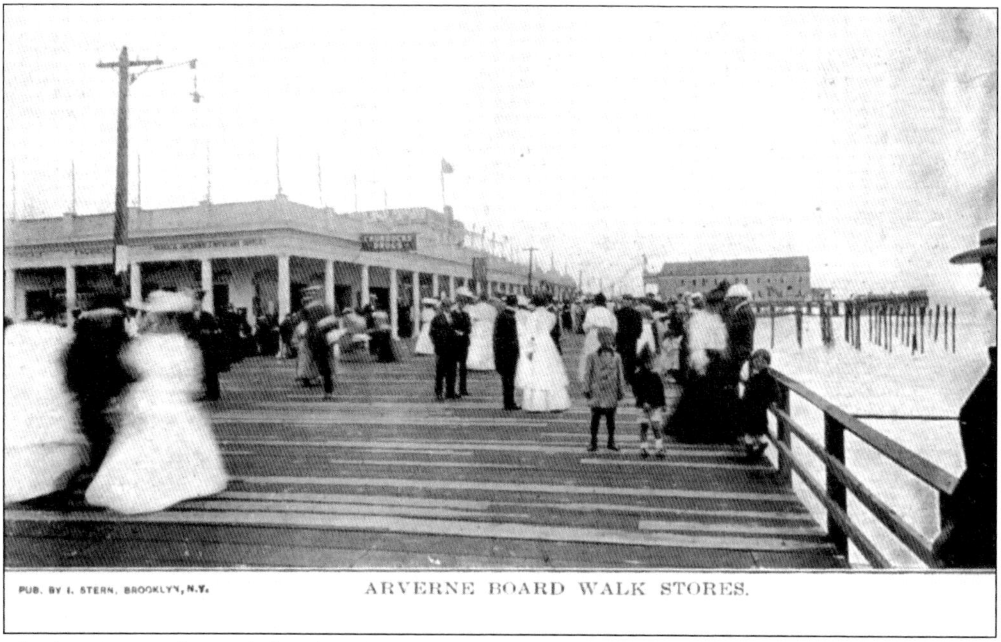

The hurricane of 1903 left only pilings of a business venture on the beach side of the Arverne boardwalk. The walk itself suffered damage, as did the stores on the left between Beach 70th and Beach 68th Streets. The Arverne Pier Theatre (in the background to the right) opened for the 1904 season at Beach 67th Street.

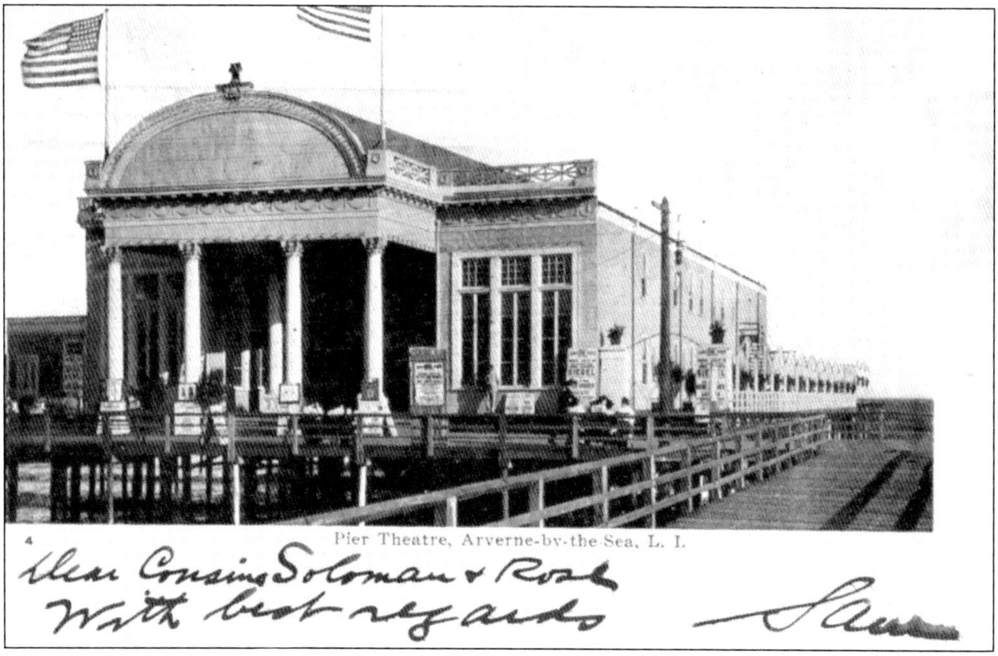

The Arverne Pier Theatre, built out over the beach (over water at high tide), opened for the 1904 season at the foot of Vernam Avenue (Beach 67th Street). Comparable to a city theater at times, the building featured a wraparound porch, a partially covered veranda, bars, a restaurant, and a dance floor. A storm in 1914 took the entire structure out to sea.

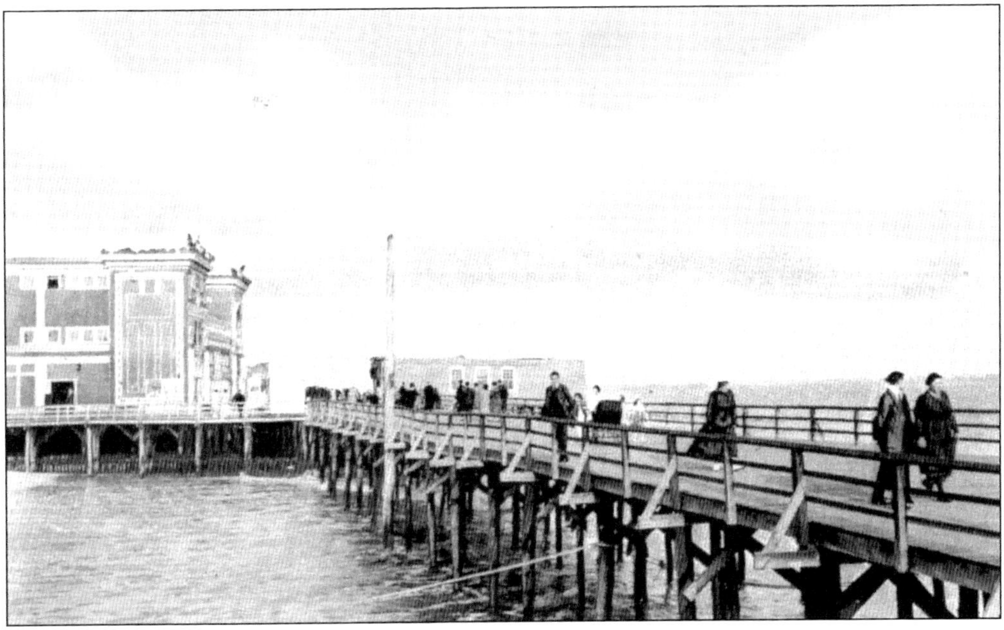

The new boardwalk open-air movie theater was opened in the early 1920s at Beach 67th Street. Silent movies were shown complete with an organ player and subtitles. Sophisticated pile supports and bulkheads supported the building, which was specifically tailored to hold off beach erosion and undermining. Talkies came to the theater in 1928.

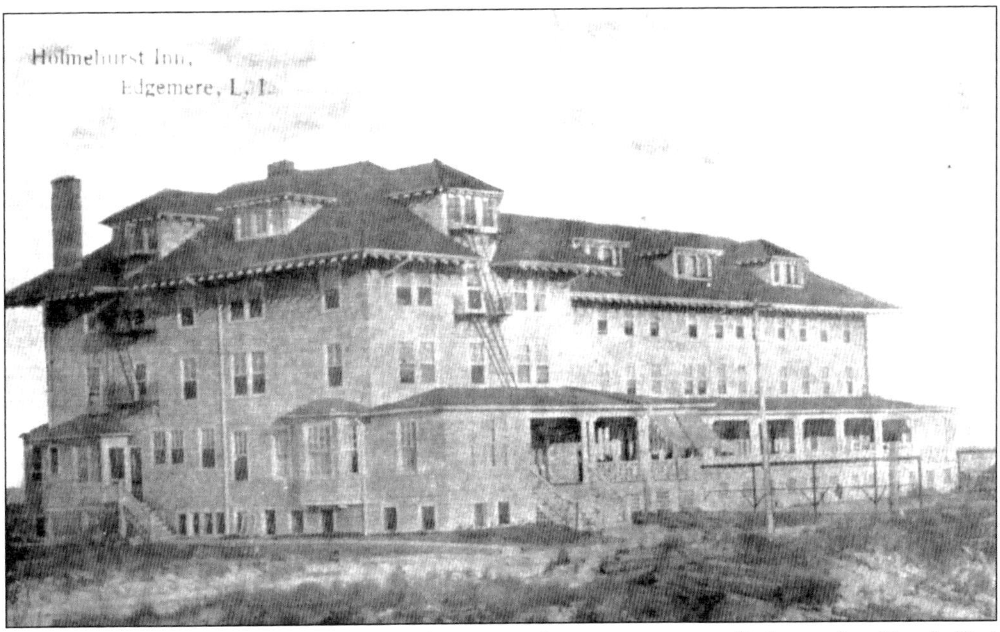

The Holmehurst Inn, although noted as being in Edgemere, was actually located on Beach 63rd Street in Arverne. First noted as the Cottage Hotel in 1908, it was next written of as the Holmehurst when it burned to the ground in 1909. It was the first great hotel fire in the Rockaways. Guests were roused from sleep in the early morning hours and some exited the hotel naked.

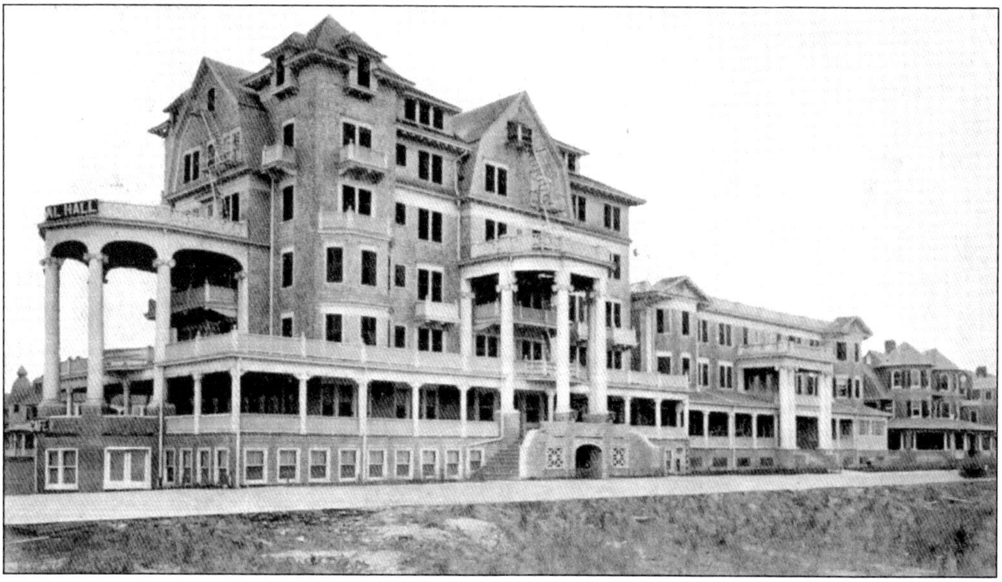

The multilevel Colonial Hotel, located on Beach 64th Street in Arverne, was built by Edward Waldman in 1904. The huge building with columned entrances contained 150 rooms and catered to theatrical prominents staying in the summer. Sol Choen's Black Kat Jass Band appeared at the Colonial Hotel in the 1920s when Herman Greer was the manager. A six-alarm fire destroyed the hotel in 1929.

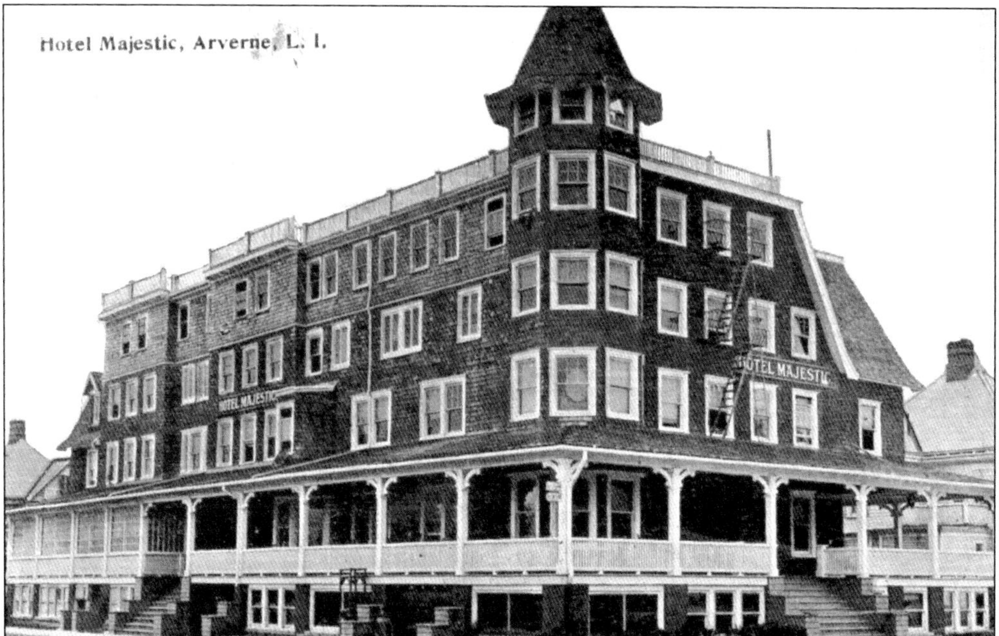

B. Ludwig of Ludwig Brothers Retail Dry Goods in the city built the Hotel Majestic on the southeast corner of Remington Avenue and Rockaway Beach Boulevard in 1893. The hotel was rented out for $6,000 a season. The Hotel Majestic was managed by Henry A. Prince for many years, until he took over the Arverne Hotel. In 1928, the hotel was replaced by an office building.

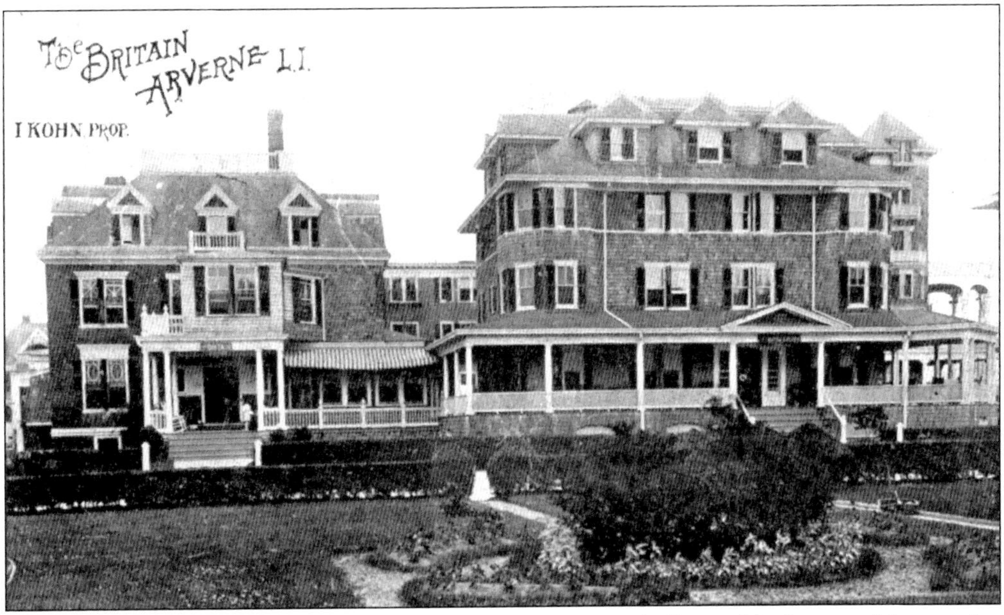

The Hotel Britain, of which I. Kohn was the proprietor, was built one block west of the massive Colonial Hotel on Beach 65th Street. Both hotels shared beach bathing facilities near the old wooden boardwalk. The Britain burned down at the same time as the Colonial as collateral damage. A new Britain Hotel was built at Beach 70th Street near the boardwalk with a large inground saltwater pool.

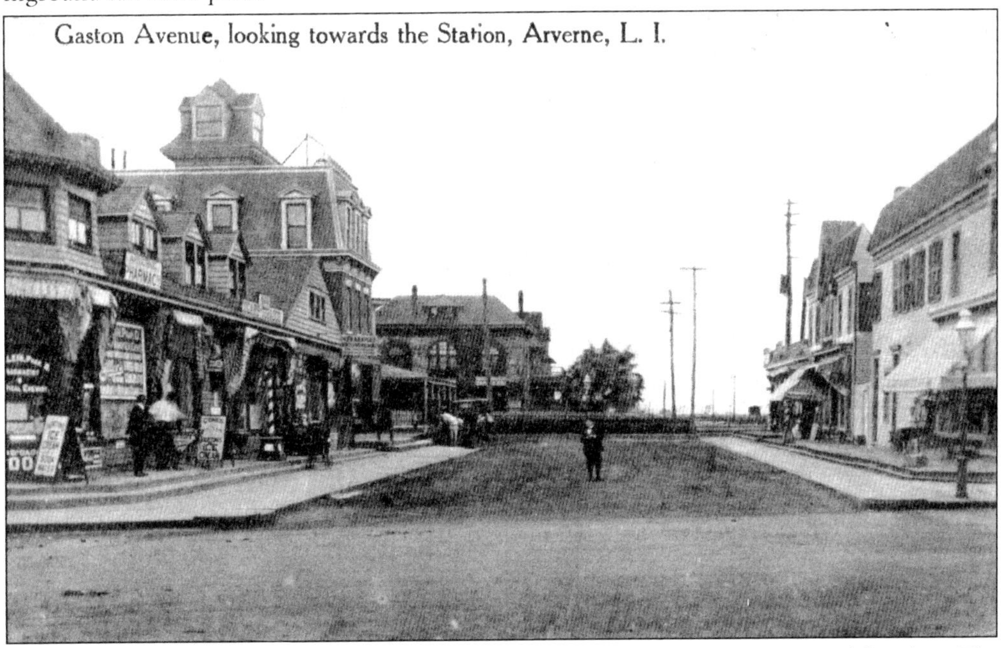

Gaston Avenue (Beach 66th Street) was named in honor of Remington Vernam's brother. The cameraman set up on Rockaway Beach Boulevard looking north toward the tracks of the Long Island Rail Road. The station tower is on the left, and Gaston Vernam's stone house, which still remains, is on the north side of the railroad. The stores and offices shown are typical of a station area.

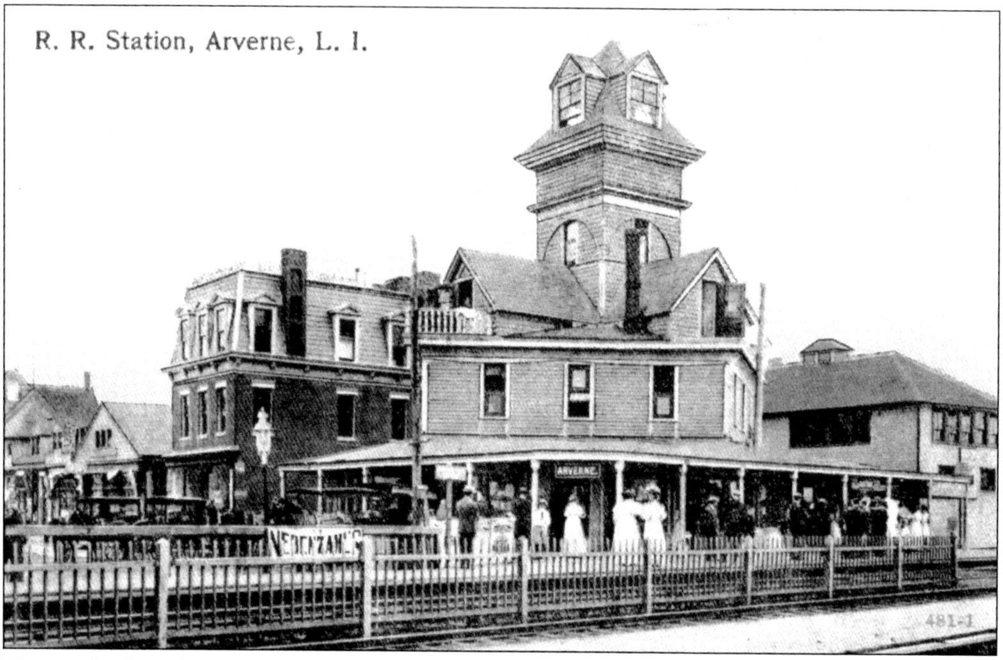

The nicely shaped Arverne station was an architectural delight set on Gaston Avenue in 1888. No pictures of the station at Beach 59th Street (Straiton Avenue) have ever been found. This station was replaced by a new station in 1912, which had a central platform for east–westbound trains.

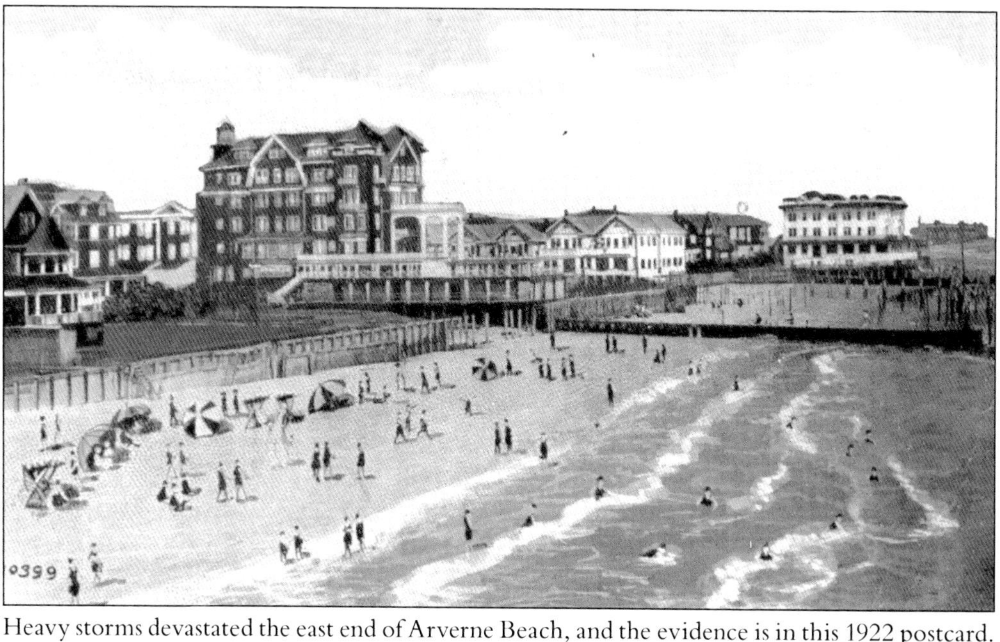

Heavy storms devastated the east end of Arverne Beach, and the evidence is in this 1922 postcard. Jerome Bibo's Hotel Jerome is now an island in itself, the boardwalk is gone, and bulkhead seawalls have been erected by hotel and cottage owners. Wooden jetties are out into the surf, and empty pilings can be found where bathhouses once stood.

Four

Hammels
Beach 79th Street to Beach 88th Street (Old)

Before the railroad from Far Rockaway passed through the Hammels section in 1872, access was by boat or the hazardous Bay Side Road for wagons from Far Rockaway.

"Aunt Abby" Ryder ran a small chowder house and saloon for boaters and fisherman on the bay near old Beach 88th Street in the 1850s. When her only daughter, Matilda, married Garrett Van Winkle Eldert, the husband assumed all responsibility for his wife's holdings, left to her by her mother. Eldert then built a large hotel and restaurant in his new Eldert's Grove, and a new dock was extended into Jamaica Bay at Beach 87th Street.

Louis P. Hammel of Staten Island arrived in 1869 and leased Eldert's Grove facilities. After a few profitable years, Hammel bought a narrow strip of beach, ocean to bay, just to the east of Eldert's Grove, the center of which was between Beach 84th and Beach 85th Streets. On the west side of Beach 85th Street near the bay, Hammel built and opened his new Hammel's Hotel with a steamboat dock out to Jamaica Bay at the foot of Beach 85th Street. The hotel was enlarged a few times, and the dock was later lined with clubs of all sorts related to bay activities. Food and drink were not forgotten for steamer passengers arriving and going from the dock at Hammels. Rowboat rentals were also available.

The Eldert Hotel was ravaged by fire in 1875, and it was rebuilt almost as large as Hammel's place, but both did well. Eldert's was lost totally in 1911 and never rebuilt. In 1880, the bay railroad to the big hotel in the west end landed at Beach 84th Street and turned west around Hammel's Hotel. A station was built on the east side of the hotel and this made two, as the other station closer to the beach was called Eldert's Grove.

When the big hotel failed shortly after the new Rockaway Beach Boulevard from Far Rockaway to the hotel was built, the hotel's railroad also failed and was taken over into the Long Island Rail Road system, which owned and operated the rail line closer to the beach. When the line from Far Rockaway was connected to the bay trestle, the right-of-way left west of Hammels was taken up. Now one line operated on the peninsula east to west.

Hammels station was rebuilt inside a wye that the railroad constructed so that trains could be diverted east or west from the landing at Hammels. At the bottom of the wye, a crossover was built that later served as a trolley station and a switch off for the boulevard trolley in 1904. Trolleys ran from Far Rockaway to the west end from 1897 to 1929.

Louis Hammel sold his hotel to Gottfried Westernacher in 1896, and he went into real estate here. Westernacher ran the hotel superbly until it was destroyed by fire in 1906. The first Rockaway Beach Hospital was constructed on the site in 1908.

Development quickened with more hotels, bungalows, homes, a church, a synagogue, and a newspaper called the *Wave*. In the 1920s, Western Union Atlantic cables were brought ashore and entrenched to the cable building on Beach 84th Street. The city boardwalk was built along the beachfront, and bathing places cluttered the beach on one side only. Hammels station also had a small freight yard in the center of the wye.

When the railroad went up in 1943, Hammels station became history, and Beach Channel Drive was now straight from Beach 77th Street to Beach 84th Street. The building of the Hammel Houses high-rise in the 1950s eliminated the new movie theater built in 1914, stores, homes, and Young's Chevy showroom, and several viable businesses had to move elsewhere. A decade later, more high-rise construction on the beachfront destroyed the old and good neighborhood, just as shorefront parkway did in 1938. In 1965, a small Dayton Shopping Plaza was opened to replace dozens of mom-and-pop stores that lined the boulevard in the past. At present, new housing is filling empty lots.

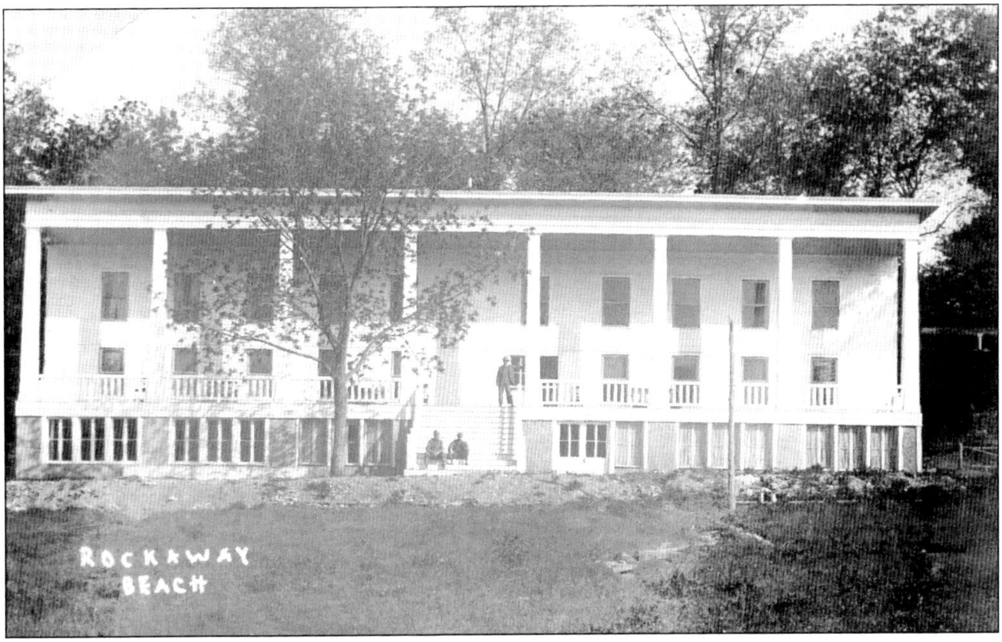

Louis Hammel's hotel on Beach 85th Street started out as shown here, and it was enlarged a few times to wind up as an L-shaped building, two stories higher with the top in a mansard-type roof. A small shed was the first house of the Rockaway Beach Volunteer Fire Department, storing a ladder and bucket wagon pulled by manpower to a fire.

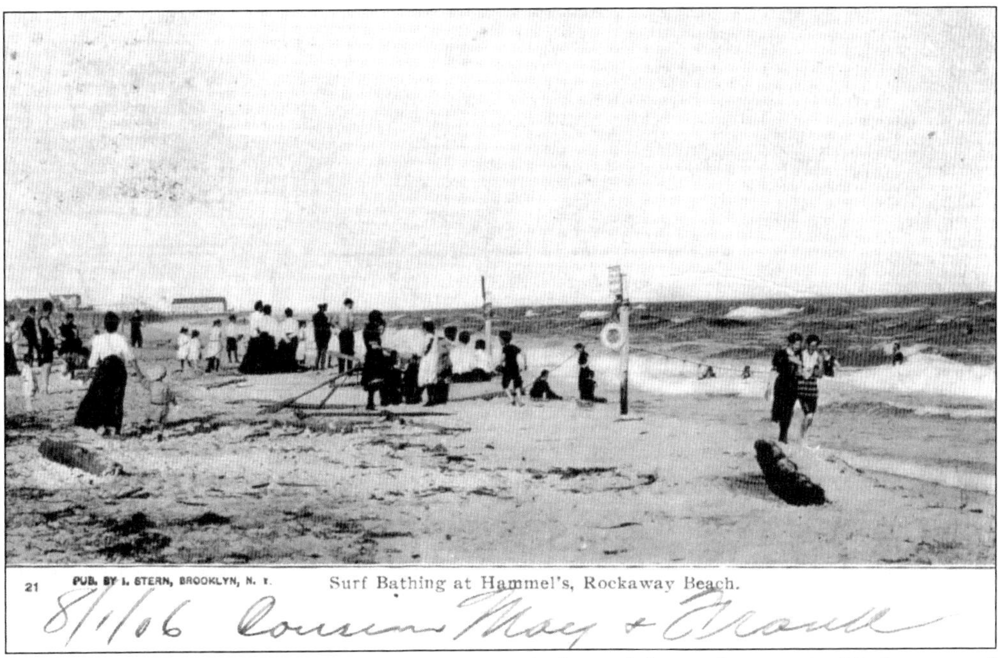

Almost every photograph of the beach at Hammels showed the sand covered with flotsam and jetsam, and more fully dressed people were visible than bathers. The end of the boardwalk is at right center, and the pier theater thereat is in the distance The Hammels Beach was void of a boardwalk until the mid-1920s.

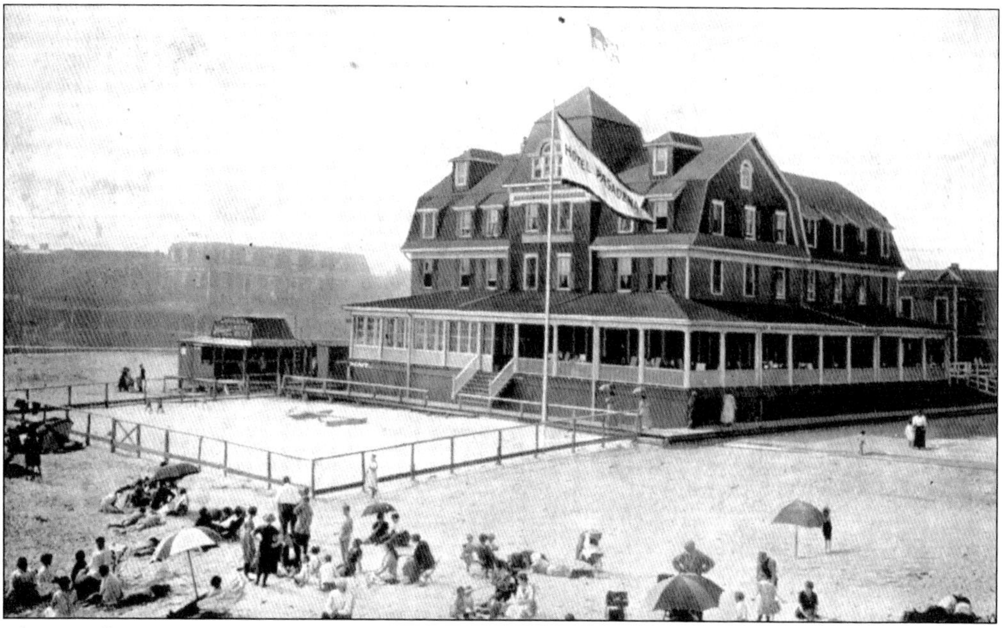

The Hotel Pasadena replaced the West End Hotel that succumbed to fire in 1904. As soon as the spot was available, the Pasadena went up at the beach end of Beach 86th Street. Built three and a half stories high, inside was the biggest saloon in the area. During the winter storm of January 1920, the Pasadena was undermined and collapsed.

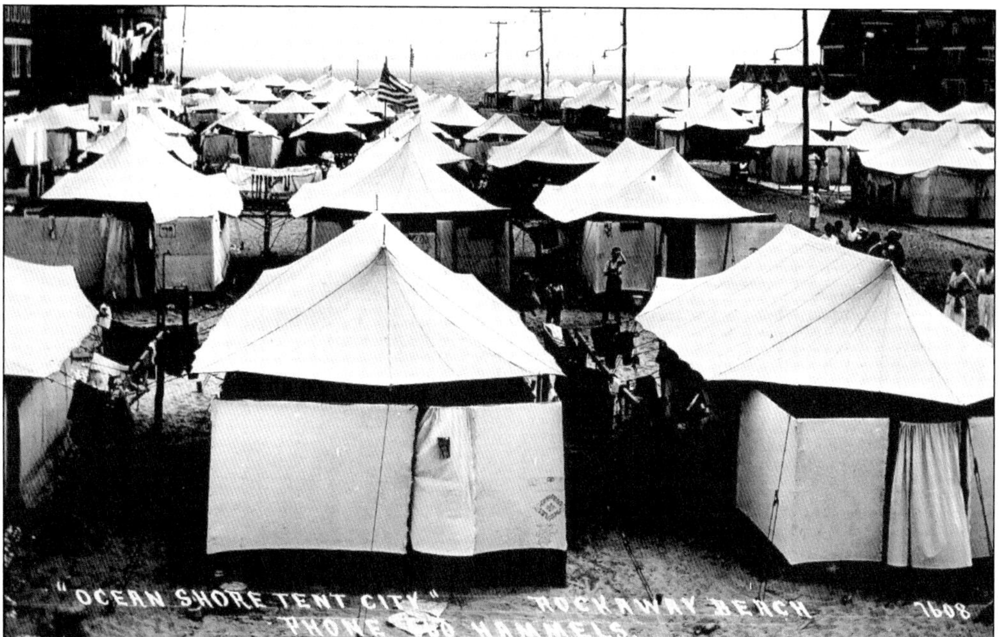

Surrounded by hotels east, west, and north, the Ocean Shore tent city was located on both sides of Beach 76th Street between Rockaway Beach Boulevard and the beach. Built in 1912 with 111 tents, the number rose to 300 in the following year. Although built in West Arverne, the telephone number was Hammels 660, in Rockaway Beach, Queens.

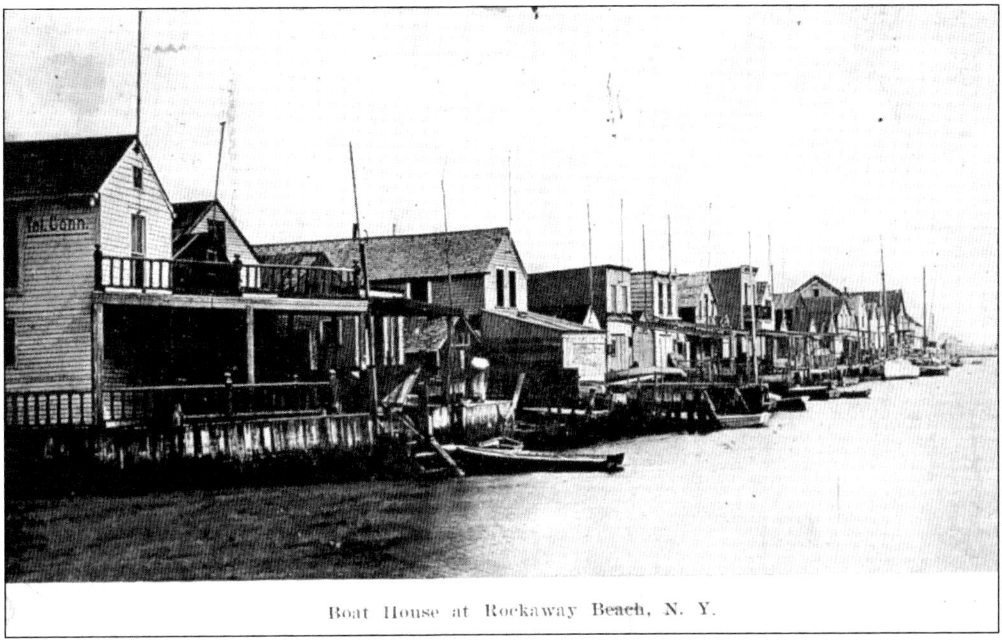

The bay side of Hammels was filled with long rows of summer facilities for fishermen and summer renters. Over the last century, storms and fire have reduced the bay front clusters to a handful on the west side of the bay trestle. These are surrounded by empty pile foundations standing upright in the bay waters off Beach 85th Street.

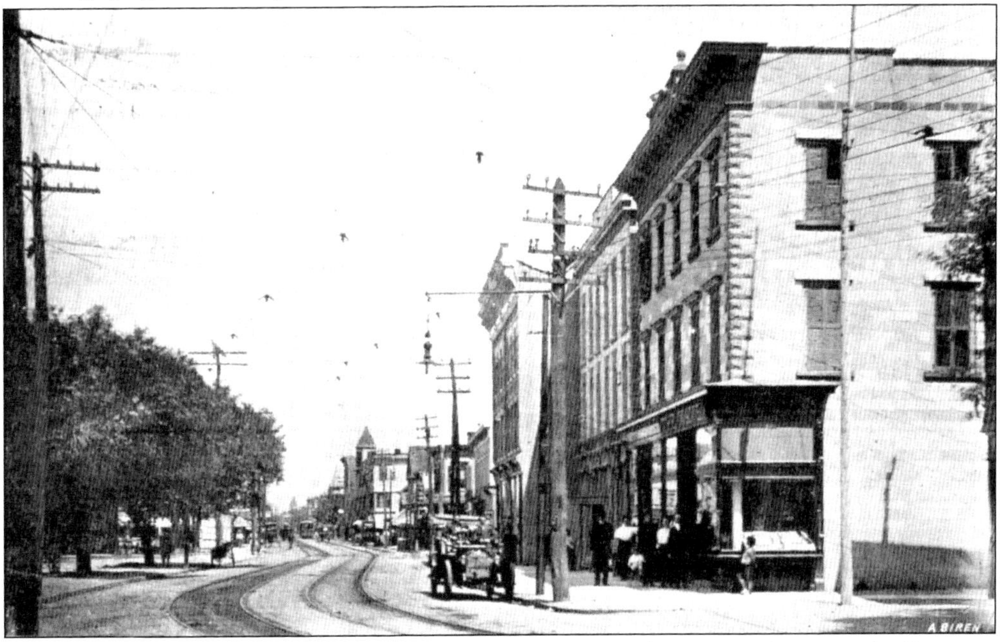

After renting a few locations, the Rockaways' newspaper, known as the *Wave*, built a new building in 1905 on the south side of Rockaway Beach Boulevard at Beach 88th Street. Next door was the Oceanus Post Office at first (later changed to Rockaway Beach). To the right and not shown is the volunteer hook-and-ladder firehouse. The trolley tracks were put in during the 1904 season.

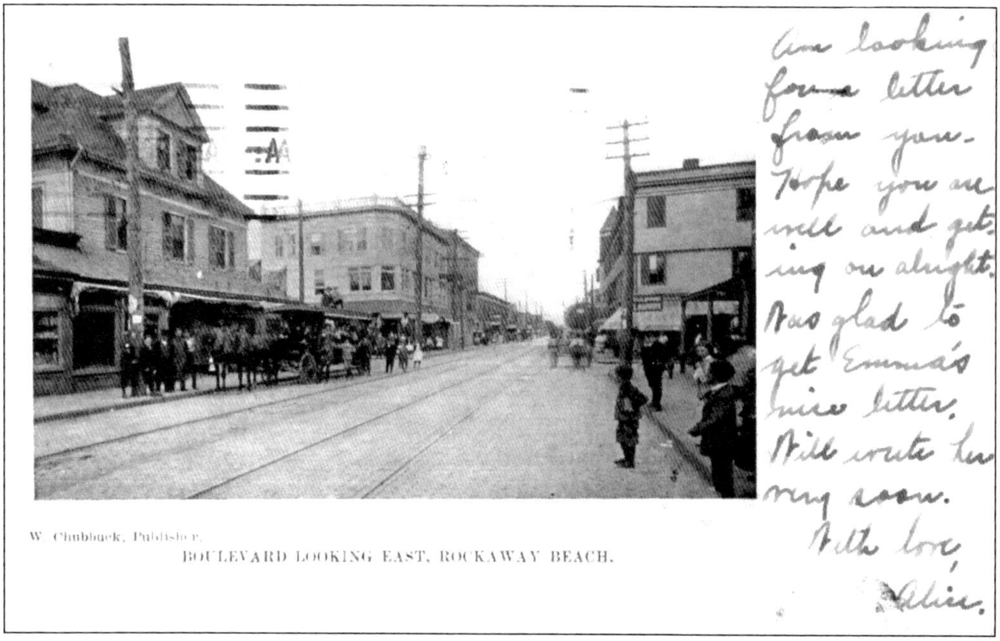

Despite the fact that railroads, trolleys, and bay-landing steamboats provided transport to and from the Rockaways, horse-drawn closed stagecoaches and long open but covered passenger coach wagons (such as the one in front of the Troy house) moved people. The wagon is in front of Rosenthal's Butcher Shop on Beach 68th Street. Opposite is Chubbuck's Drugstore.

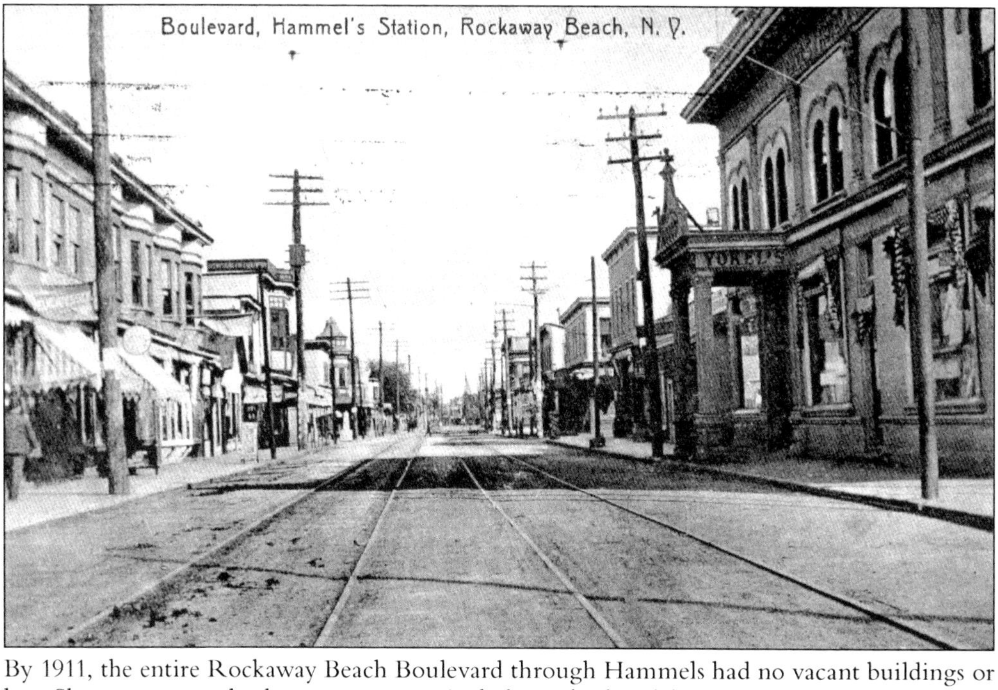

By 1911, the entire Rockaway Beach Boulevard through Hammels had no vacant buildings or lots. Shops, stores, and a department store, including a kosher deli (left), supplied residents with their needs. Beach 84th Street is behind the cameraman, and Yokel's Hotel is on the southeast corner. The first motion pictures were shown here in the early 1900s.

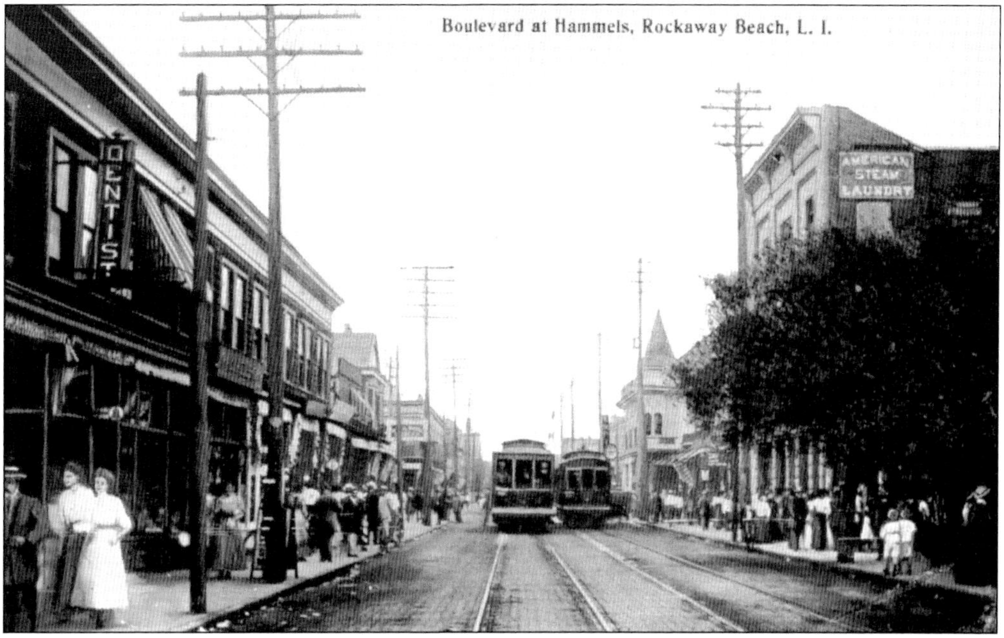

The trolley car on the left has just come down Beach 84th Street from Hammels station (on its trip from Far Rockaway) and is now heading west to Neponsit. On the right, the trolley car will turn left on Beach 84th Street to Hammels station, then turn east on tracks to go back to Far Rockaway. The trolleys ran up to the late 1920s, when buses took over.

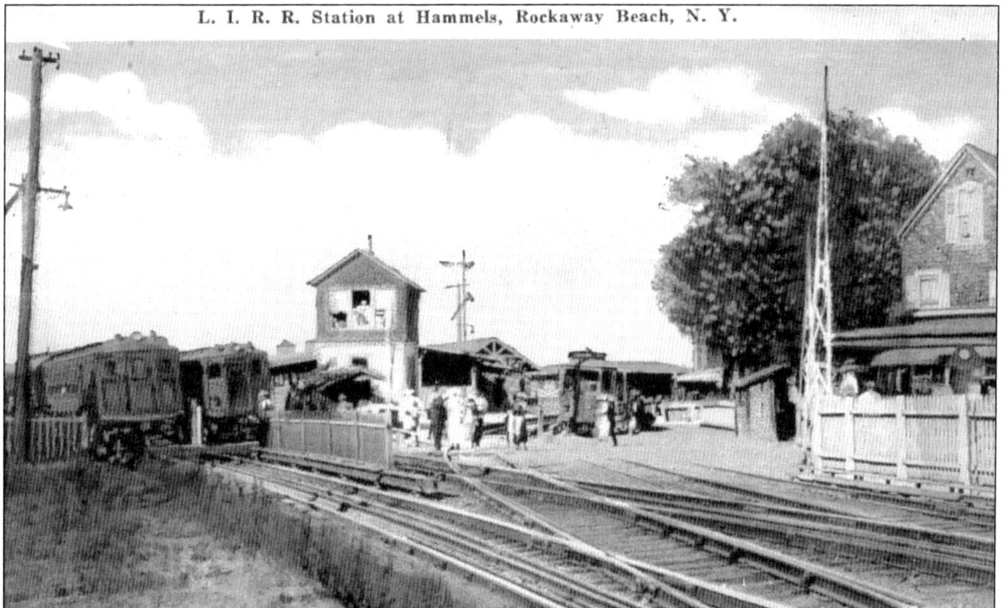

This rare view of the west side of the Hammels station wye shows Beach 84th Street over the fence on the right. A trolley car in the station can also be seen discharging passengers to catch the westbound train to the city next to the station tower or the eastbound train to Rockaway Park to the left. Far Rockaway trains used the east side.

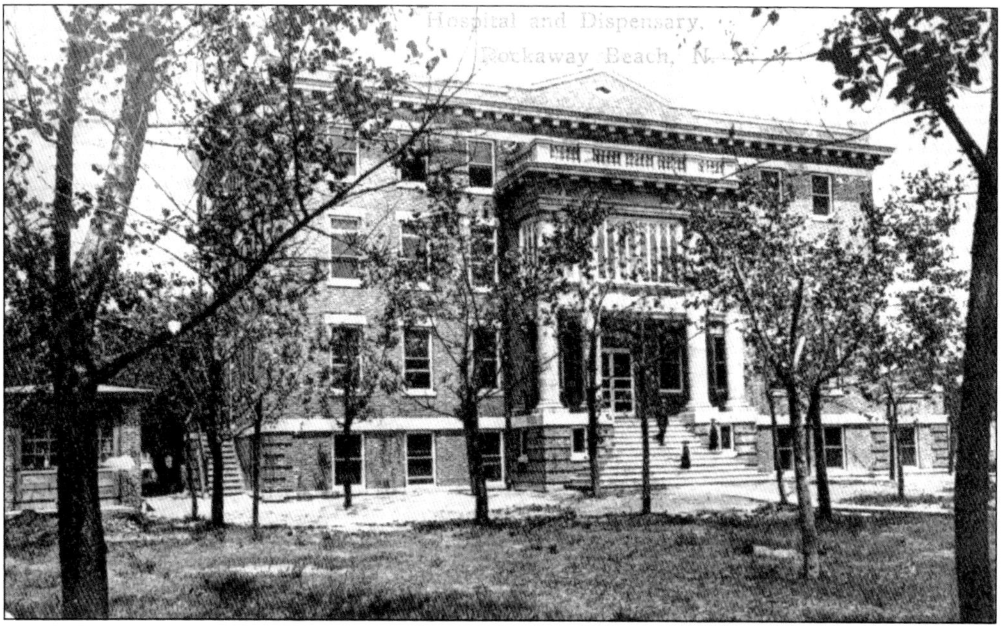

After Louis Hammel sold his Hammel's Hotel to Gottfried Westernacher in 1896, Hammel went into real estate. In 1907, the hotel was lost to fire, and the fire wreck was removed. In the following year, the construction of a hospital began on the site, and in 1911, the new hospital was dedicated. Enlargement occurred there three times.

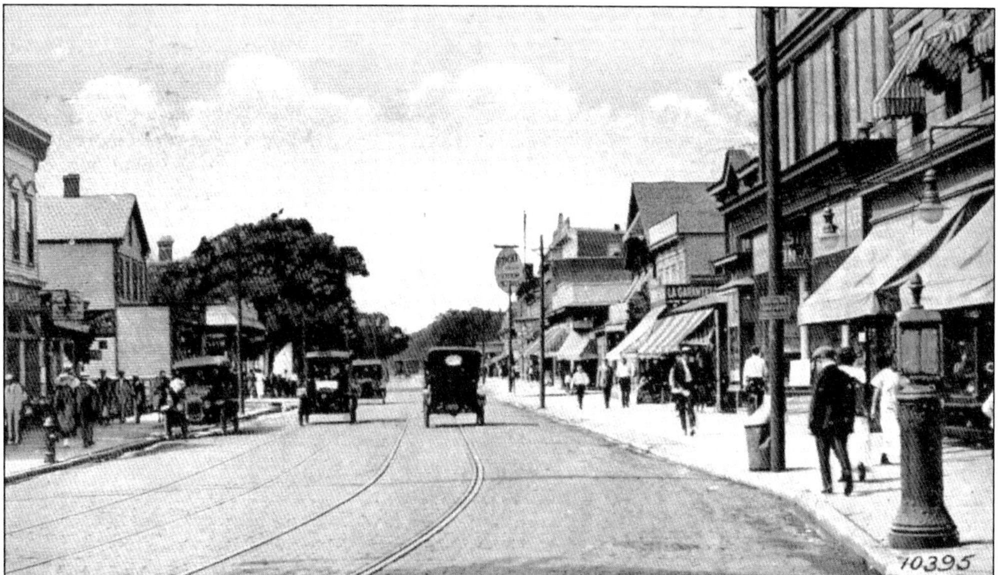

The Hammels Boulevard, as it was called by some, was steadily improved and paved with Belgian blocks to lay flush with the grooved girder trolley tracks put in during 1916. Beach 88th Street is on the right, and the borderline of Hammels on the west. The building on the right (without awnings) is the present *Wave* site, and the Rivoli Movie House (oval sign) is also shown in this 1925 postcard.

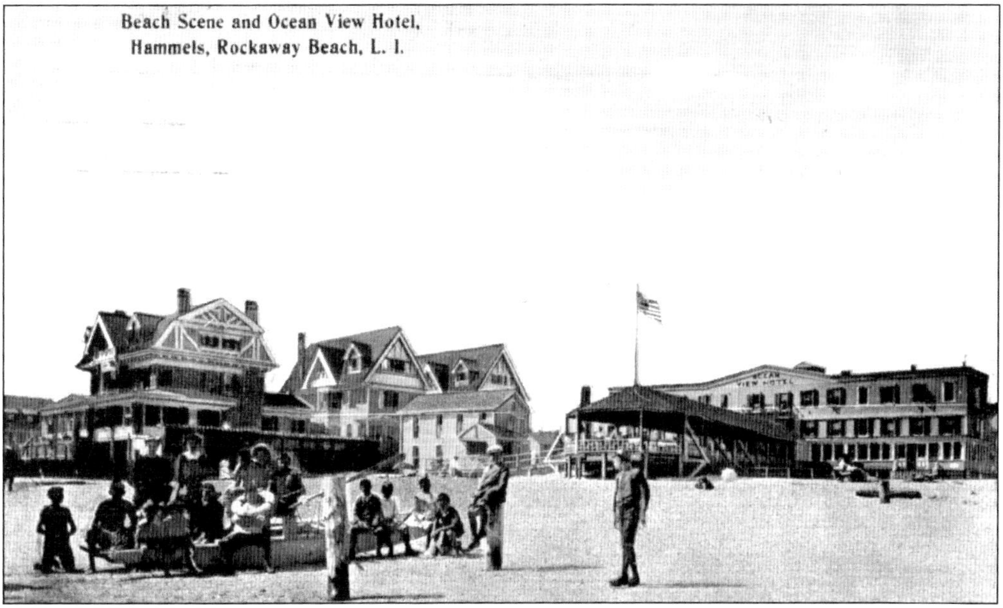

Many hotels were built near the beach in Hammels, but only a few photographs of them have survived. The old Oceanview Hotel (1884–1931) was the first, and it is on the beach at 84th Street. On Beach 85th Street are the East End Cottage, the Normandie, and the Sachsonia Hotels.

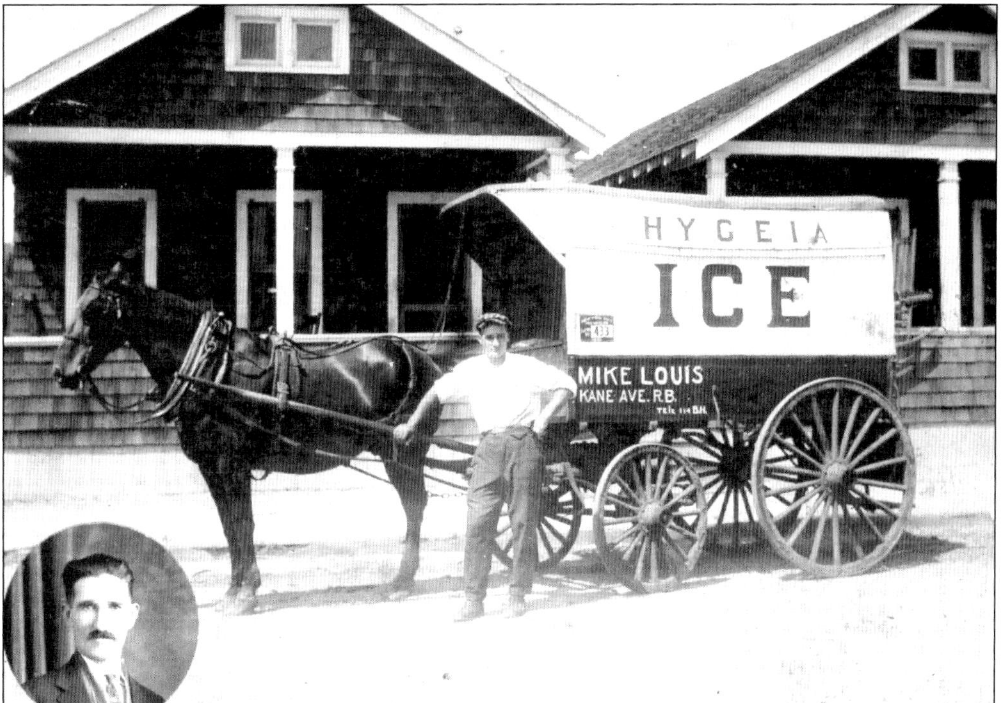

Mike Louis (inset) and his brother-in-law, Sam Ortulan, were founders of the Hygeia Ice Company in 1915. The family business lasted until after World War II when refrigerators began to replace the iceman in the Rockaways. The horse named Tony and the ice wagon were replaced by a Ford Model T truck in 1927.

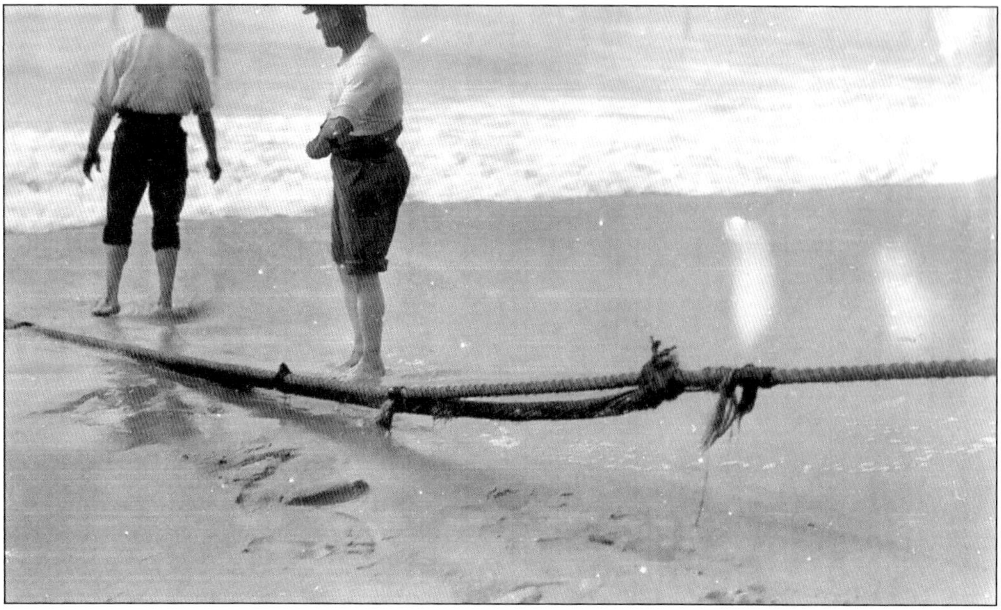

Western Union telegraph workers are shown assisting in the landing of the company's Atlantic cable from the Azores in 1924. The cable was buried in a trench to the Western Union cable building near the Hammels station under Beach 84th Street. A few more underocean cables were landed a few years later. (Courtesy of Mrs. Fred Magic.)

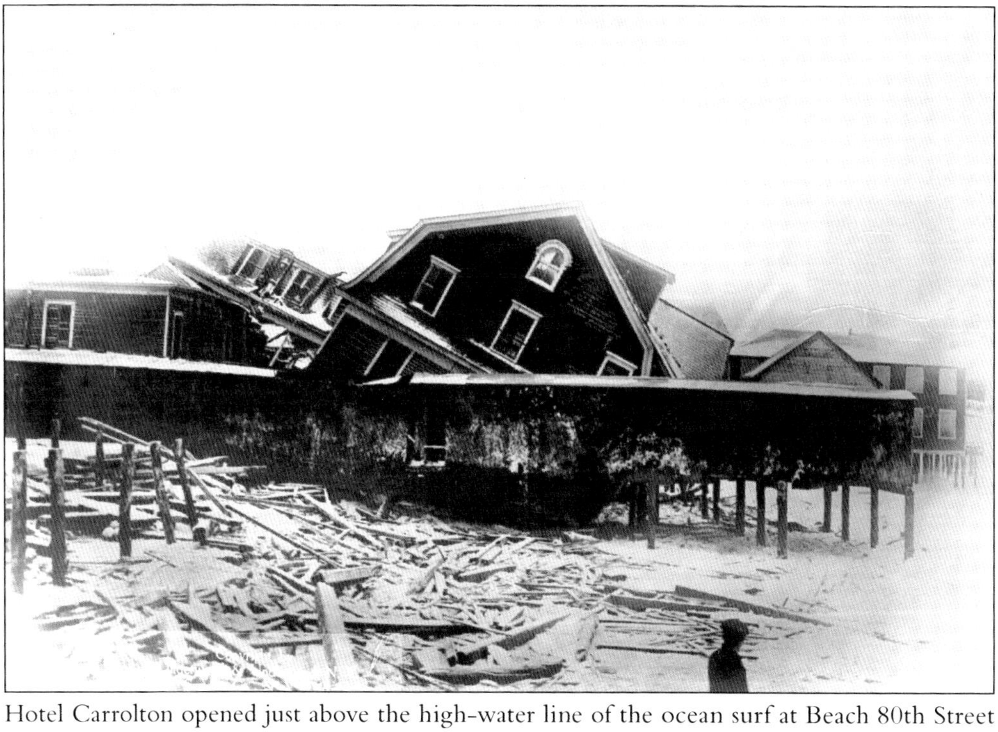

Hotel Carrolton opened just above the high-water line of the ocean surf at Beach 80th Street in 1909. A fire in 1914 damaged the four-story building, and six years later, the wrath of King Neptune ended the career of this beachfront edifice by undermining the brick and concrete basement. Hammels was once West Arverne.

Five

Holland
Beach 88th Street (Old) to Beach 100th Street

The Holland family arrived at their land in the Rockaways by boat on October 3, 1857. Originally from Jamaica, Queens, Michael P. and Fannie R. Holland planned to reopen the old Carhart Hotel on their beach property (at Beach 92nd Street) as their Holland Hotel. The senior Holland died in 1859, leaving his wife with eight children, and young Michael P. assumed most of the fatherly duties at age 11.

A small boat landing was built on the bay side, where the Bay Road entered Holland. The hotel succeeded, especially when the railroad was extended down the peninsula in 1872 and Holland Hotel became a station. Top soil was imported from Far Rockaway, and a good quantity was laid in thickness over the sand, creating a small farm for the hotel. Rainwater was collected in cisterns. The family sold small lots of beach to newcomers, and Fannie built the first Holland steamboat dock 800 feet in length out to Beach Channel so visitors could safely land.

When the bay railroad came in 1880, another station appeared close to the bay side and, together with the completion of the new Rockaway Beach Boulevard several years later, the Holland section experienced severe growing pains. A schoolhouse, a church, hotels, homes, and a post office were added to the increasing bathing facilities.

During the winter of 1884, the Holland dock was carried away by bay ice and was rebuilt with clubs, residences, and hotels lining both sides. Other landowners did not balk at the use of the Holland name as a selling point for property as far as Beach 100th Street because Holland realty was the big kahuna.

After the failure of the big hotel to the west and the bay railroad being absorbed into the Long Island system, the beachside track was taken up after a connection was made to the trestle from Far Rockaway.

After the fire of 1883, Holland Hotel was enlarged by building a new hostelry near the elevated Holland boardwalk in 1901. On the bay front, big yacht clubs and fishing stations appeared, as well as homes and summer-only places. Public School No. 44 was built on the west side of the old boulevard site of the First Congregational Church, and a new church was built where the doughboy monument now stands.

Where there was no more room to build, the bay front west of old Beach 88th Street was bulkheaded, and landfill behind it provided more solid land to build. A year later, the Crossbay

Bridge opened to Broad Channel, Bay Road (now Beach Channel Drive) appeared, and Crossbay Road to Howard Beach opened in 1926. The landfill left all boat clubs and their counterparts high and dry. They were all converted to other uses, and when the stock market crashed in 1929, many lots remained empty for years, but new streets were opened along the bay front to the railroad.

The now empty courthouse was built in the early 1930s, as was the famous Grogan's Restaurant, and for the next several decades, empty lots on the bay side filled with homes and commercial places.

Shorefront parkway construction in 1938 chopped 200 feet off the beachfront north of the boardwalk, opened a decade before, and did the same to all amusement park sites on Holland's west side. More than 800 structures were demolished for a road built by Robert Moses. Rockaways' Playland, the former L. A. Thompson Amusement Park, and Rockaway's Steeplechase Park suffered losses.

In the 1960s, what was left north of the boulevard was demolished for Title I high-rise housing. Playland survived until closing in 1985, and thereafter until the present day, housing of all types has saturated the old Holland section. Police and fire department buildings stand where the first Holland school was built in 1884, and Madelaine Chocolate's firm stands where the old Jamieson and Bond/Weissman Lumber and Building Supply Company pioneered almost a century ago.

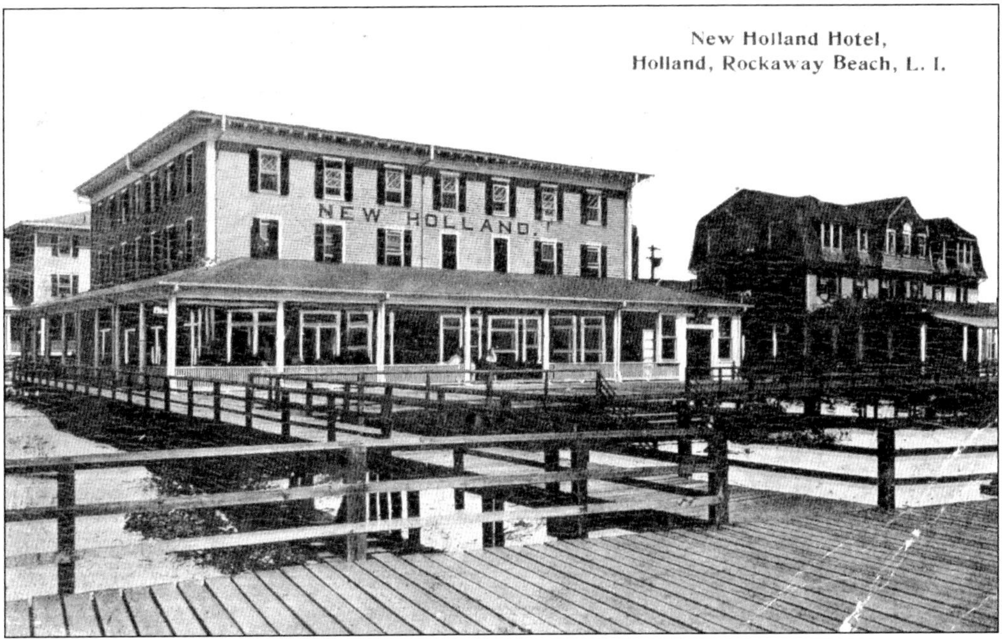

The two earlier Holland Hotels had been built beside the railroad track from Far Rockaway (Holland Avenue) on Beach 91st Street. At Beach 94th Street, the railroad turned northwest up to Seaside. The third Holland Hotel was built near the new Holland boardwalk in 1901. Next to Holland's was McCarthy's with connecting walks around.

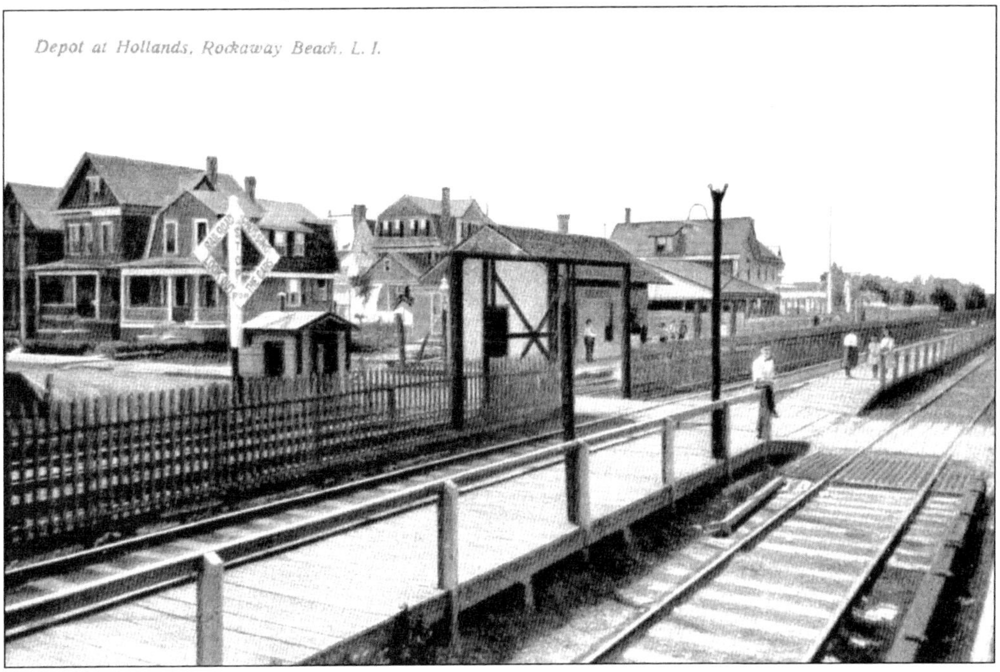

Holland's station was on both sides of the Beach 91st Street crossing, with freight sidings on both sides. The station building (center) has riders awaiting the eastbound (to the city) train, and the four people on the right are going to Rockaway Park. Behind the building is Emmerich's Hotel and Pavilion at Beach 92nd Street.

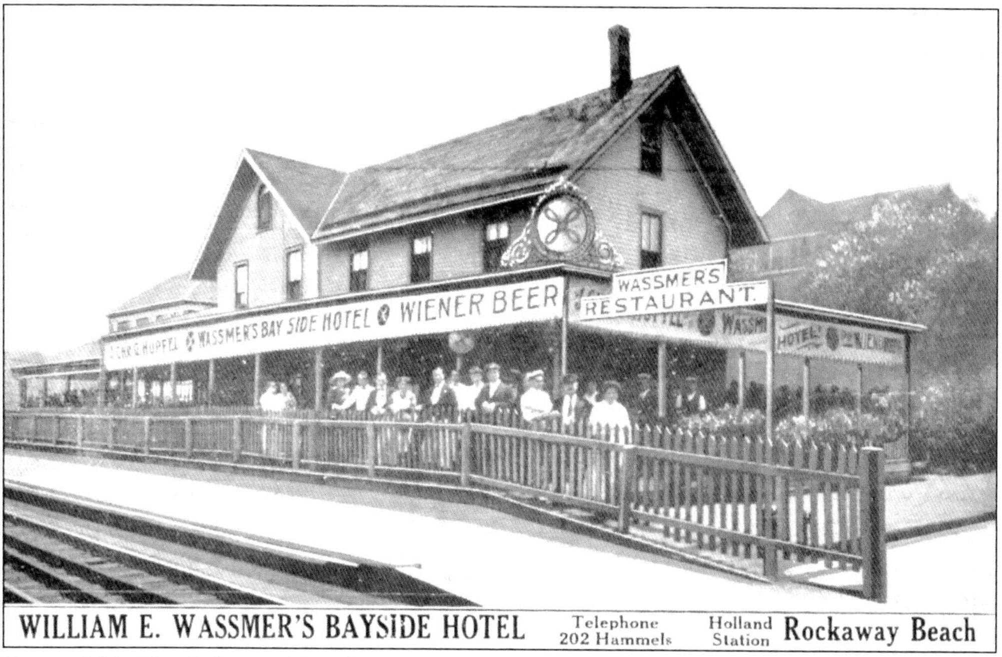

Emmerich's Hotel changed hands in 1916 and became the new Bayside Hotel of William E. Wassmer at the Holland station. On draft was James Christian George Hupfel Weiner beer. Old Brush Place, now Desota Road, is to the right and the station building to the left. The track was elevated in 1943, with the Rockaway Freeway under it.

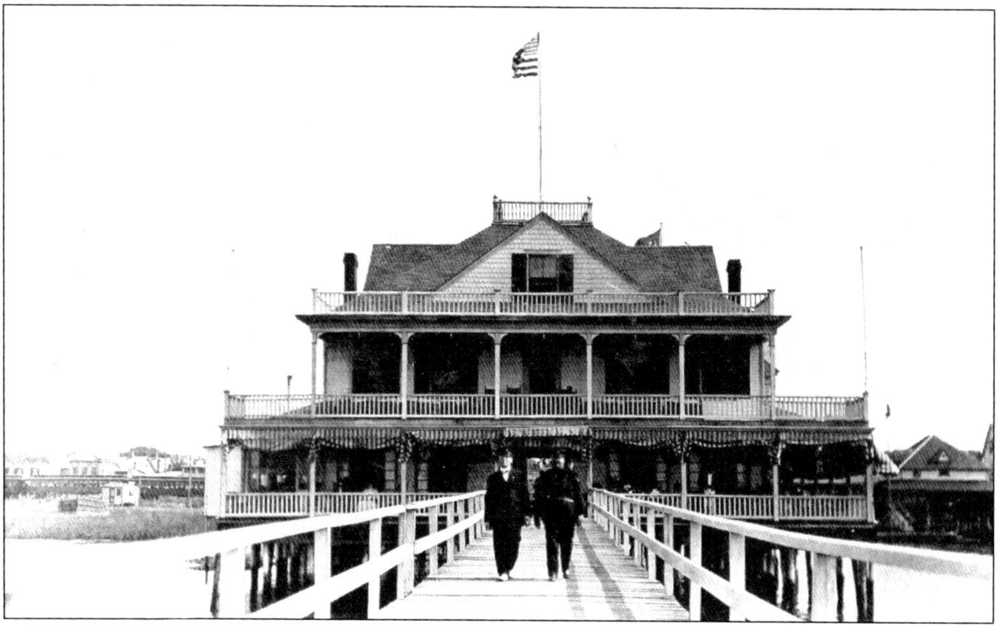

Before the landfill of 1923, the Jamaica Bay Yacht Club jutted out into the bay for several hundred feet. The club's float was on the deep water of Beach Channel. A train is on shore at the left, and the Bayview Club is on the right. After the fill, the club became the Jambay Casino and Restaurant on Beach 90th Street.

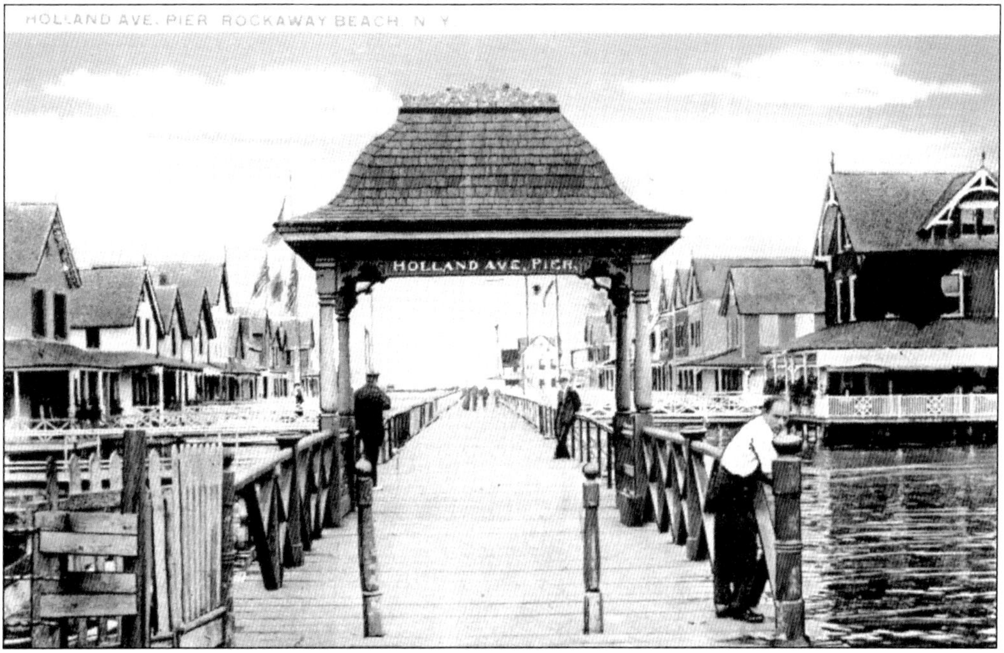

The Holland Avenue Pier was built out into Jamaica Bay in 1885, and after the fill of 1923, Beach 92nd Street was laid out and paved from the railroad to the bulkhead at Beach Channel. The camera is on the railroad's planked crossing and is showing sportsmen's clubs, boat clubs, and residences. At the head is Frey's Hotel (Pier 92).

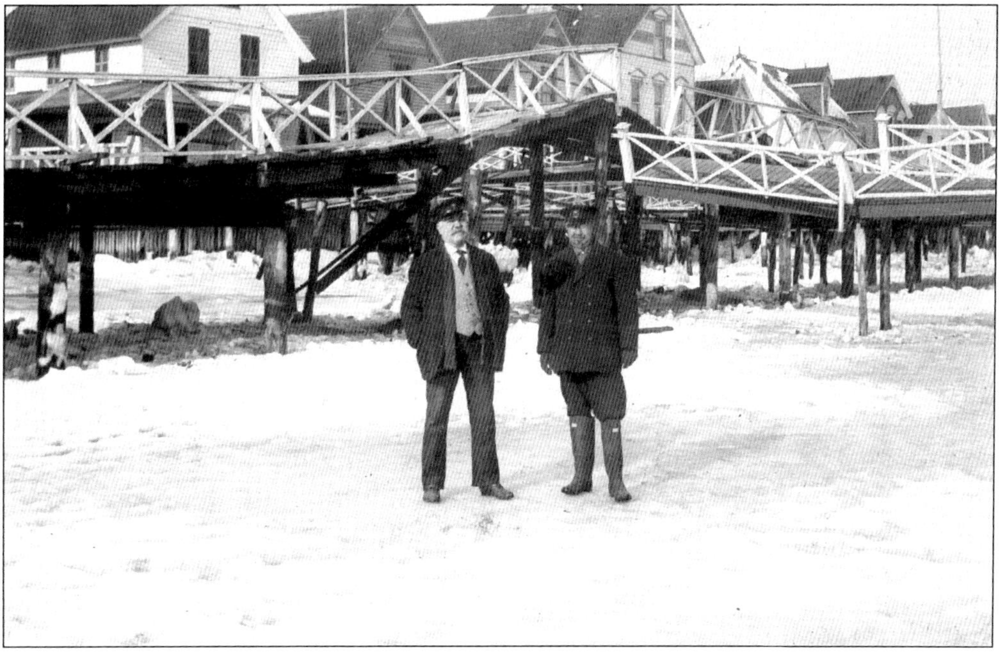

Two city dock inspectors pose for a photograph after a check and report concerning winter ice damage to the Holland Pier at Beach 92nd Street and the bay front. The dock and walks to all side structures look like graphs on paper. It is low tide in this January 1918 photograph, and when the tide comes in, ice frozen to the pilings of wood will raise the structure a bit more.

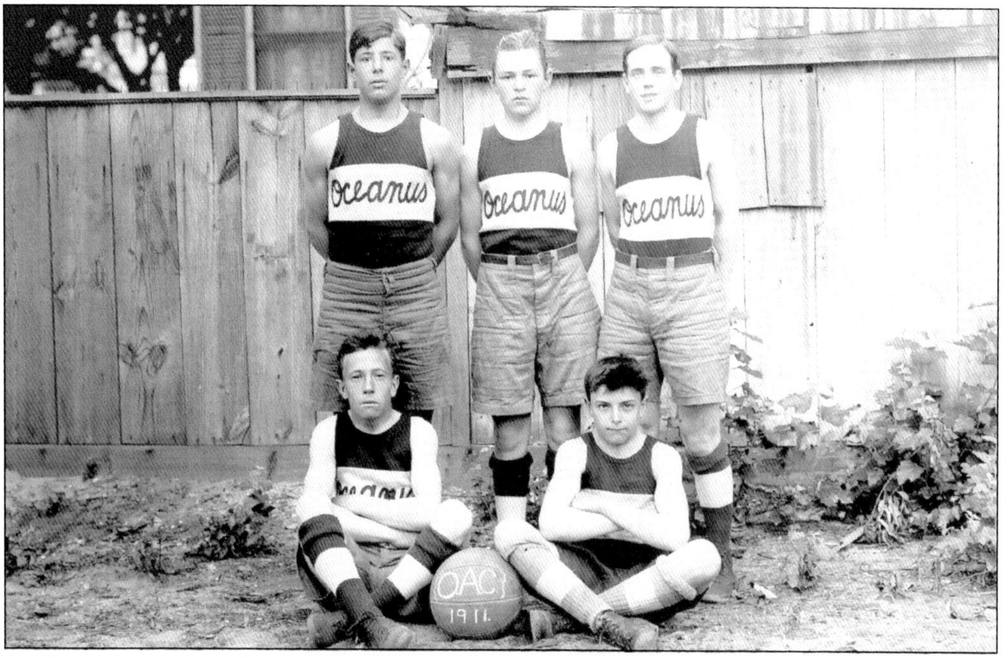

Rockaway Beach was known as Oceanus until the post office changed it in 1905. However, the Oceanus Athletic Club kept the name. Members of its 1911 basketball team, from left to right, are (first row) ? Featherson and ? Rogers; (second row) ? Sabatino, John W. Rogers, and ? Gallagher.

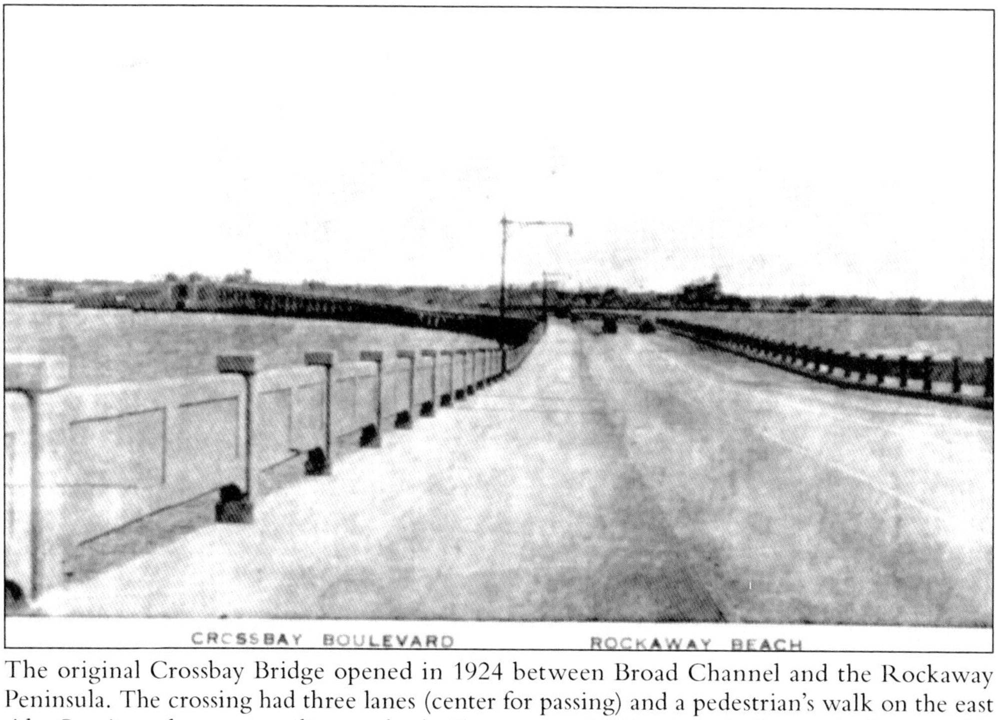

The original Crossbay Bridge opened in 1924 between Broad Channel and the Rockaway Peninsula. The crossing had three lanes (center for passing) and a pedestrian's walk on the east side. Granite and concrete railings on both sides prevented falling into the bay, and rebars provide strength. The bridge was widened in 1938 and rebuilt in 1970.

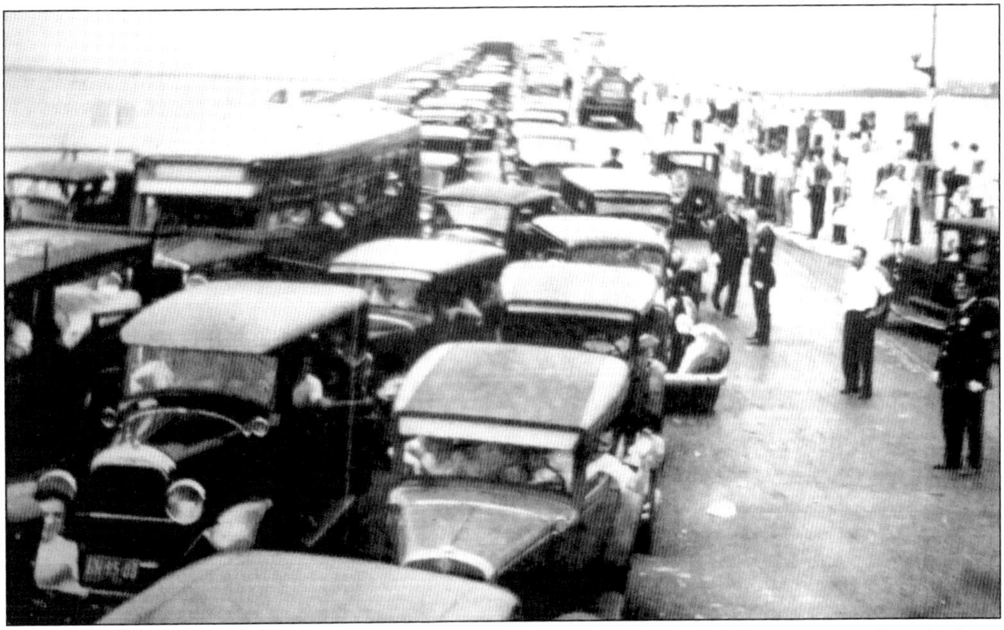

During the summer, especially on weekends and holidays, Crossbay Bridge traffic filled all three lanes during the morning and evening commutes. Shown here is the evening traffic gridlock as throngs of tired and sunburned visitors are backed up from the Broad Channel end over to Rockaway. It is likely that the line is bumper-to-bumper up to Woodhaven and Old Shepherd's Bridge on today's Belt Parkway. (Courtesy of the Chamber of Commerce of the Rockaways.)

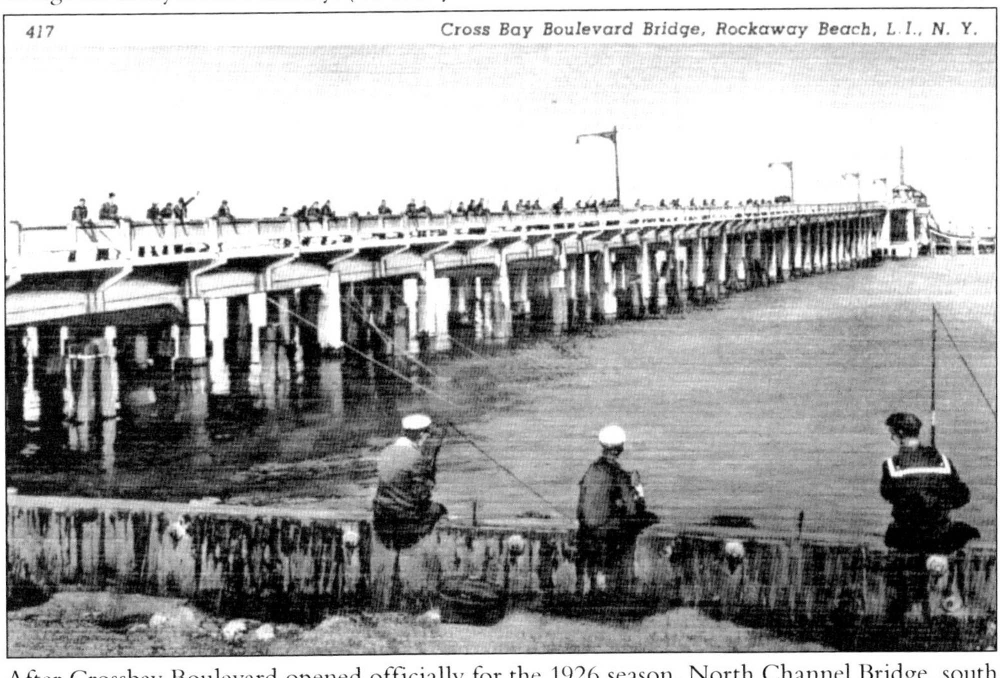

After Crossbay Boulevard opened officially for the 1926 season, North Channel Bridge, south of Howard Beach, and Crossbay Bridge, from Broad Channel to the Rockaways over Beach Channel, became a paradise for fisherman who lined up along the railings to drop their lines into the bay. The new bulkheading also provided seating for anglers and crabbing with scoops.

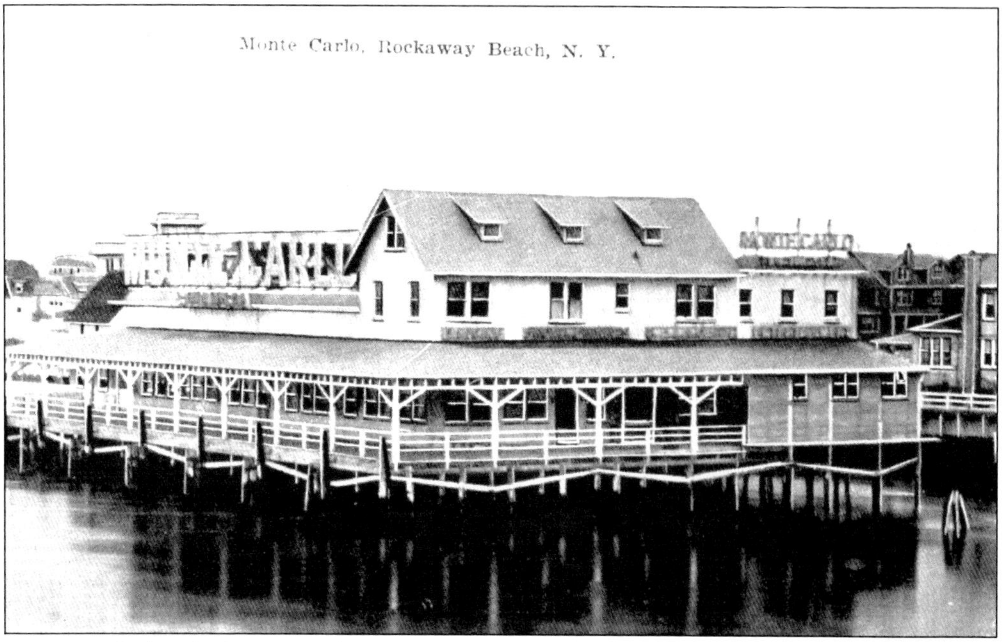

Monte Carlo by the Sea opened in 1926 just west of the Crossbay Bridge landing in Holland. It was the finest nightclub in town, featuring top acts and entertainers. A $3 beefsteak dinner was worn away by music and dancing. The hot spot, at Beach 92nd Street and the bay, bragged at having the first jukebox in the Rockaways. The name was later changed to Moulin Rouge before being torn down in 1937.

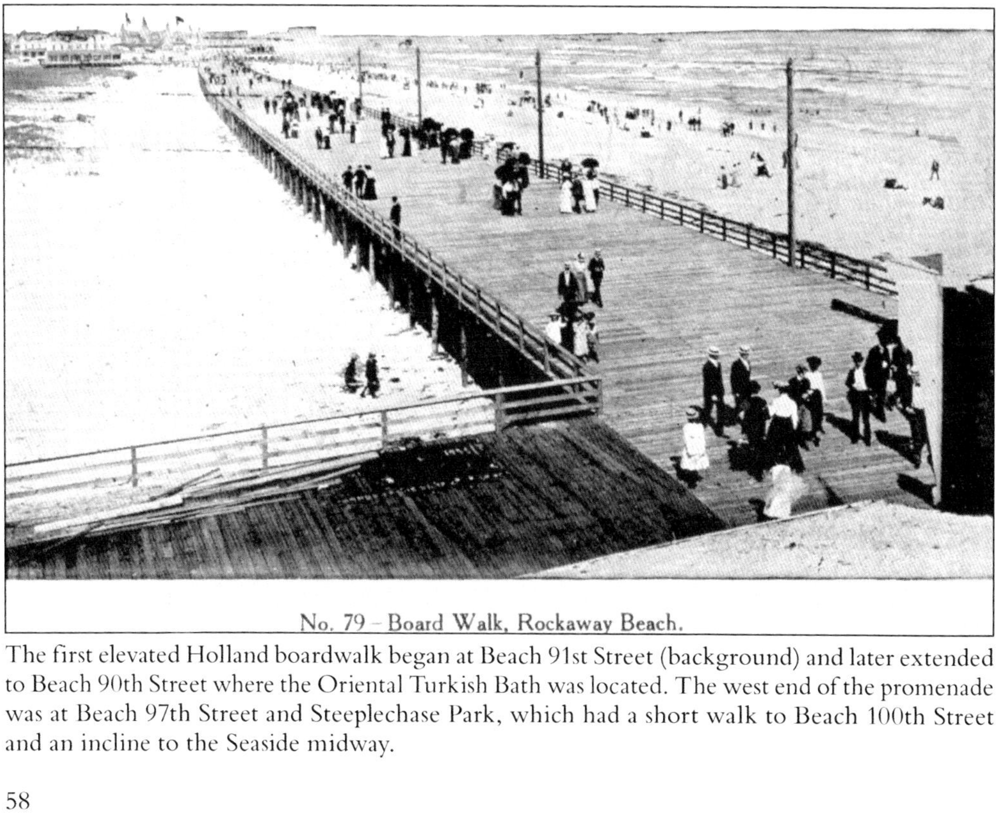

The first elevated Holland boardwalk began at Beach 91st Street (background) and later extended to Beach 90th Street where the Oriental Turkish Bath was located. The west end of the promenade was at Beach 97th Street and Steeplechase Park, which had a short walk to Beach 100th Street and an incline to the Seaside midway.

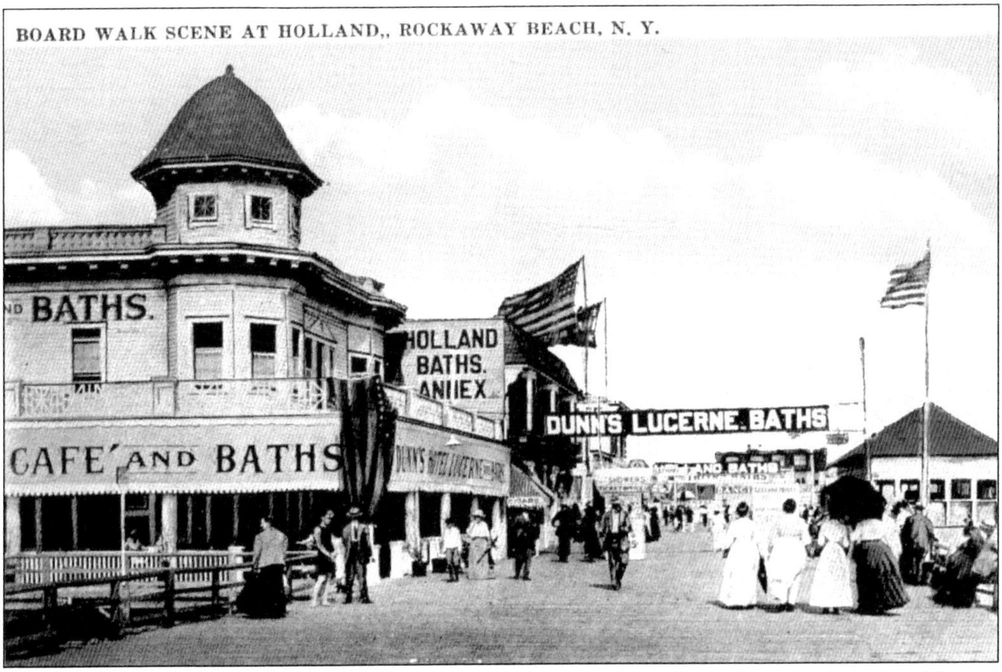

Looking east toward the Oriental Turkish Bath from Beach 95th Street, a myriad of bathhouse signs can be seen, proving that business was excellent. Even the small lunchroom on the right did well. The Hotel Lucerne and café and baths were a favorite, as were the Holland Baths until they were torn down for Shorefront Parkway in 1938.

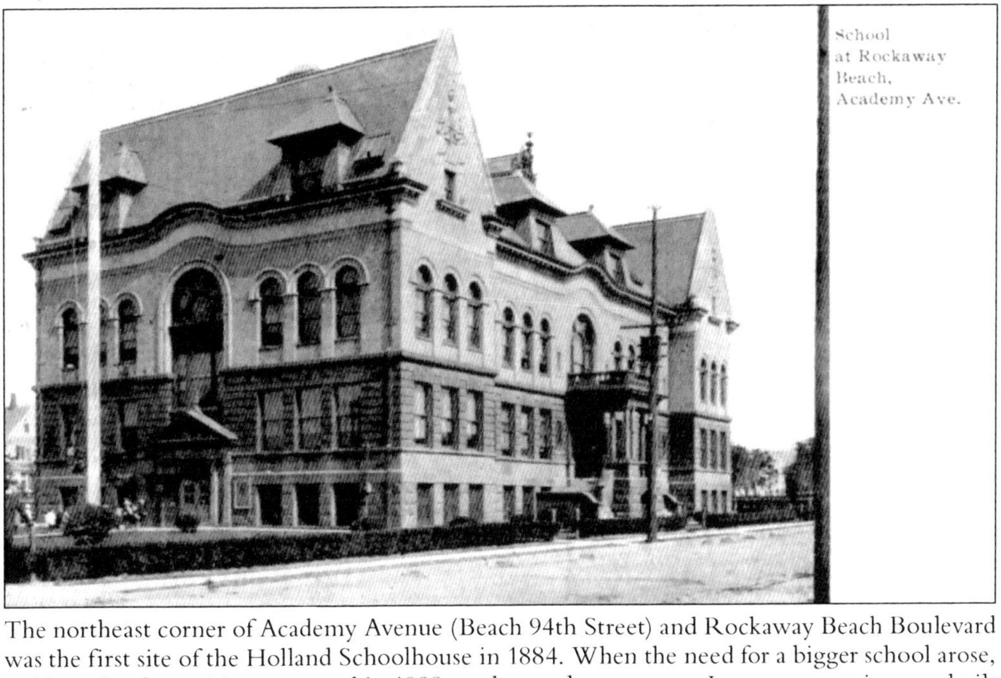

The northeast corner of Academy Avenue (Beach 94th Street) and Rockaway Beach Boulevard was the first site of the Holland Schoolhouse in 1884. When the need for a bigger school arose, Public School No. 44 was opened in 1898 on the southeast corner. Later an extension was built for the populace. The old schoolhouse became a police station, and the peninsula library now occupies the site shown.

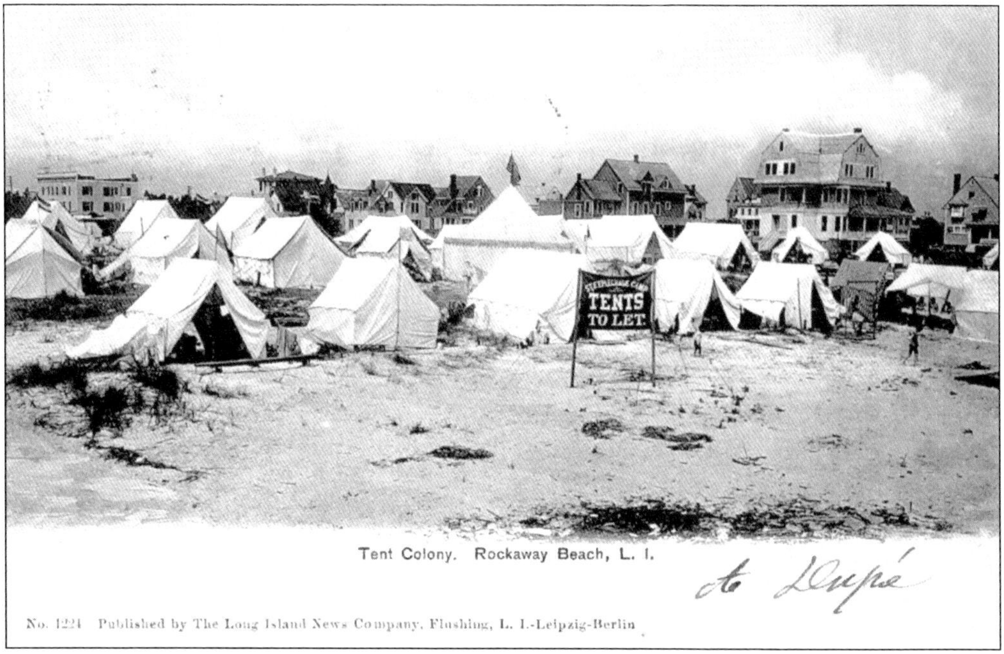

George C. Tilyou of Coney Island opened his amusement park on the west side of Holland in 1901. Steeplechase Park in the Rockaways had the same features as Coney Island between Beach 97th and Beach 100th Streets. The tent camp of 1901 became the L. A. Thompson Amusement Park in 1902, and the L. A. Thompson Scenic Railway was built on the site along with a carousel, restaurant, and bathhouse. (Courtesy of Philip Nybo.)

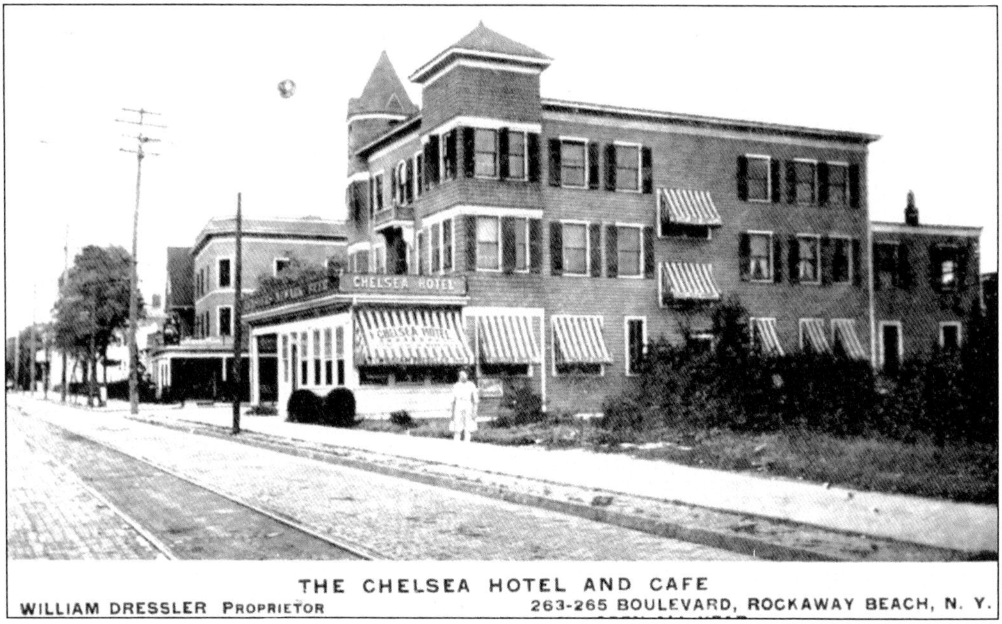

William Dressler's Chelsea Hotel opened in 1907 in front of the L. A. Thompson Scenic Railway on the southwest corner quad on Beach 97th Street and Rockaway Beach Boulevard. It was later known as Thomas Howley's Hotel, which lasted to 1987. Trolley poles are seen on the sidewalk, but overhead wires have been washed out for clarity of the scene.

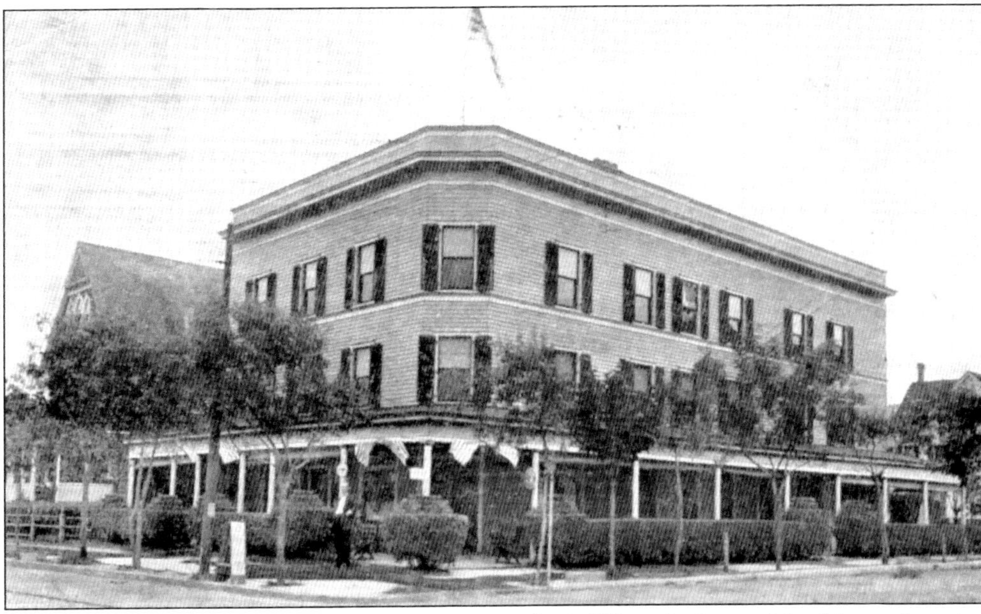

Stacom's Narragansett House was built in 1901 as the William A. Barnes Hotel in conjunction with George C. Tilyou's new amusement park called Steeplechase. Barnes also had a bathhouse and some attractions in the park. Stacom took it over in 1909, but most fans of Irishtown remember it as Hickey's and the Fiddler's Green. The building collapsed in the late 1990s and was removed.

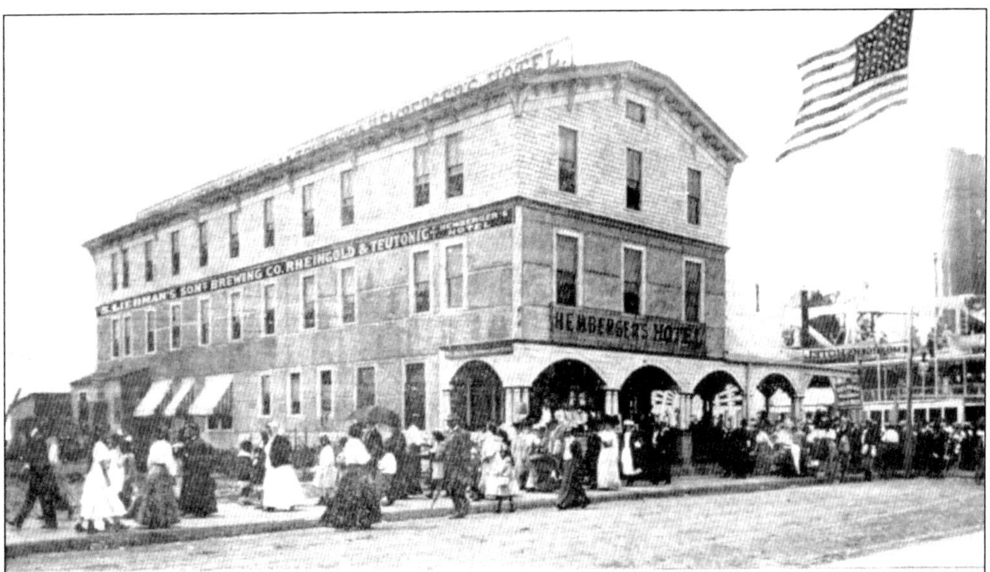

After Thompson, Tilyou, and John Jamieson built the new steamer dock at the foot of Beach 98th Street for the 1905 season, Louis Hemberger built a singe-story hotel and pavilion. By 1910, the place was three stories high and had the advantage of steamer passengers both going to and coming from the beach and amusement areas. A program for the removal of old buildings in 1944 demolished some.

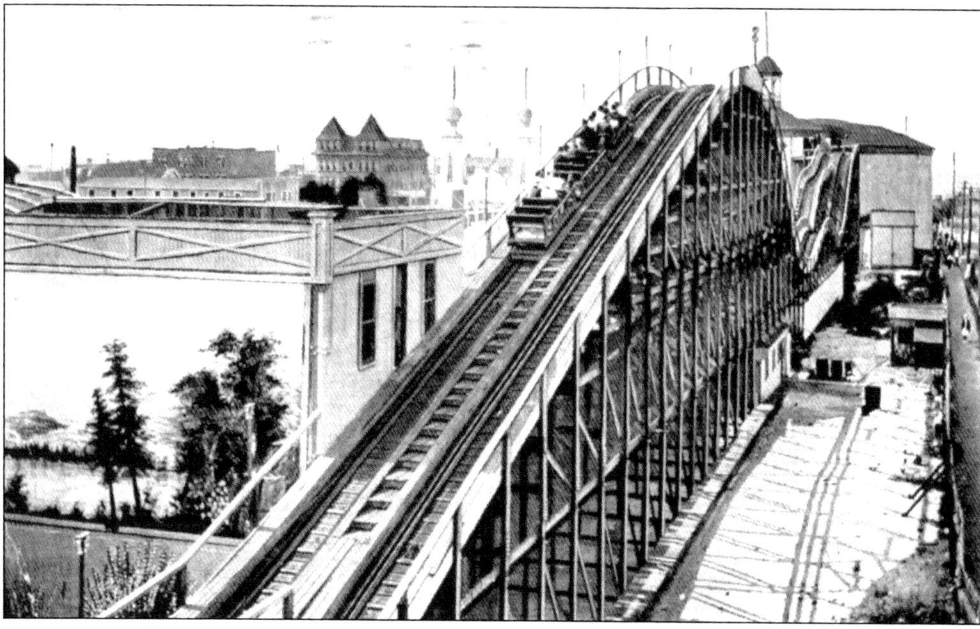

LaMarcus A. Thompson invented the roller coaster in 1884 and ran what was called a switchback—a ride on an up and down rail system where cars full of people went out and back. Rockaway's Seaside had two such rides in 1888. The coaster evolved into a scenic railway where cars rode through buildings filled with colorful scenes.

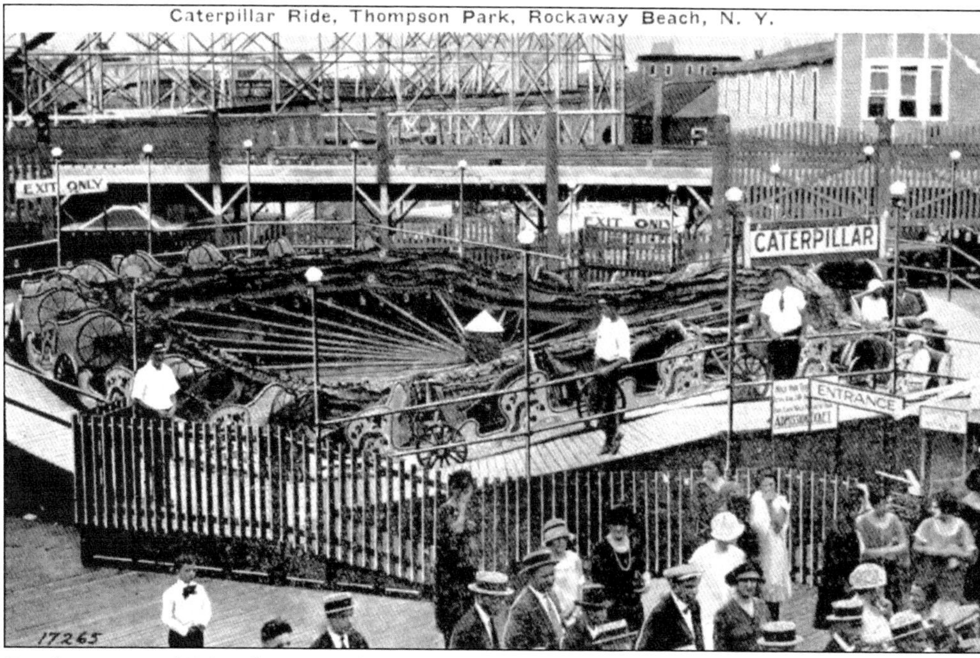

For the season of 1924, the L. A. Thompson Amusement Park opened after a massive rebuilding featuring a giant of a coaster called the Whirlwind but dubbed the Hurricane by the riders. The first dip was seven and a half stories high. Kiddie rides were featured, as well as a glowworm caterpillar ride, a fun house, and circle airplane swings. The Thompson park surpassed the other parks, Steeplechase and Seaside.

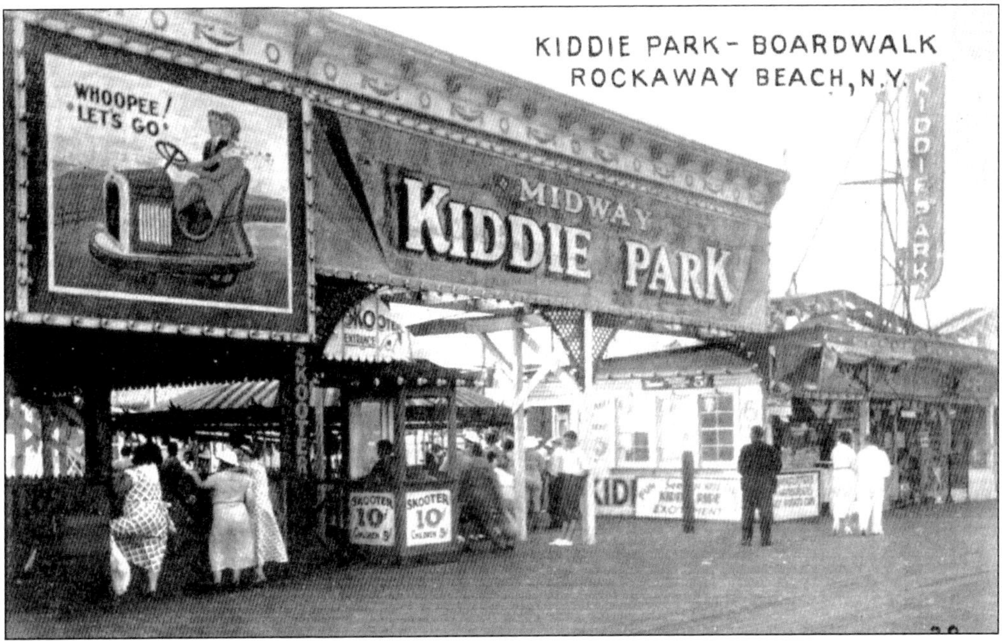

When the Thompson park was built, William Auer lost his small tent rental concession inside the park. He then joined forces with Morris Kraus, who ran a kiddie ride park nearby. Together they opened a new kiddie park and tent city along the boardwalk on Beach 97th Street. The building of Shorefront Parkway in 1938 by Robert Moses reduced the park's size by two-thirds.

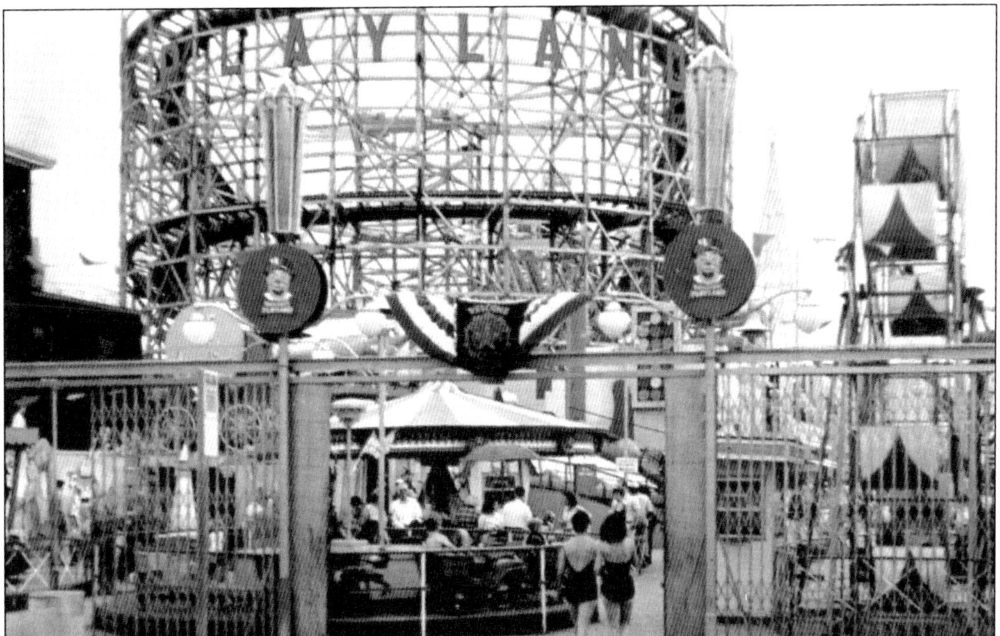

The L. A. Thompson Amusement Park was sold to the Geist Group of local men in 1928. The park was rebuilt and opened as Rockaways' Playland with an Olympic-size swimming pool, a giant theater and boxing area, a scooter ride, and a leftover Dentzel carousel. A. Joseph Geist and family ran the park until it closed in 1985.

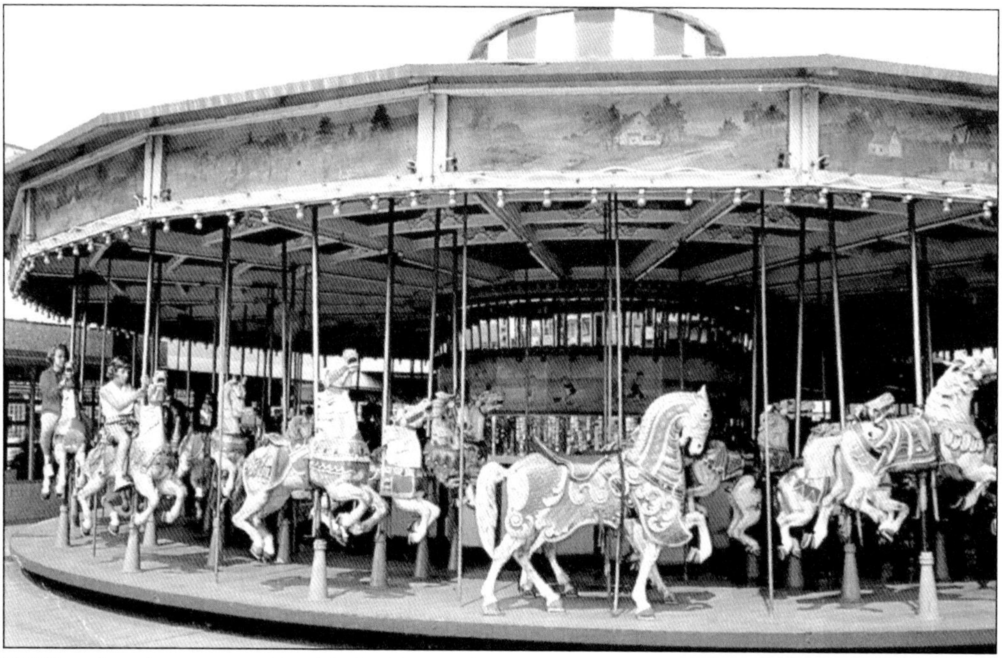

William Nunley came to Seaside in 1914 and ran this four-abreast carousel with outside horses that went up and down for brass ring catchers until 1938. A move was made into Rockaways' Playland, which also lost 200 feet of its park when Robert Moses built Shorefront Parkway. Then years later, Nunley's moved out of Playland to a new boulevard site on Beach 98th Street where it stayed until 1959.

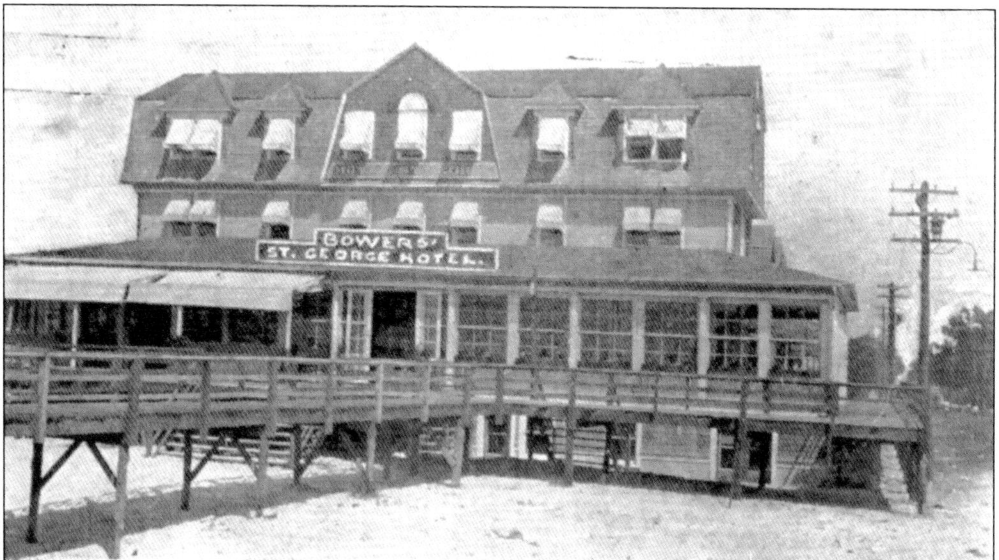

BOWERS' ST. GEORGE HOTEL, HOLLANDS, ROCKAWAY BEACH, N. Y.

McCarthy's Hotel on Beach 91st Street was built in 1905, and the Ben Mark, in 1907, was the new name. After four years, the hotel changed hands again to become Bower's Prince George with a Russian restaurant. Bower's, like Holland's, was connected to the old Holland boardwalk. Both were demolished for Shorefront Parkway in 1938.

Six

SEASIDE
BEACH 100TH STREET TO BEACH 108TH STREET

Seaside, founded by James S. Remsen, started after the Civil War. George C. Tilyou of Coney Island fame started his Steeplechase Park at Rockaway in 1901; LaMarcus A. Thompson started his amusement park in 1902 as part of Steeplechase Park and was on his own in 1905. The Thompson park became Rockaway's Playland in 1928.

When Remsen acquired his terra incognita at Rockaway Beach from Beach 94th Street to Beach 126th Street, people at the auction thought he was crazy to buy a place that the ocean, with a storm, could take away in a heartbeat.

There was a small chowder house and boat landing visited by boaters and fishermen at Beach 103rd Street on the bay front, close to Bay Road from Far Rockaway.

With the Civil War (1861–1865) coming to a boil, materials essential to the war effort prevented any capital construction at what Remsen called his seaside park. In the meantime, he sold some small lots in the area of Beach 108th Street near the bay, and in doing so, improved his hotel, Seaside House.

At the war's end, Remsen traded his land, excepting a portion from Beach 100th Street to Beach 107th Street (Seaside Park) to have a railroad built from east New York in Brooklyn to Canarsie Pier on the Brooklyn bay front, as well as a steamboat line from Canarsie to his Seaside dock via the waters of Jamaica Bay. The Brooklyn and Rockaway Beach Railroad and Steamboat Line began operating in 1867, bringing passengers to the new two-story Seaside House Hotel, which featured first-class hotel accommodations, fine cuisine, entertainment, libations, or just plain clams and beer. Bathing facilities were at the beach end of a plank road laid on the sand. This was Hicks Street (later Hollywood Avenue and now Beach 101st Street).

The railroad from Far Rockaway came west to Seaside in 1872, and a few more steamers were added to the run from Canarsie. In 1876, William Wainwright, Remsen's new partner, established a system that allowed more steamers to come to the Seaside dock from the city through the treacherous and constantly changing Rockaway inlet. The system worked well, and all of the bay side docks of the Rockaways benefited by the increased steamer traffic in summer. In 1880, the new bay railroad passed through on the way to the big hotel just to the west, and a second railroad stop or station appeared by Seaside House Hotel.

The beachside facilities expanded rapidly as many more hotels and baths were built and catchpenny amusements were added, as were a rifle range and an ocean pier built of iron out into the ocean at Beach 105th Street for 1,080 feet. In turn, Seaside House Hotel was enlarged also.

After the failure of the big hotel and railroad, the latter was taken over by the Long Island line, which removed the track it had closer to the beach. The old right-of-way became Grand Central Boulevard, lined with many hotels.

"Uncle Jim" Remsen rarely sold land outright, and he rented every square foot he could squeeze out of the sand. When he died in 1887, he left a good-sized fortune to his heirs.

The *New York Times* Rockaway column in the summer of 1888 reported that among all other amusements, two switchback coasters were thrilling riders at the Seaside amusement section. The switchback ride was invented by LaMarcus A. Thompson in 1884, who is known as the "inventor of gravity" and whose Rockaway Amusement Park became Rockaways' Playland in 1928.

The whole of Seaside from ocean to bay was reduced to steaming ashes after the season of 1892 closed in September. The great holocaust could be seen for miles, but the train station was saved by firemen who constantly hosed it down as more equipment was coming from afar by train. The rebuilding began while the ashes were still steaming. It was not long until Seaside was back in full swing, and in 1896, the giant Shoot-the-Chutes water ride thrilled thousands of riders who asked for rerides. Two bigger switchback coasters at the beach side had long lines, as did the chutes on the bayside across the street from Seaside House. An amusement midway was built at the beach side (a plank walk about 20 feet wide), and the bulk of attractions were built here, with carousel band organs cranking out nice but loud music.

At the start of the 20th century, Steeplechase came to Rockaway in 1901, L. A. Thompson Amusement Park opened out of Steeplechase in 1905, thus making the Rockaways a serious competitor of Brooklyn's Coney Island for many years to come. The switchbacks gave way to scenic railways that gave way to higher and longer roller coasters, of which Rockaway Beach had four—the Hurricane, the Jackrabbit, the Thunderbolt, and the Thriller. It would fill an encyclopedia to tell of the many attractions that appeared here over the following years. Outstanding was the giant 400-tent camp Chaffee at the west side of the section boulevard to Beach 106th and Beach 109th Streets. By 1914, bungalows began to replace tents to saturate Seaside ocean to bay.

Rockaways' Playland outlasted all, including Coney Island, closing in 1985 and finally torn down for housing in 1987.

Playland's management had stayed the course, surviving even Robert Moses's attempts to be rid of it, by the Geist family adhering to the old colonial saying "Mind your business." Moses called Rockaway a "cheap amusement area," ditto for Coney, which he also chastised as cheap thrills. High-rise buildings and roads are his legacy here, and a rash of housing now excites the realtors on the peninsula. Beach Channel High School and a sewage treatment plant, plus new and bigger schools, were also built by the city.

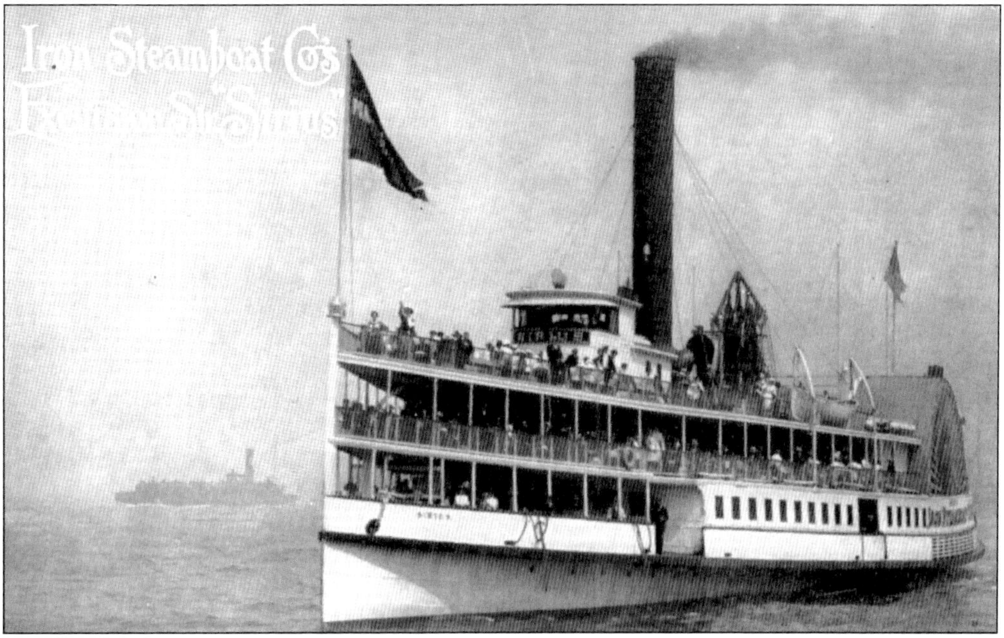

The Iron Steamboat Company's fleet of boats brought passengers to the Rockaways from the early 1880s to 1926. Each boat in the fleet of a dozen was named for a star constellation. Seen here is the *Sirius*.

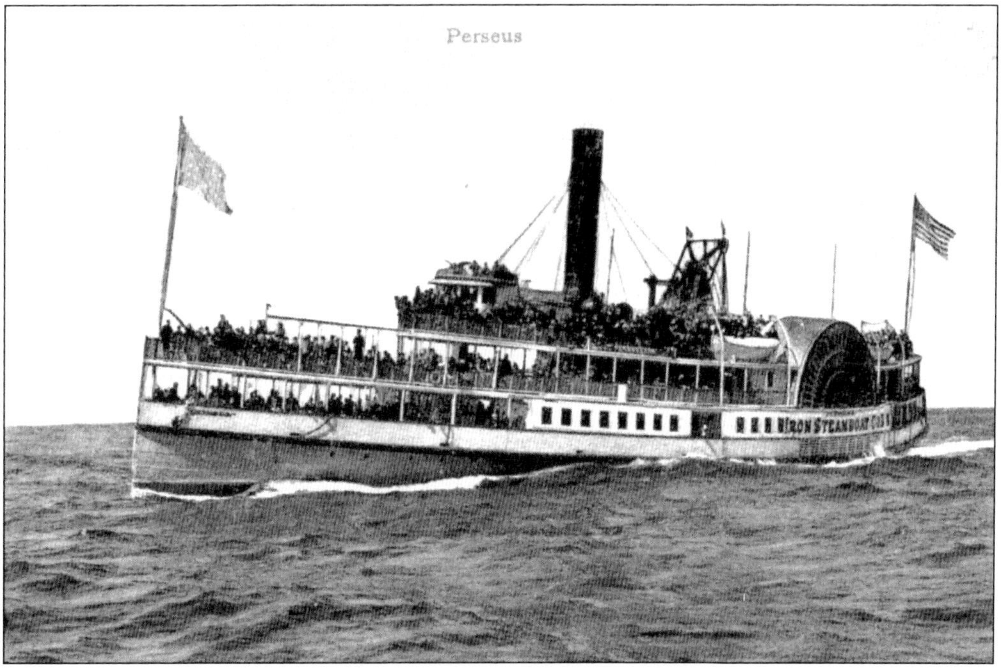

The steamboat *Perseus* is another of the Iron Steamboat Company vessels that came to the Rockaways almost a century ago. When Crossbay Road was opened in 1926, cars came loaded with people. The steamers waned, and companies went into bankruptcy. The iron steamers were auctioned off in 1931 at a severe loss of worth.

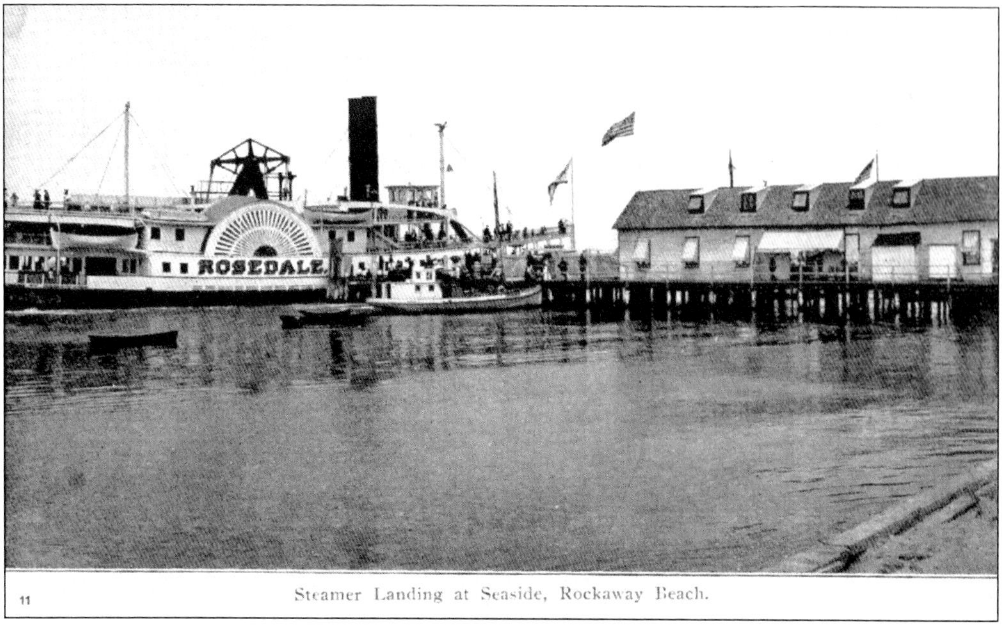

The steamer *Rosedale* takes on passengers at Seaside dock No. 1, one of the three docks built on the bay side by Seaside House Hotel. Looking back in retrospect, the dock would be across Beach Channel Drive and the vessel in front of Beach Channel High School.

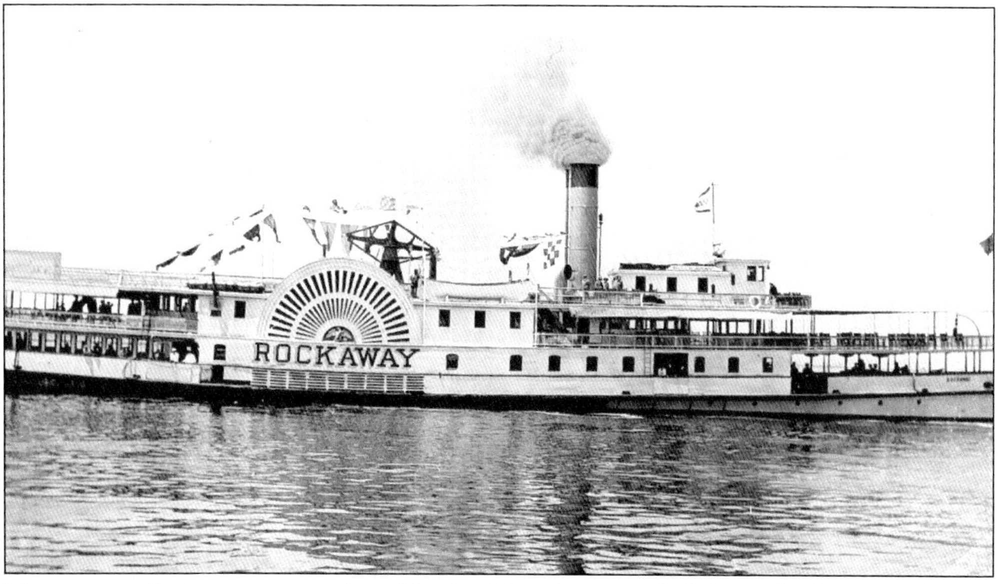

The steamer *Rockaway* was purchased by local hotel men and christened after a refit by the daughter of William Wainwright, who was responsible for getting the boats to come to the Rockaways through Rockaway Inlet. It was a symbolic gesture, for the boat only made several trips for the lack of interest by the public in 1925.

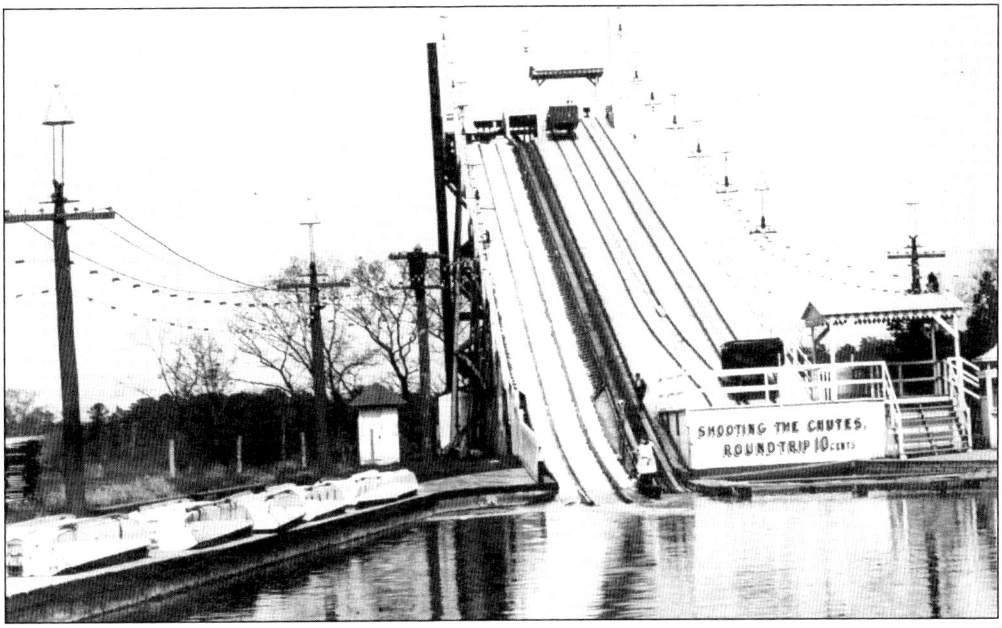

Shoot-the-Chutes was the largest water ride built in Seaside across the way from Seaside House Hotel. Riders went up the 80-foot tower on an inclined rail-type elevator, and they came down the sluice chute in a boat that fishtailed across the artificial lake. Built in 1896, the Shoot-the-Chutes closed in 1902 as amusements nearer the beach drew the crowds.

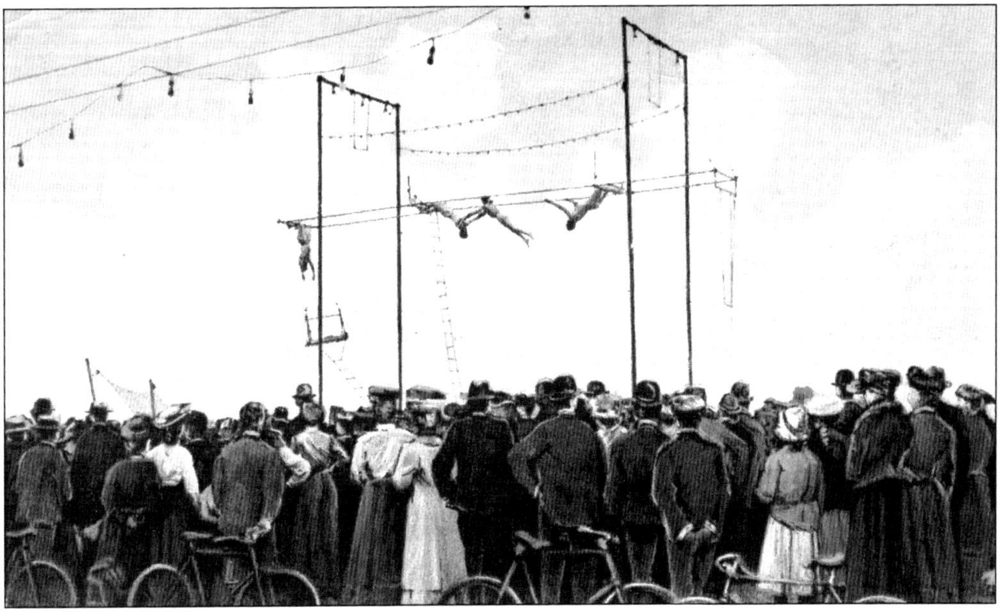

Many outdoor shows such as this trapeze act appeared at Seaside, and souvenir cards such as this one were sold by the performers after the show. Prof. F. Baldwin made balloon ascensions and parachuted into the bay where he was fished out by his crew. Two girls walked on a net upside down like human flies.

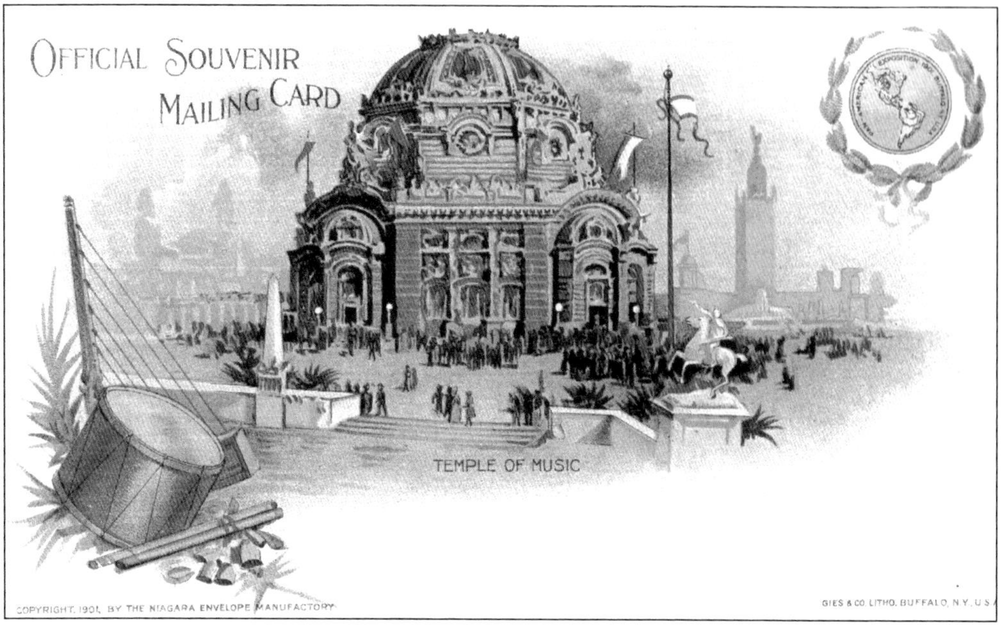

The assassination of Pres. William McKinley, seen here in this attraction at the Buffalo Exposition of 1901, caused LaMarcus A. Thompson to move his midway amusements to Rockaways' Steeplechase Park. By 1905, Thompson opened his own amusement park on the same site, and the park became Rockaways' Playland in 1928.

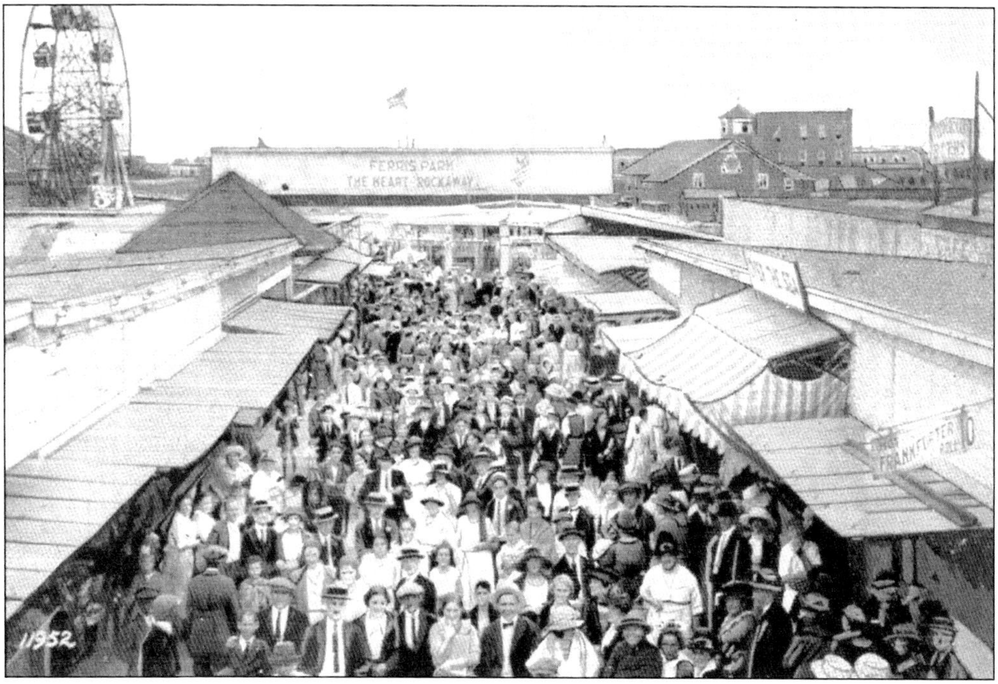

An incline walk led people from the old Steeplechase boardwalk down to the Seaside amusement midway. Numerous concessions of all types lined the way, and at the small Ferris Park shown, a left turn led to the heart of Seaside. St. Camillus Church and Steeplechase Park are to the right. Entrepreneur Nels Rasmusson operated Ferris Park from 1911 to 1925.

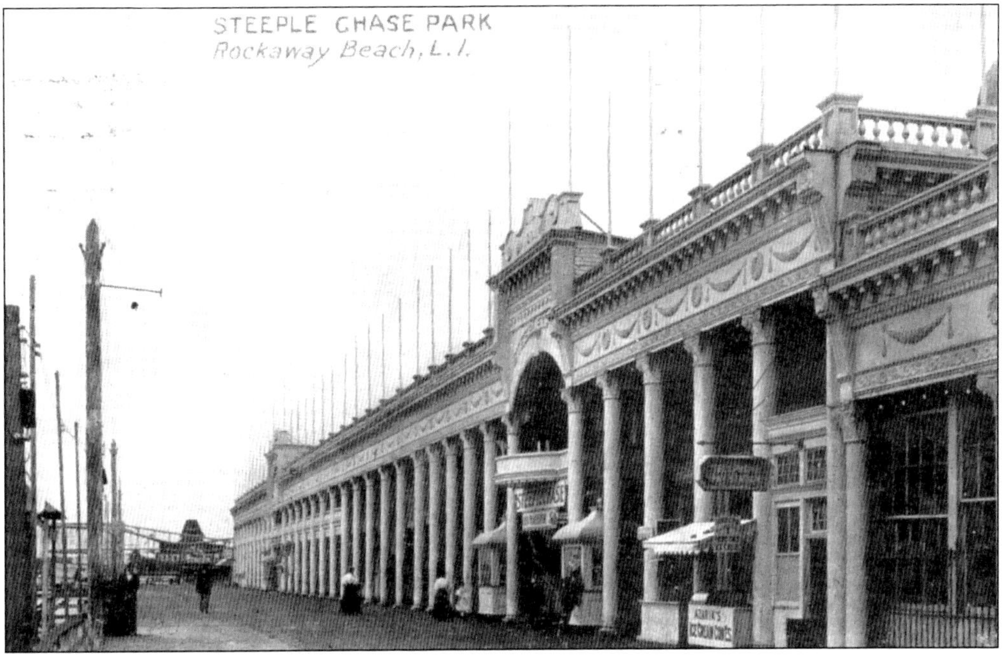

The Rockaway Beach Steeplechase Park boardwalk had a small ice-cream concession run by Arthur Azarik of Rockaway Beach. Azarik was in contention during a great controversy over who first folded a waffle into a cone shape, filled it with ice cream, and invented the famous ice-cream cone in 1904. Unfortunately, he had no witnesses.

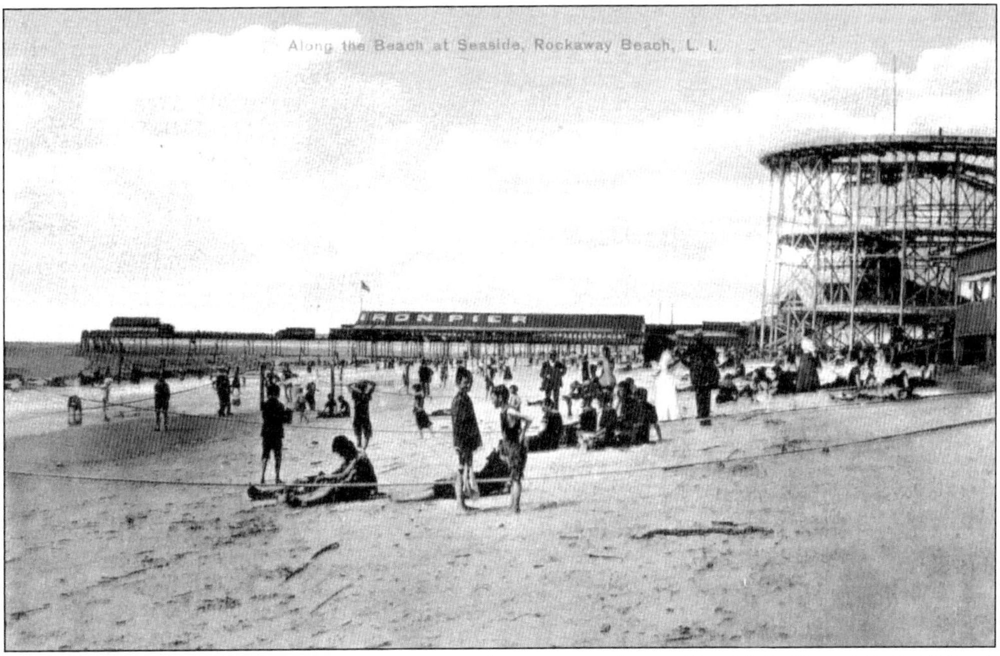

Sitting between the bathing lifelines is a group of patient people awaiting high tide, while Schilling's Pavilion and Grant's Switchback Coaster at Beach 102nd Street add to the surf sounds. The Seaside Iron Pier at Beach 105th Street, 1,080 feet long when built in 1880, has been shortened by storms since. Safety lines for bathers were installed in 1876 at Seaside beaches.

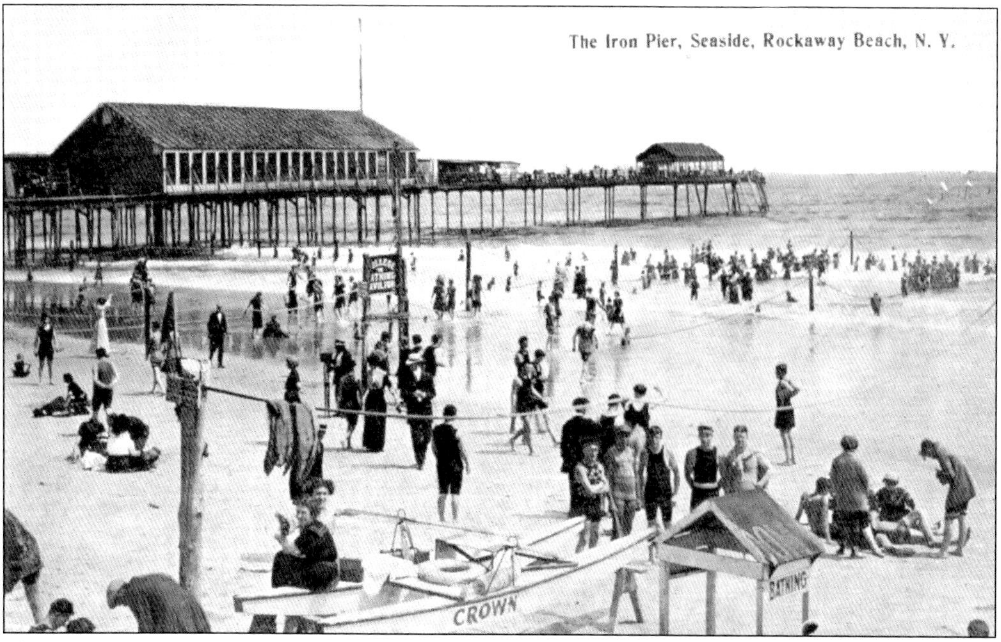

The Seaside Iron Pier was battered by the big winter storms of 1914 and 1920, and new smaller pavilions and concessions were built to replace those carried away by a raging sea. It was once a grand showcase of activity in Seaside, containing a restaurant, ballroom, barbershop, steamer landing, and fishing facilities. What remained was torn out for the new 1926 boardwalk construction.

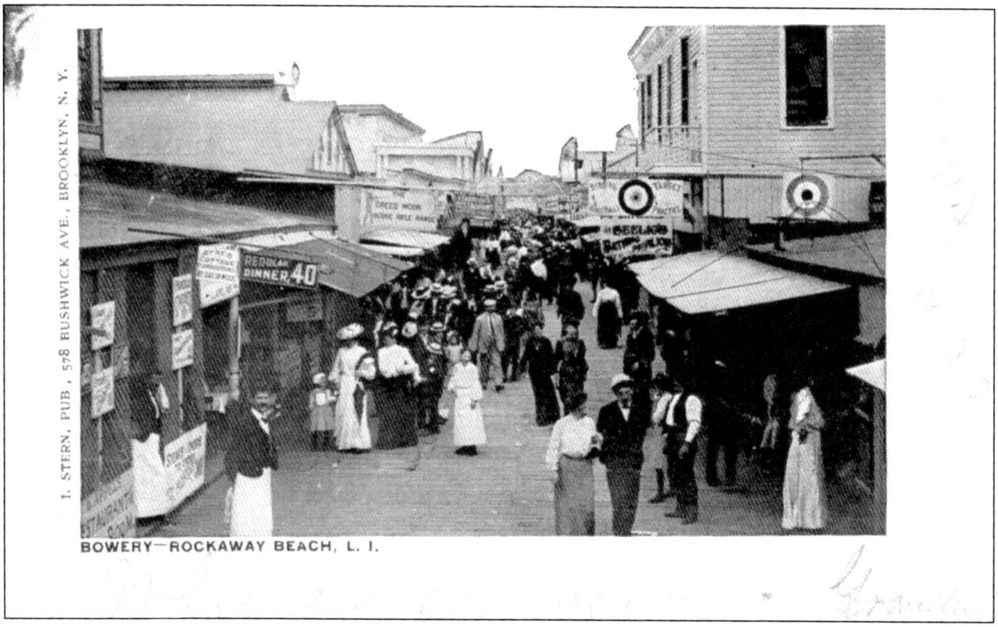

Taken from a moving stairway, or people conveyor, that transported bathers from the second floor of Wainwright and Smith's bathhouse directly to the beach (over the Seaside amusement midway), this 1906 view faces east from Beach 103rd Street. It shows much activity, including shooting galleries, hotels, baths, restaurants, and souvenir photograph booths.

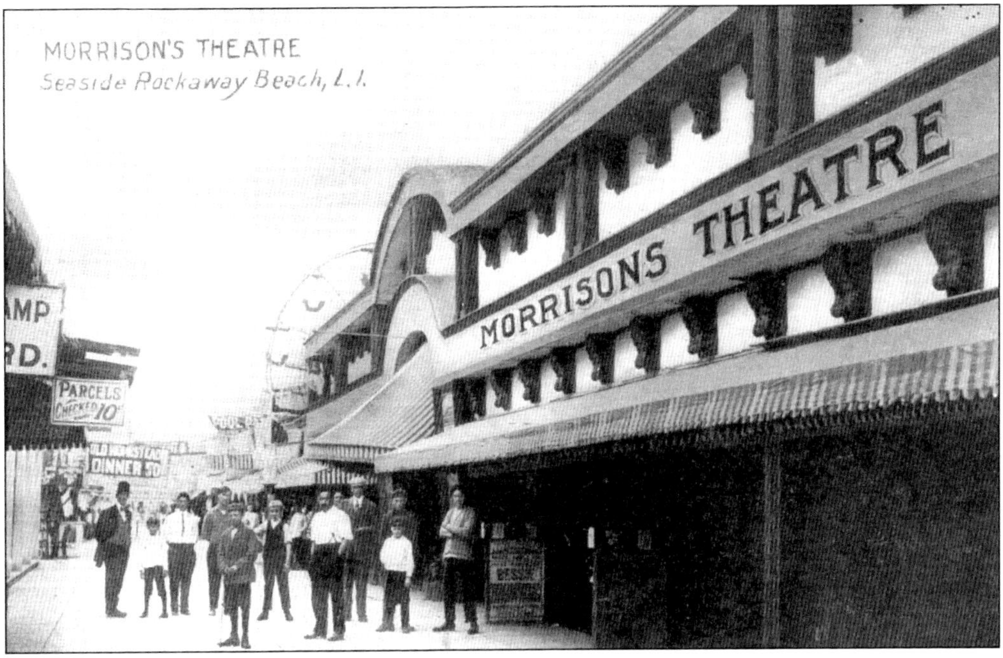

The Edgar Morrison Theatre dates back to the old 1890s Seaside, and it was rebuilt in the early 1900s by Morrison's son, Patrick. The auctioned contents of a New York theater consisting of red velour-covered seats, as well as red carpeting, were put into the Seaside theater. The lobby was mirrored and 100 feet long. Top vaudeville acts were always featured at the Beach 102nd Street site.

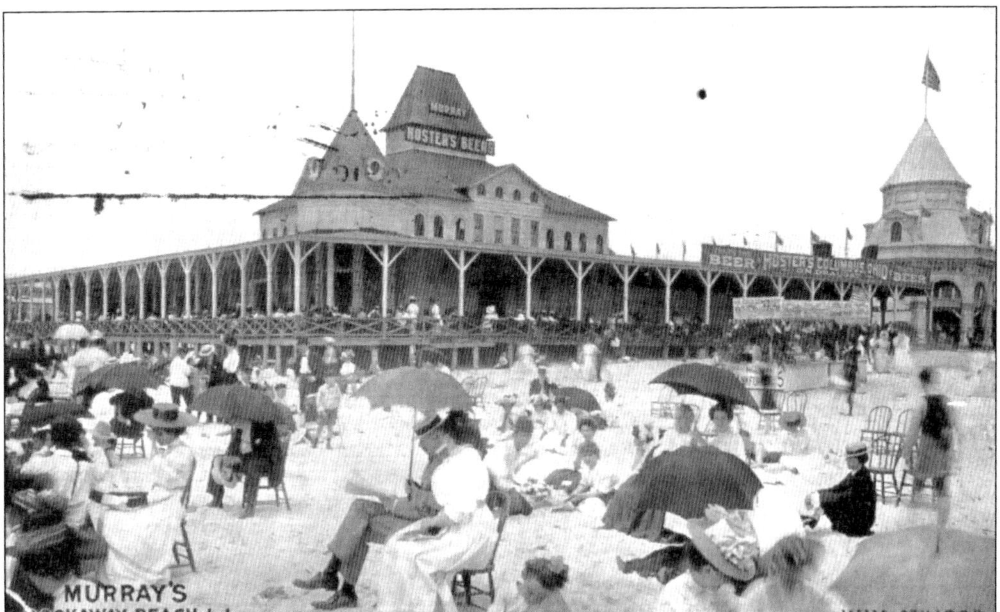

Sanford Murray's dance hall, restaurant, hotel, and bar were among the largest of attractions in Seaside. Located at the foot of Beach 103rd Street on the Seaside midway called Ocean Avenue, Murray's Grand Ocean Pavilion was taken over by the Wainwright and Smith Baths Company before the 1920s.

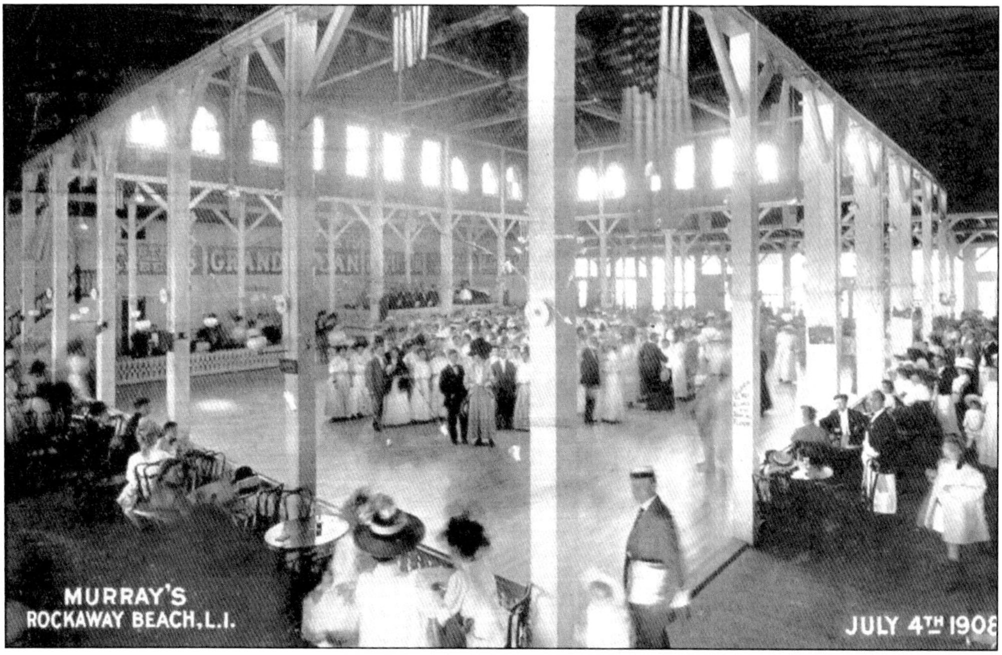

Murray's had the finest dance floor on all of Long Island, so the advertisements said, and it was big. Highly waxed and made of longleaf pine, the 120-foot-by-120-foot floor held many terpsichorean artists. There was seating on three sides, and the fourth was used for the orchestra. On occasions, a band organ would fill in for the orchestra in times of need.

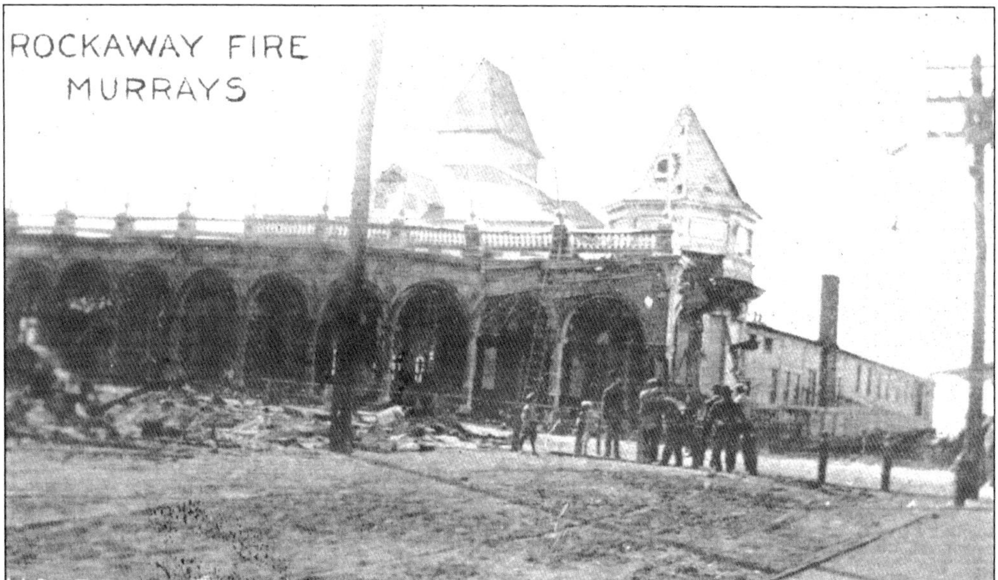

The Seaside fire of 1911 was so intense that the cast-iron colonnades of Murray's dance hall warped from the heat. The place was rebuilt after the fire, although the Old Mill water ride, the Lion Restaurant, and the decade-old Hurdler's Carousel and Pavilion were not. Murray's continued for years until the disastrous fire of 1923.

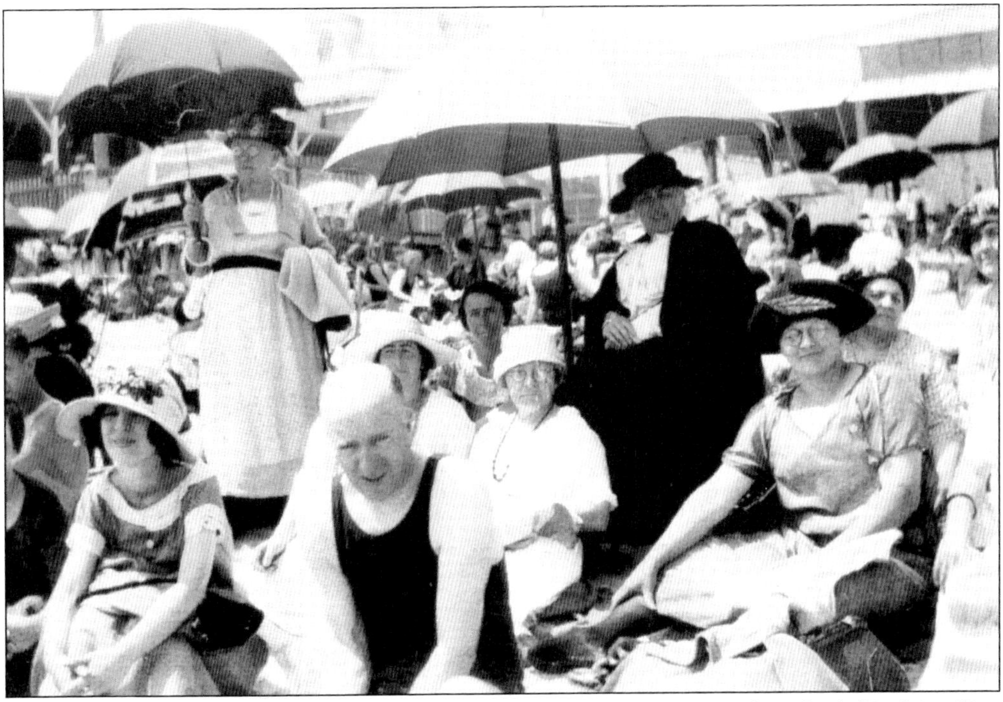

It appears to be ladies day on the beach at Murray's Grand Ocean Pavilion (left) and Schilling's Pavilion (right). "Mother Superior" and the "Grand Duchess" are under cover of the umbrellas.

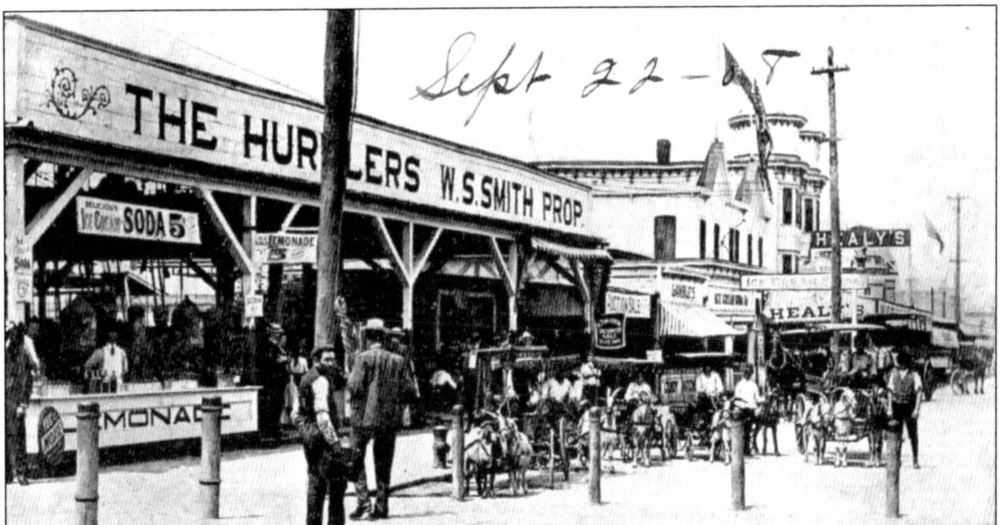

At the intersection of Beach 103rd Street and Seaside's midway stood the W. S. Smith Hurdler's carousel and its refreshment pavilion, as well as Healy's Place, which is still in business but at a different site. This carousel burned in 1911 and was replaced by William Nunley's carousel in 1914. Note the goat cart touring vehicles in this 1906 image.

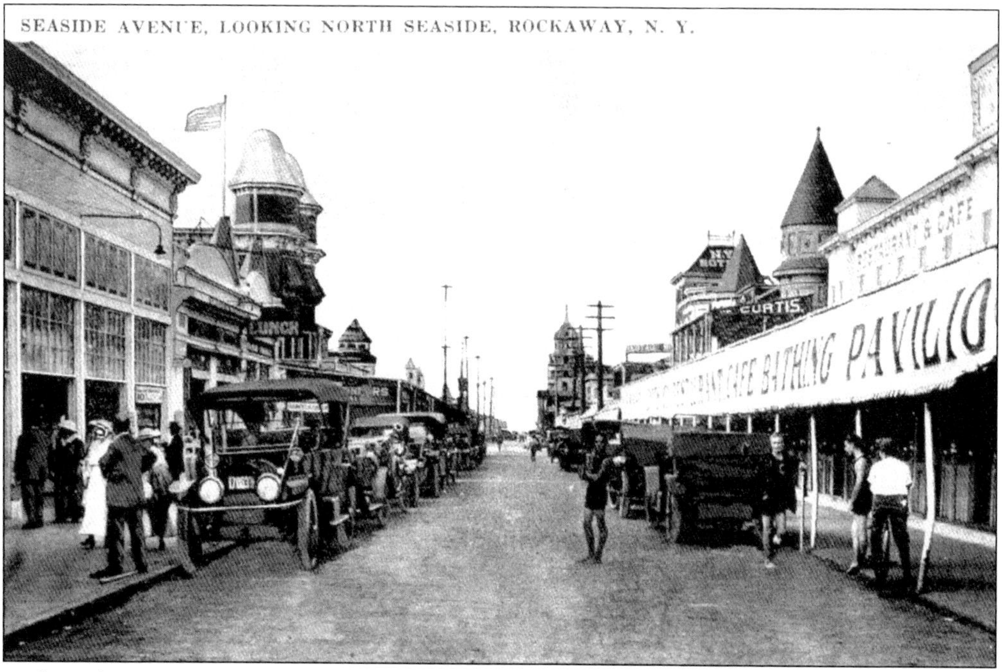

In the early 1920s, Seaside Avenue, or Beach 103rd Street, had developed into a grand thoroughfare from Ocean Avenue (foreground) looking northward toward the bay where the tower of the mighty Seaside House Hotel can be seen. William Nunley's large carousel is on the left, and a dozen hotels line the avenue.

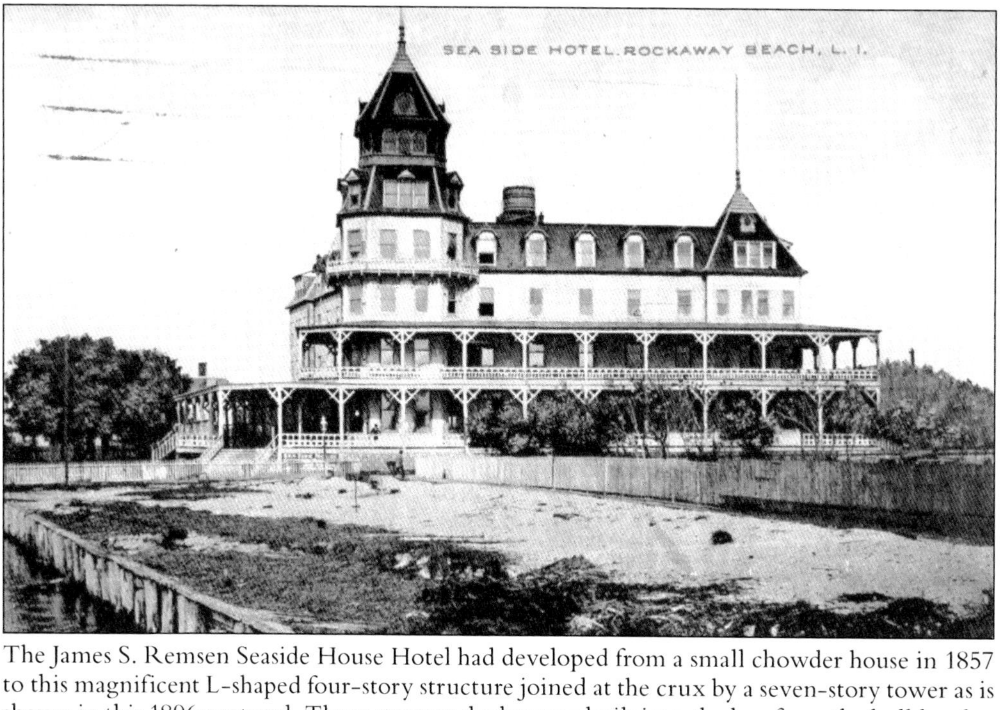

The James S. Remsen Seaside House Hotel had developed from a small chowder house in 1857 to this magnificent L-shaped four-story structure joined at the crux by a seven-story tower as is shown in this 1896 postcard. Three steamer docks were built into the bay from the bulkhead at lower left. The building was torn down in 1941 after having been closed for some time.

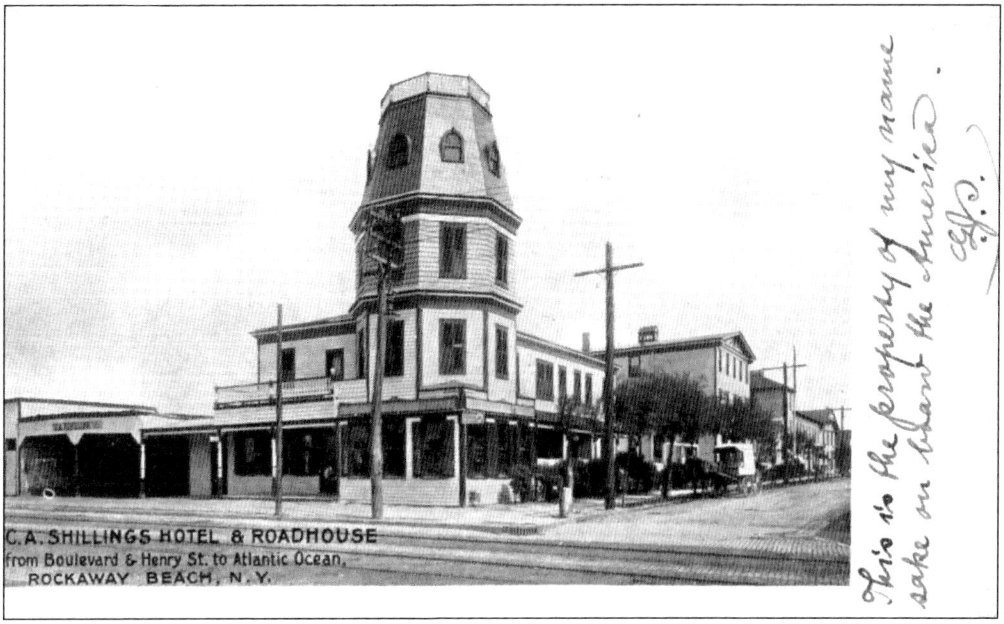

Charles Augustus Schilling built his roadhouse on Beach 102nd Street and Rockaway Beach Boulevard in 1893. The hotel building at the beach end of the street survived the great 1892 fire that destroyed all of Seaside. At that time, it was Curley's Hotel, which was built in 1876. The peaked-roof building at center was a police station built in 1900, and it is now the Crystal Hotel.

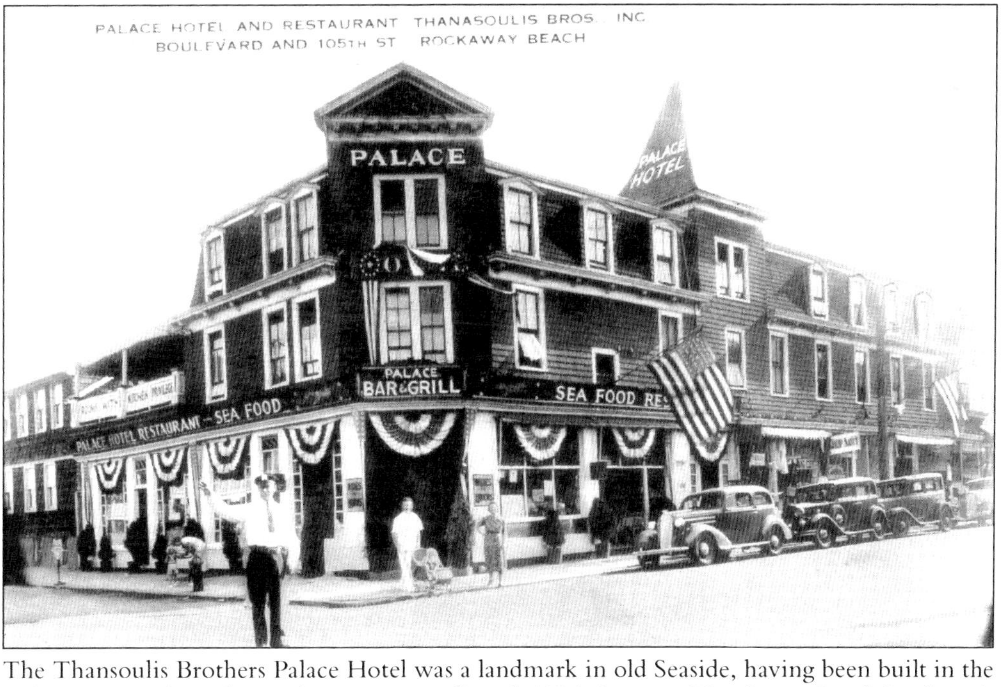

The Thansoulis Brothers Palace Hotel was a landmark in old Seaside, having been built in the early 1900s. Built on the northwest corner of Beach 105th Street and Rockaway Beach Boulevard, the Palace Hotel was torn down in the 1960s for high-rise Title I construction. It was a favorite haunt in Irishtown, Rockaway, USA, (Seaside).

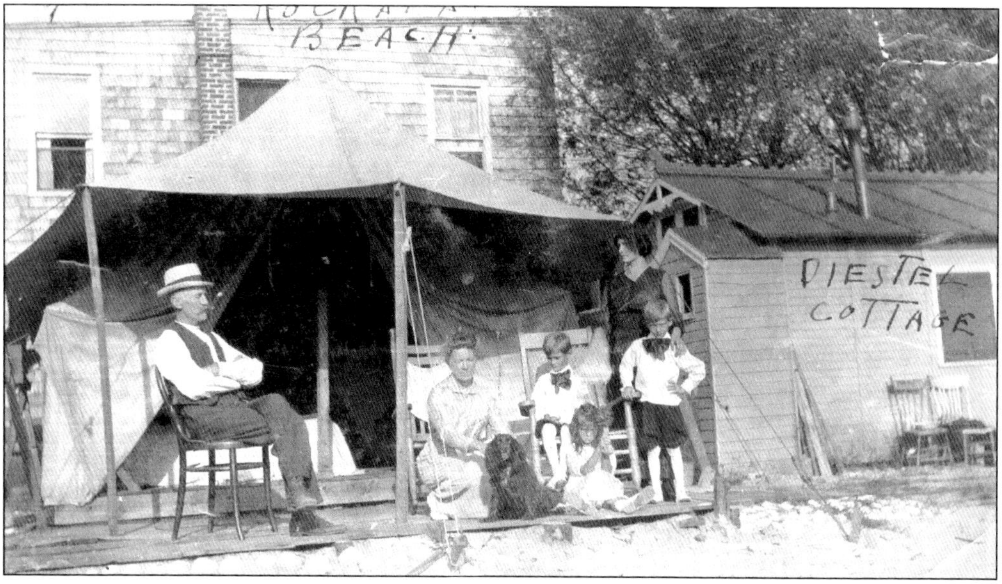

Despite the fact that wooden bungalows began to end tent camps in Seaside as early as 1902, this defiant-looking gentleman is sitting on the front porch of his canvas tent as if eviction was eminent. Seaside's big tent city was located west of Beach 106th Street from 1903 to 1913.

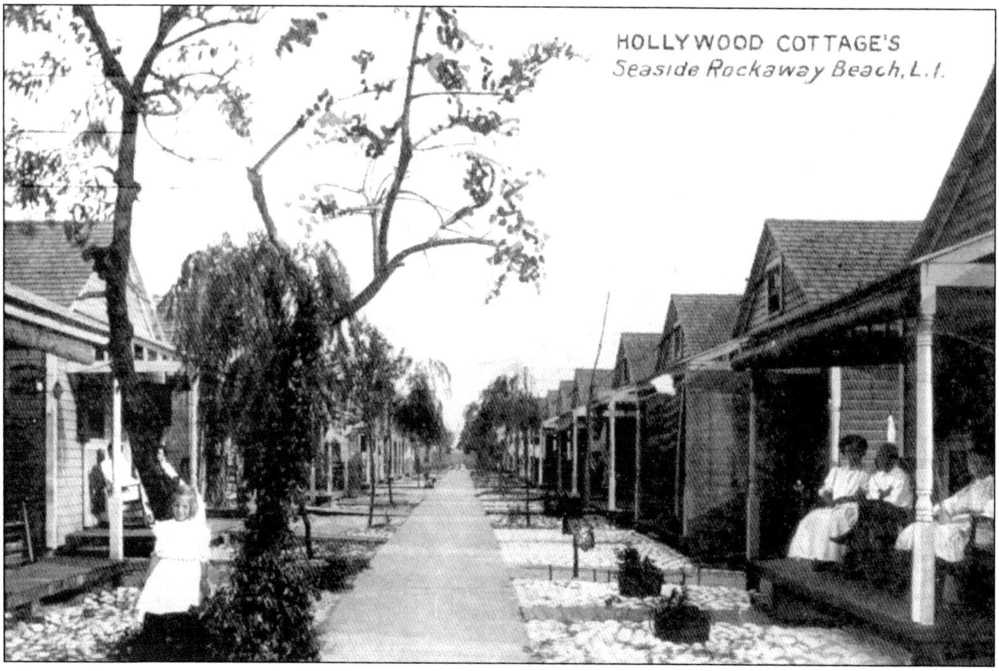

The Hollywood Avenue bungalow cottages on Beach 101st Street were built before World War I. Wooden buildings took the place of tents as many bungalow courts with practical names like Marie or Albert were being built from Far Rockaway to the point. Recently about two-thirds of this court was replaced by condominiums.

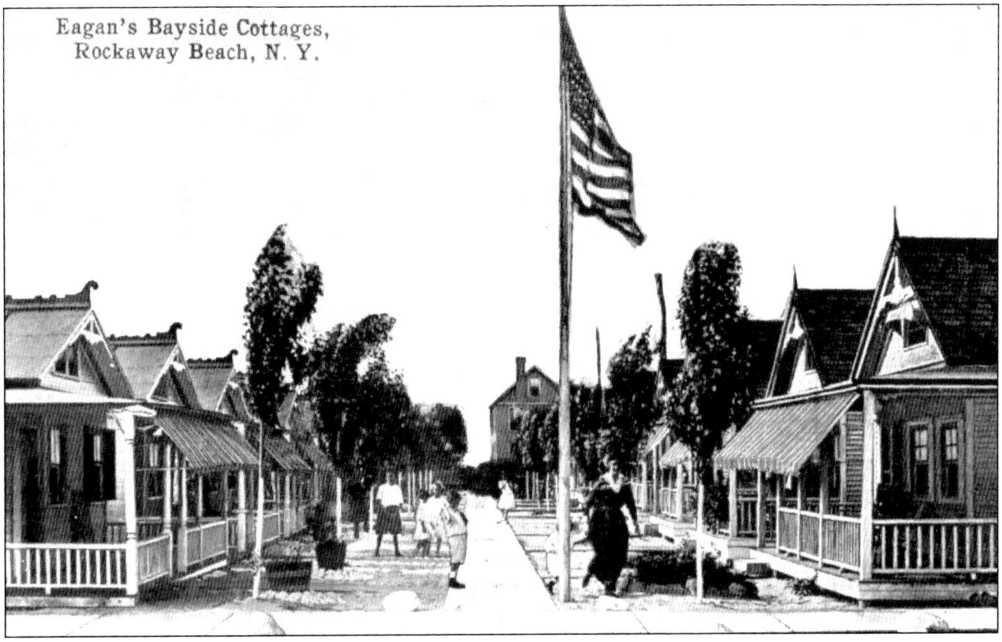

John J. Eagan built many bungalow courts in Seaside on the beach side at first, and then bay side bungalows were constructed in 1905. They arrived freight on board from Grand Rapids, Michigan, as prefab wooden structures. These were on Beach 107th Street between the old Rockaway Beach main boulevard and the railroad until the late 1930s.

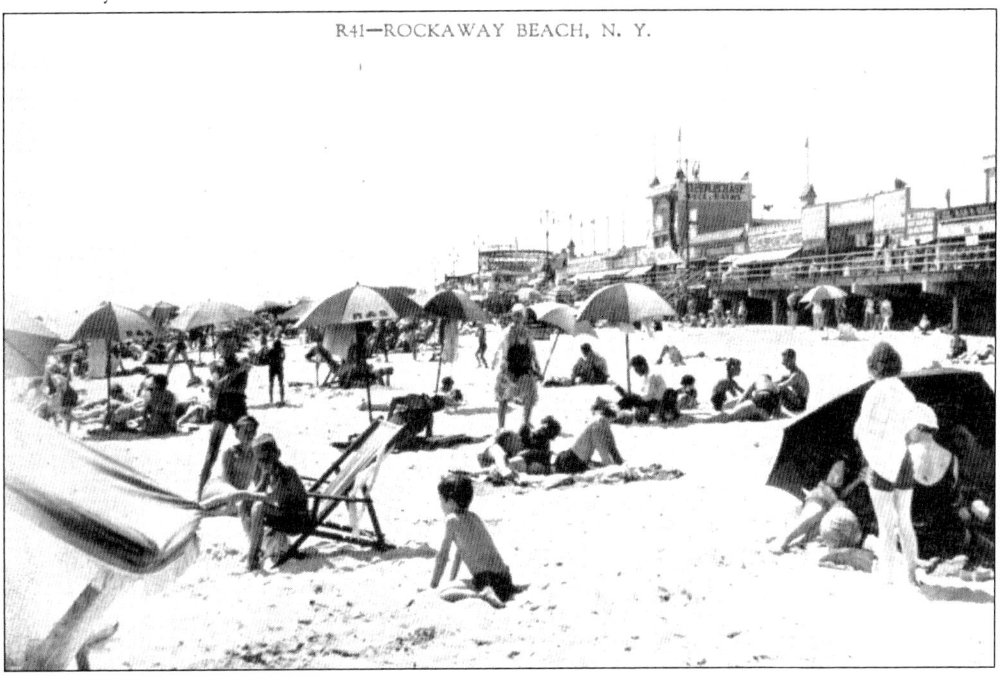

The new beach and boardwalk at Seaside was built in the mid-1920s, and no construction of any kind was to be built on the beach side by park commissioner Robert Moses. All attractions, baths, a wax museum, a coaster named the Thunderbolt, and the giant Steeplechase pool on the land side were demolished for Shorefront Parkway.

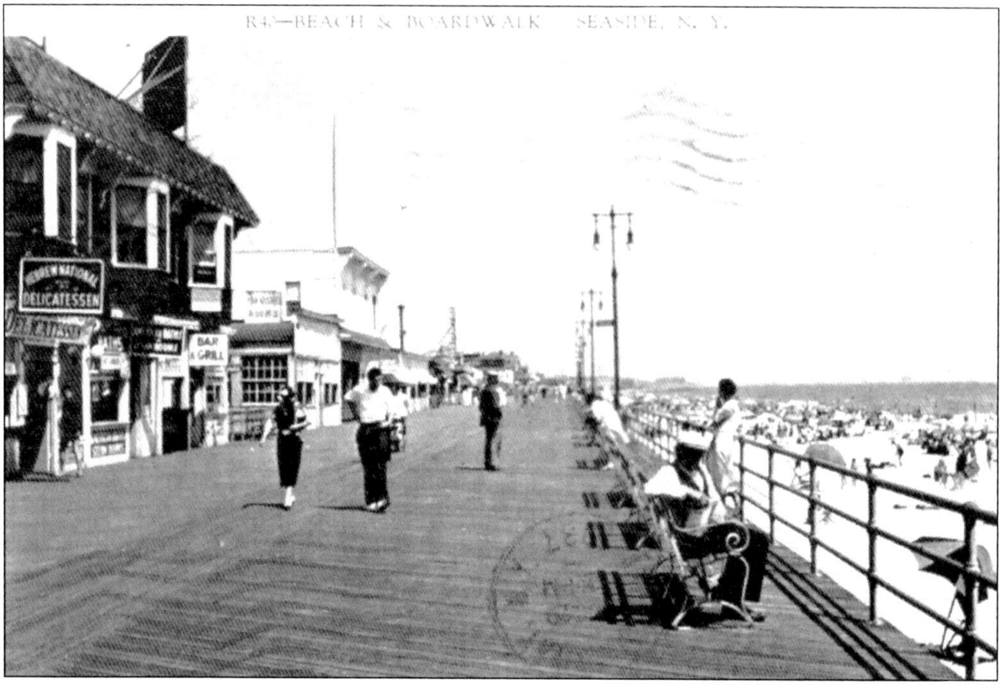

The land side of the new city-built boardwalk at the east end of Rockaway's Seaside in Holland contained many bathhouses, hotels, restaurants, and a delicatessen by Hebrew International. All this was demolished for a ribbon of concrete by Robert Moses.

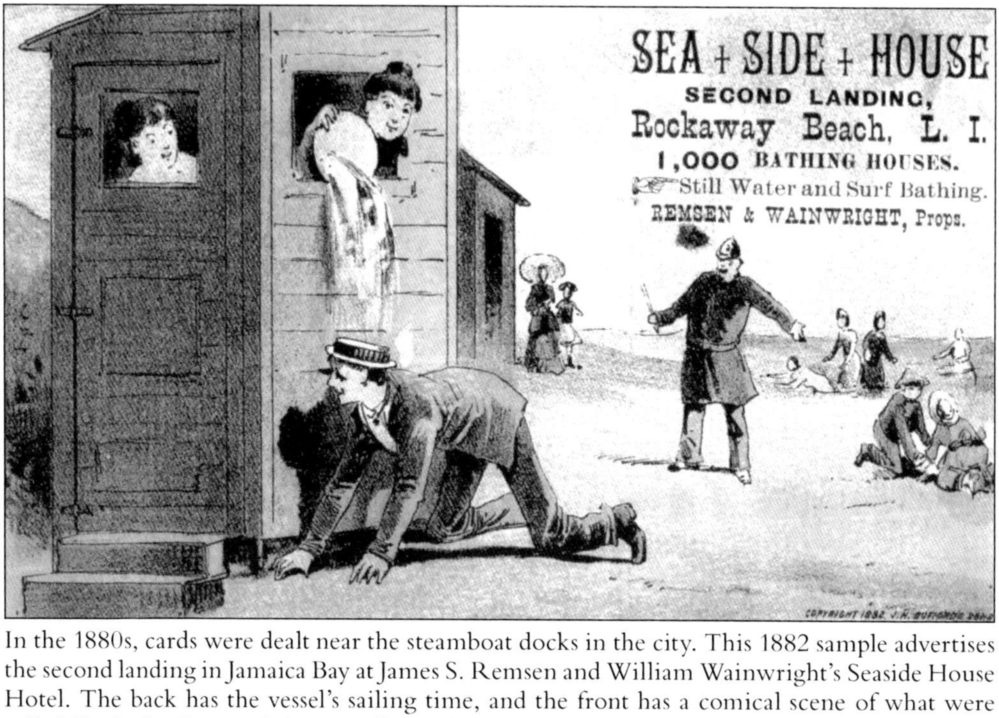

In the 1880s, cards were dealt near the steamboat docks in the city. This 1882 sample advertises the second landing in Jamaica Bay at James S. Remsen and William Wainwright's Seaside House Hotel. The back has the vessel's sailing time, and the front has a comical scene of what were called "Jack-the-Peppers" then. Stiff punishment was given out.

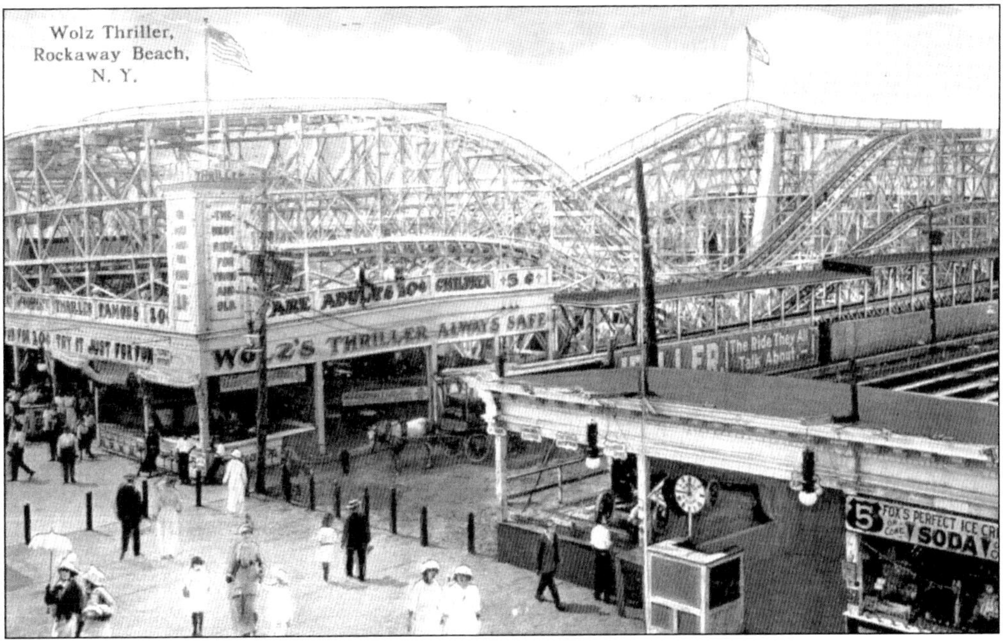

Seaside's first roller coaster was the Thriller in 1909. The Thriller replaced a scenic railway (1904) that replaced a switchback ride (1893). Next door on Beach 104th Street and the midway was a motorcycle daredevil attraction. In 1927, the Thriller was torn down, and a new electric automobile attraction was opened at its site.

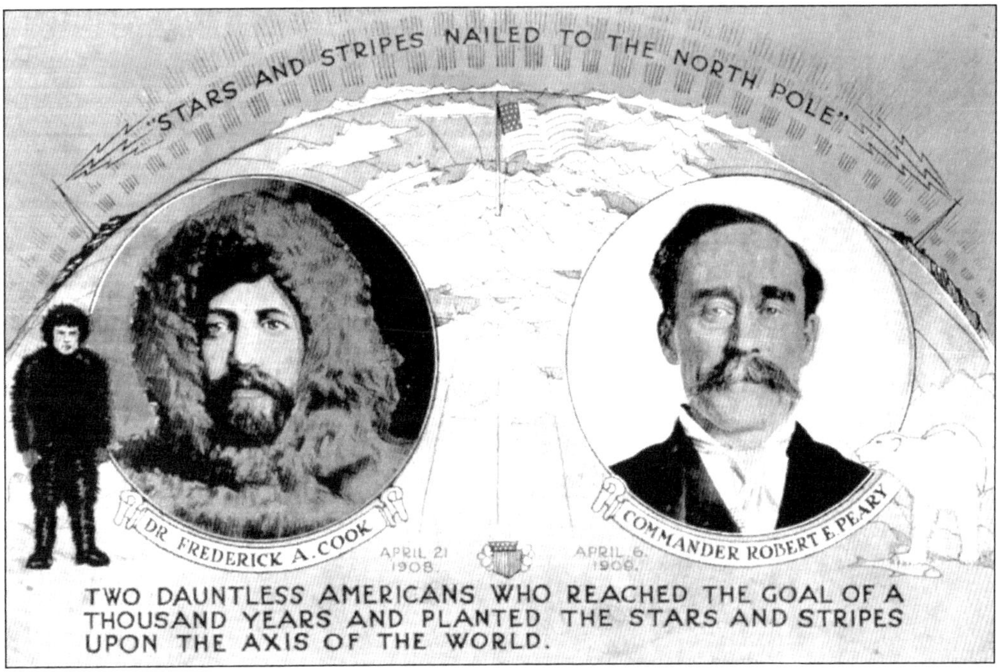

Dr. Frederick A. Cook worked at his brother's milk and dairy store in Seaside during the summer between his medical school semesters. He later was on medical staff on a few polar expeditions before he went on his own and was in contention with Robert E. Perry on the 1908 discovery of the North Pole. Cook was believed to have made the discovery first.

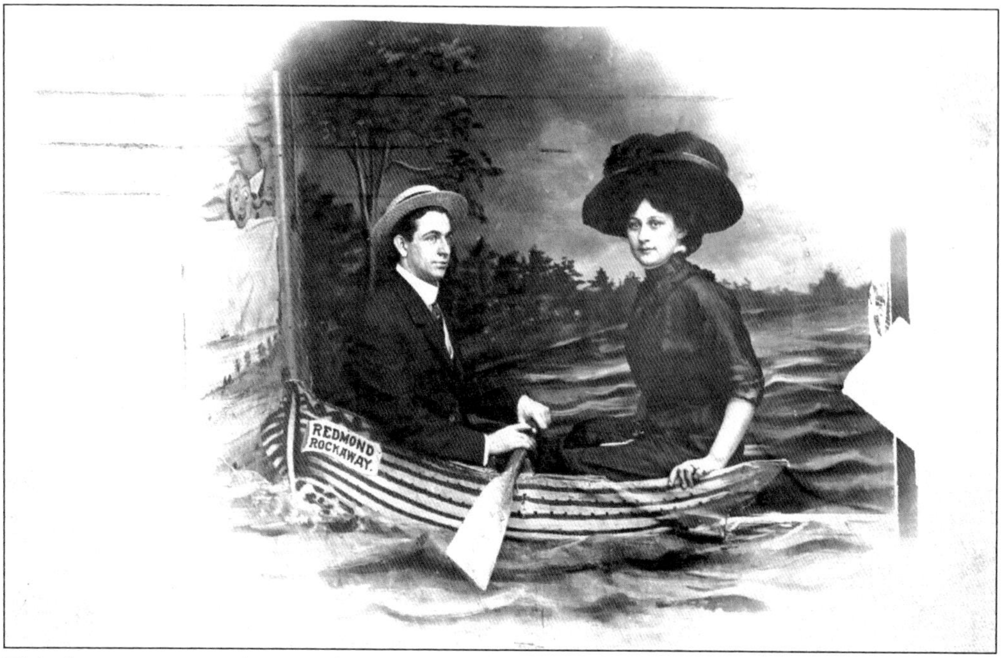

This elegant souvenir photograph, taken at Redmond's Studio on the Seaside Bowery, distinctly shows who the captain of this ship was. Both members of this crew have wedding bands on the ring finger of their left hands, so the crewman rows and the captain shouts out the orders.

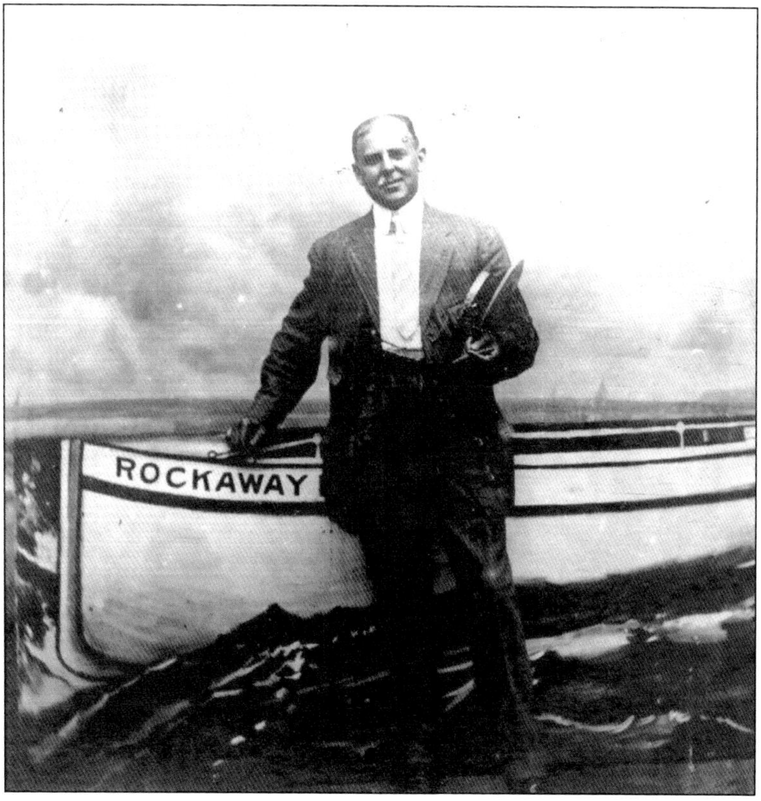

This apparently well-bred gentleman stands graciously against an open boat backdrop with his hat cradled in the crook of his arm and a cigar in his left hand.

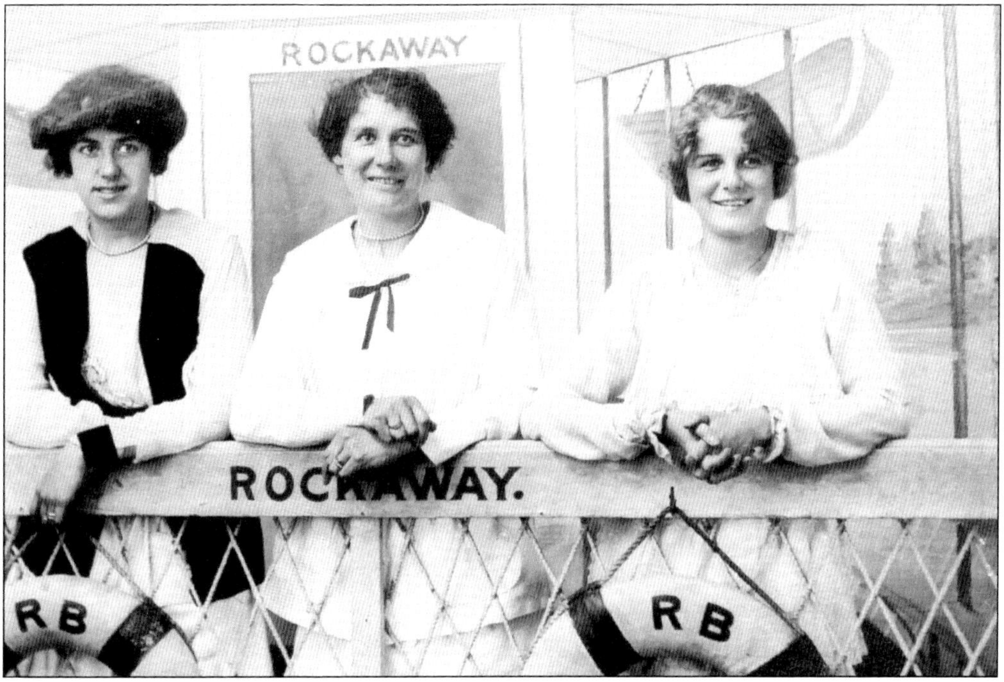

This happy threesome appears to be mother in the middle with a daughter on each side. They have chosen a boat deck scene for their souvenir remembrance of their trip to the beach in the summer of 1910.

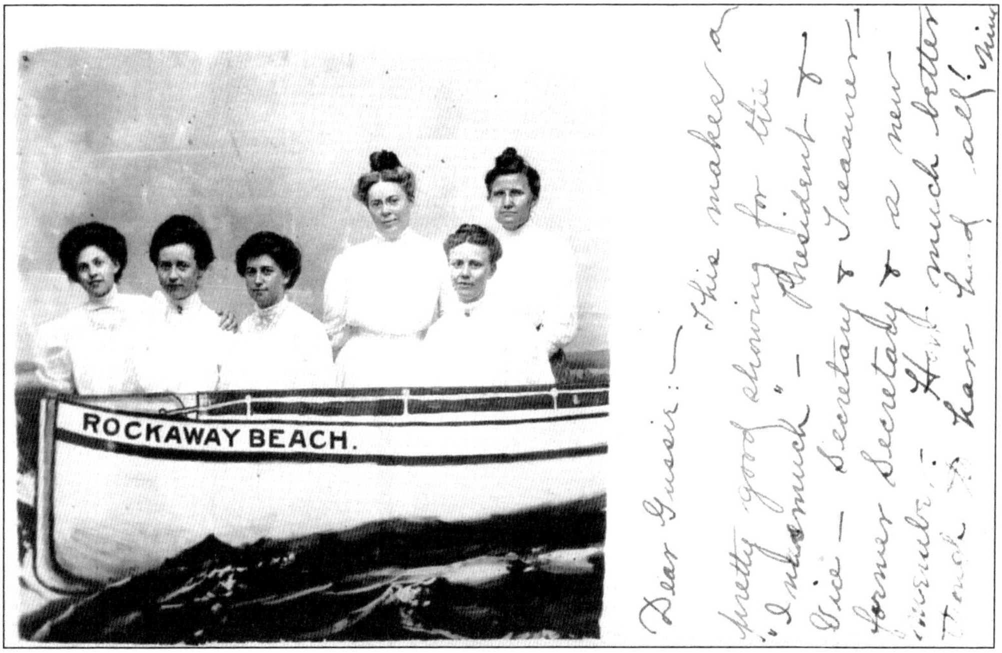

Many clubs and organizations held outings on the old Rockaway Beach peninsula, and arrangements were made with local beach owners. In modern times, one needs a permit from the City of New York to have such outings. These young ladies are members of the "Inasmuch" club, credo unknown.

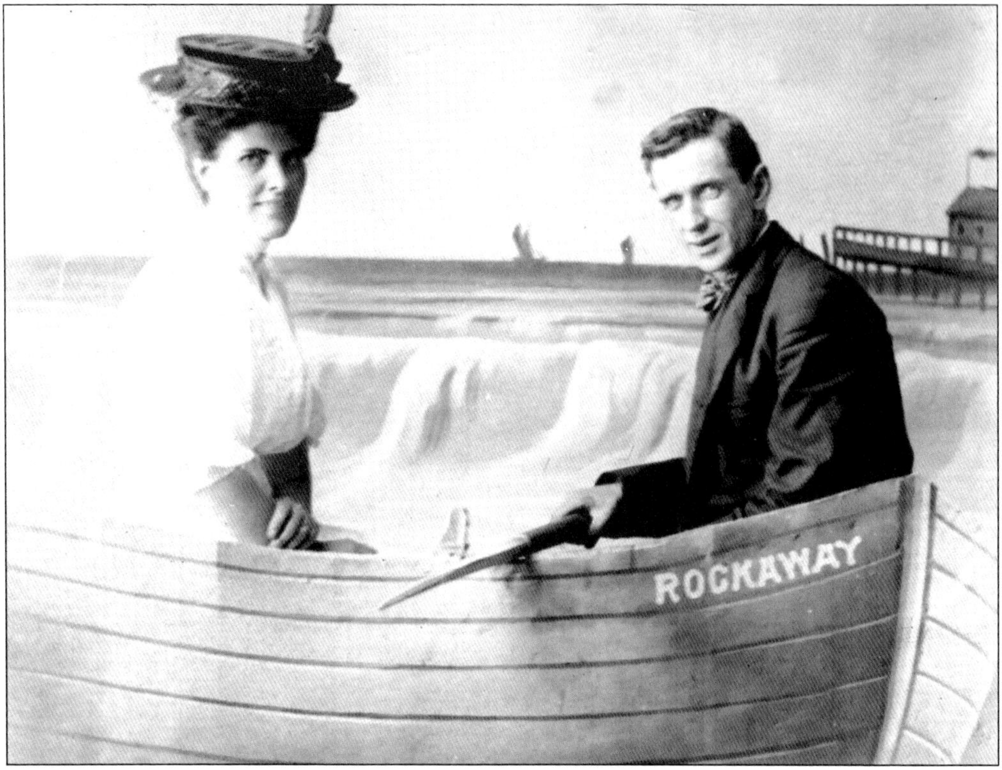

This stern-looking couple appears to be angry. She is holding a clenched fist down with her left hand, and he has the wooden oar in his right hand, seemingly ready for a slap shot. She is looking at the camera as if thinking, "Take the picture already!"

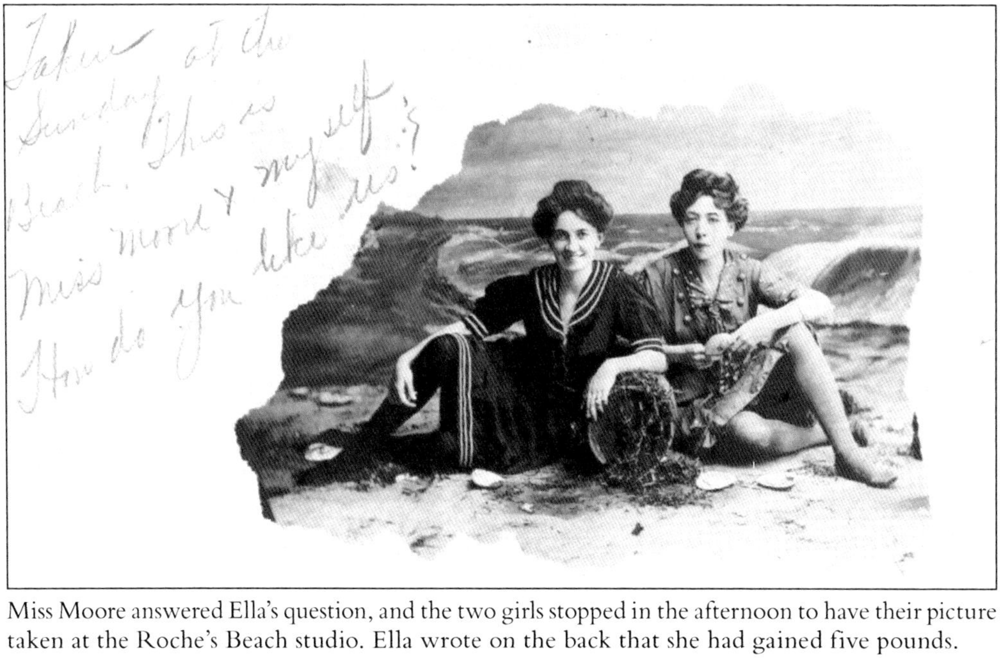

Miss Moore answered Ella's question, and the two girls stopped in the afternoon to have their picture taken at the Roche's Beach studio. Ella wrote on the back that she had gained five pounds.

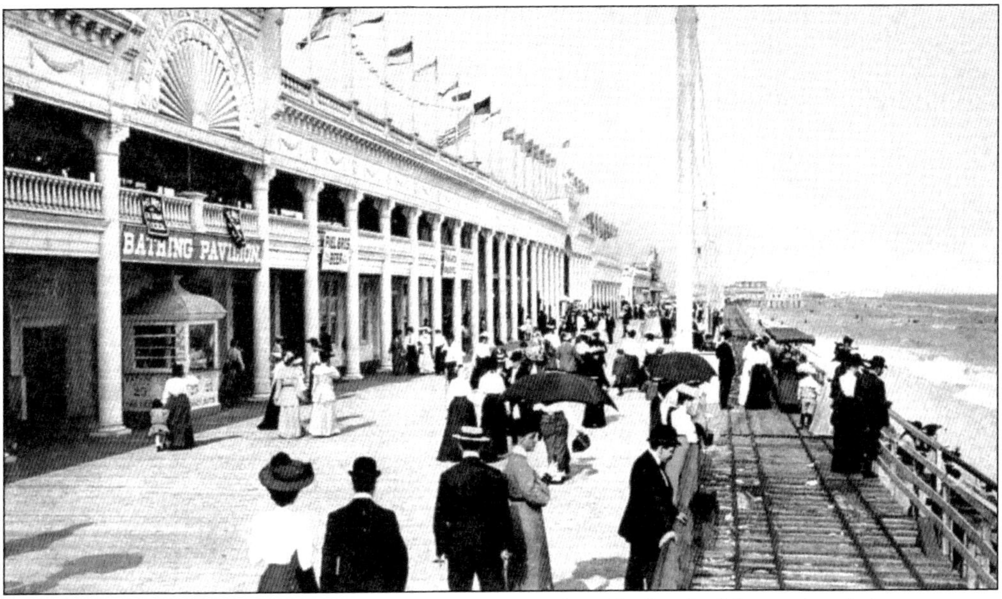

Visitors to the Steeplechase boardwalk were amazed to find a double-track miniature steam railroad that ran the length of the ocean promenade. A few times, a train derailed onto the beach, although no injuries were told of. A hurricane in 1903 ended the short run of the Steeplechase Railroad, and the ride was not rebuilt. (Courtesy of the Library of Congress.)

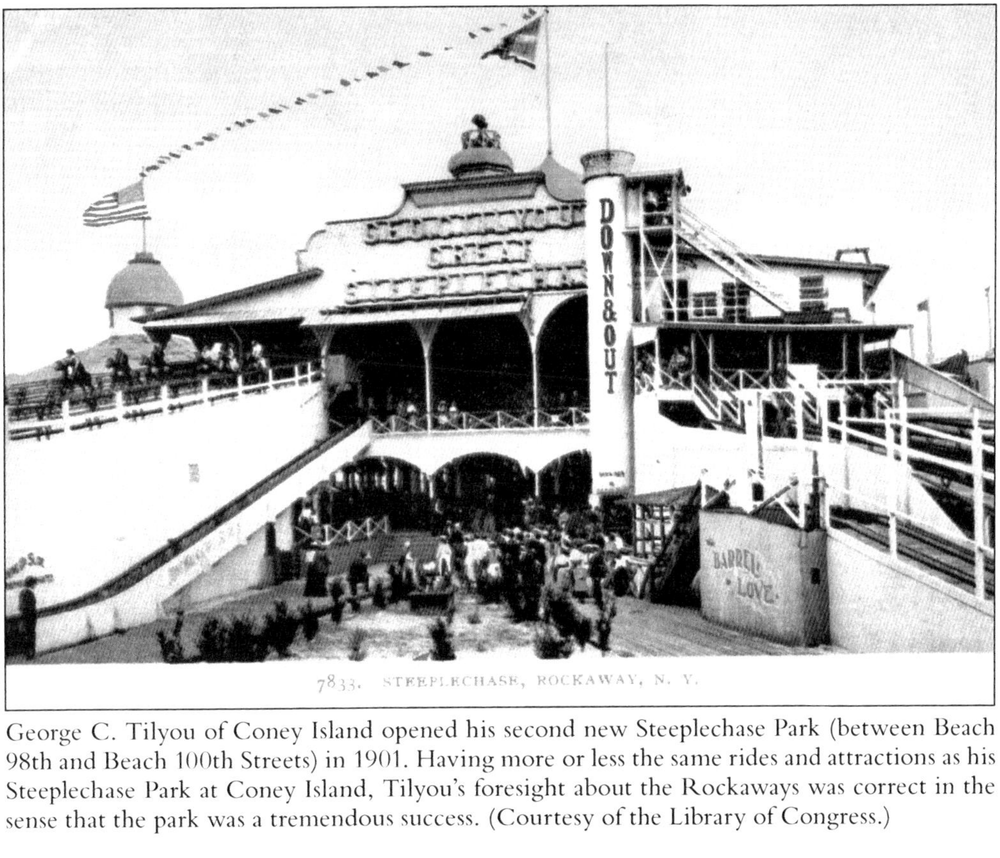

George C. Tilyou of Coney Island opened his second new Steeplechase Park (between Beach 98th and Beach 100th Streets) in 1901. Having more or less the same rides and attractions as his Steeplechase Park at Coney Island, Tilyou's foresight about the Rockaways was correct in the sense that the park was a tremendous success. (Courtesy of the Library of Congress.)

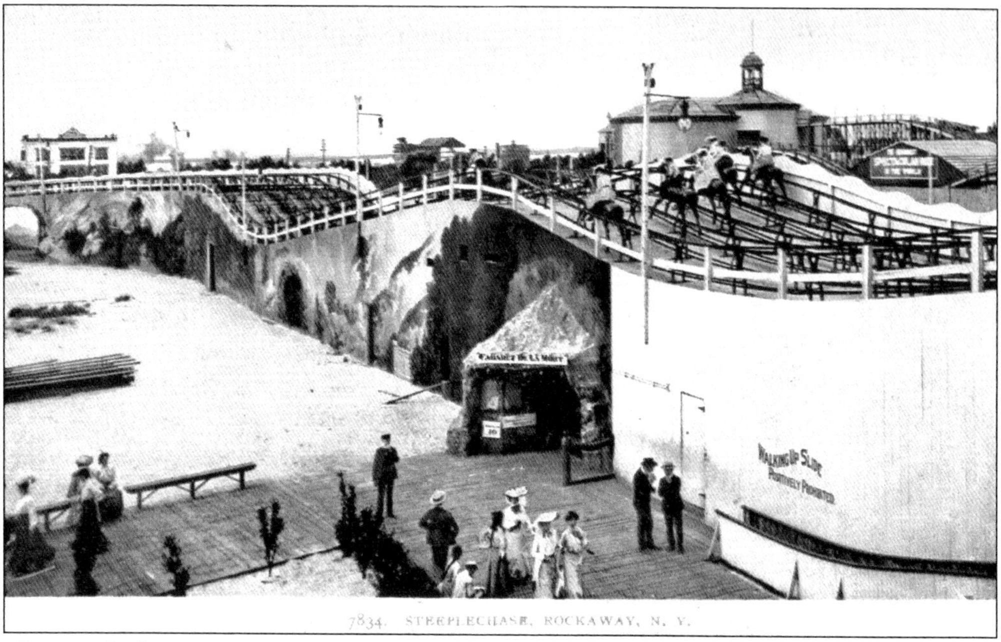

The Steeplechase Gravity Horse Ride was comparable to the L. A. Thompson Scenic Railway (background on right side) in the sense that they both operated using the same kind of natural power source. The Cabaret de la Morte, a wax museum, was located under the Steeplechase. At the bottom left, tracks for a mini-railway await installation. (Courtesy of the Library of Congress.)

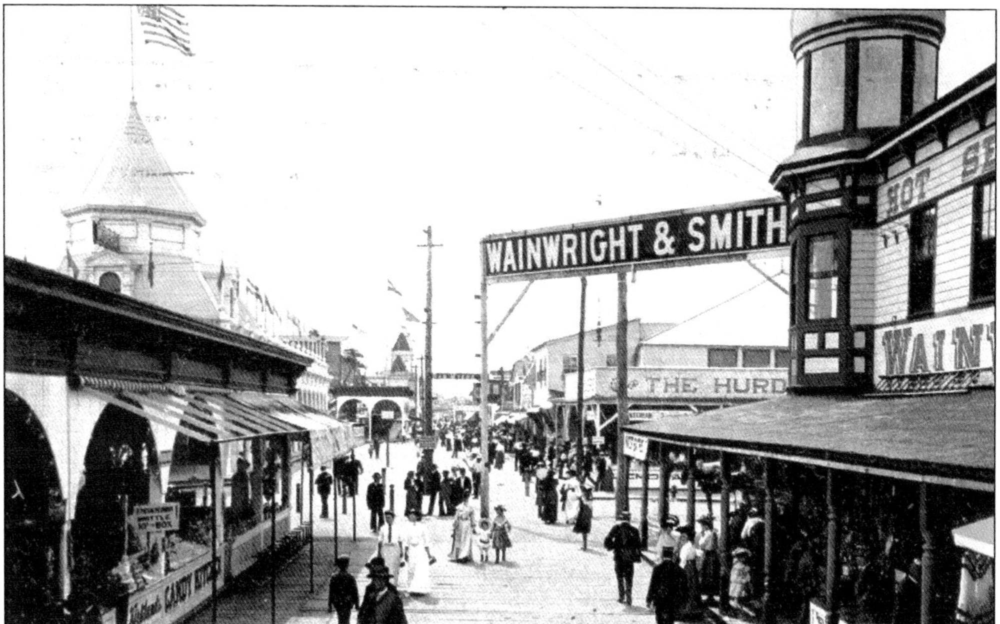

Looking westward from Beach 102nd Street, the Seaside Bowery (Ocean Avenue) featured many attractions, rides, and shops of all kinds. On the walk is a bathhouse, the Seaside Avenue crossing to the beach, the Hurdler's Carousel and Pavilion, the Lion Brewery Restaurant, and a series of hotels and dance halls. (Courtesy of the Library of Congress.)

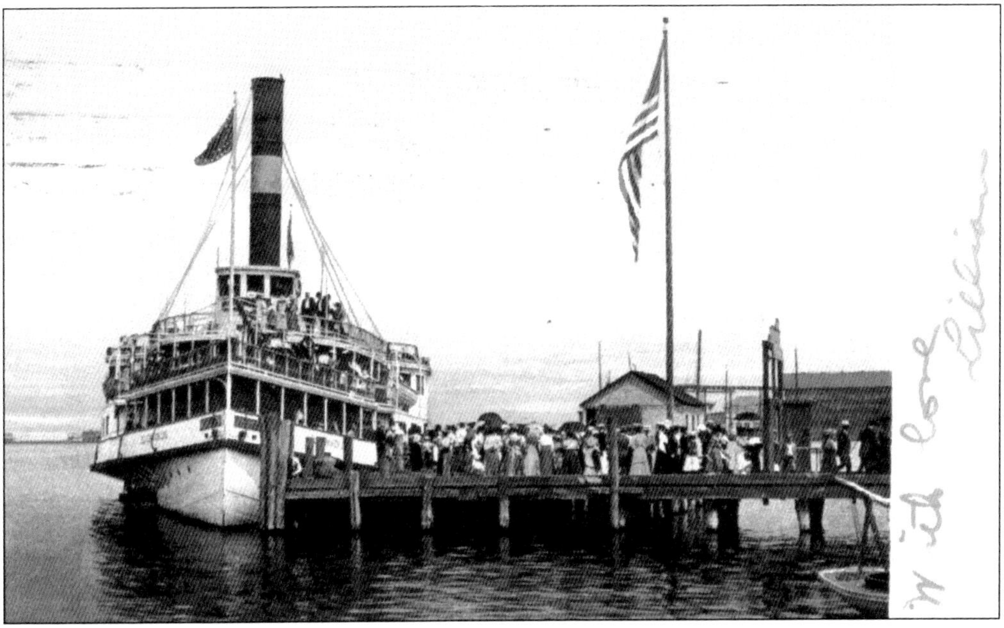

The side-wheeler steamboat *Mobjack* unloads many hundreds of passengers to the Steeplechase dock on the bay at Beach 98th Street. This dock was built by George C. Tilyou and LaMarcus A. Thompson so steamers could bring patrons to their respective amusement parks on the beach side of the Rockaways. (Courtesy of the Library of Congress.)

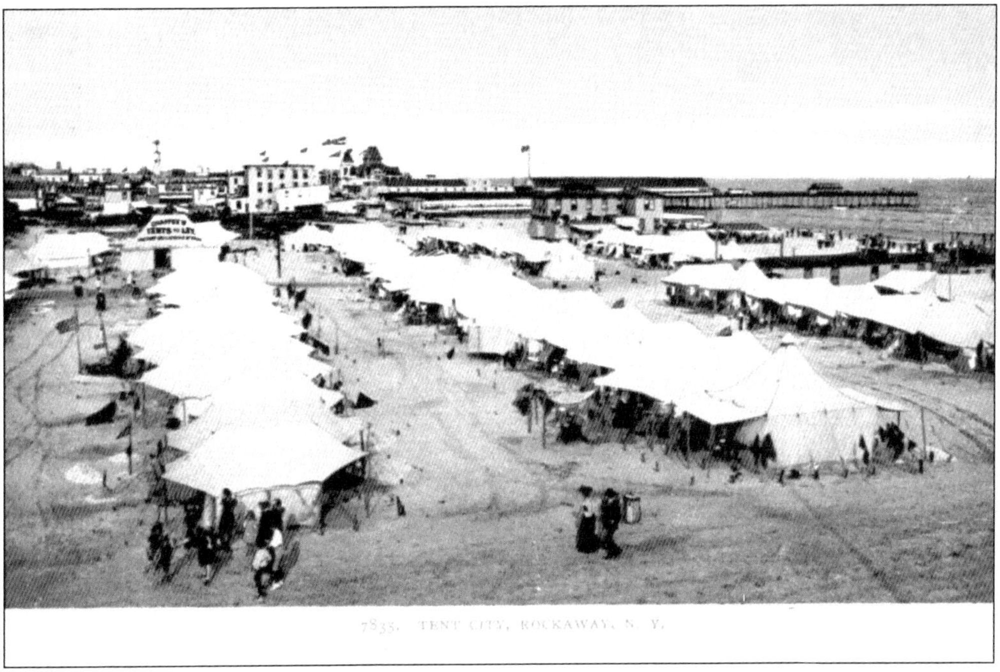

Frank Chaffee, a tent and sailmaker in the Rockaways, opened the first tent city on the peninsula, renting to tenters for the day, week, or season. Camp Chaffee had upwards of 385 canvas tents with running water and gas, but showers and sanitation facilities were communal. In 1914, wooden bungalows replaced tenting. (Courtesy of the Library of Congress.)

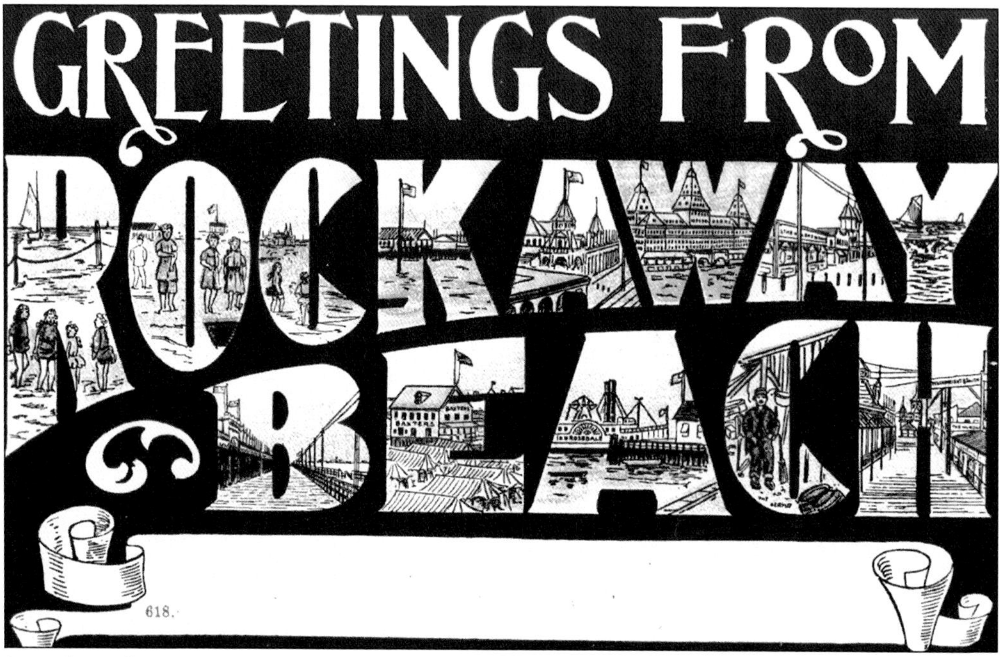

Some large-letter postcards contained small graphic images of what appeared on other full-picture postcards. This card has more than a dozen, plus a scroll at the bottom for a message on the front as well as on the reverse side. This was considered a bargain in the old days at the beach.

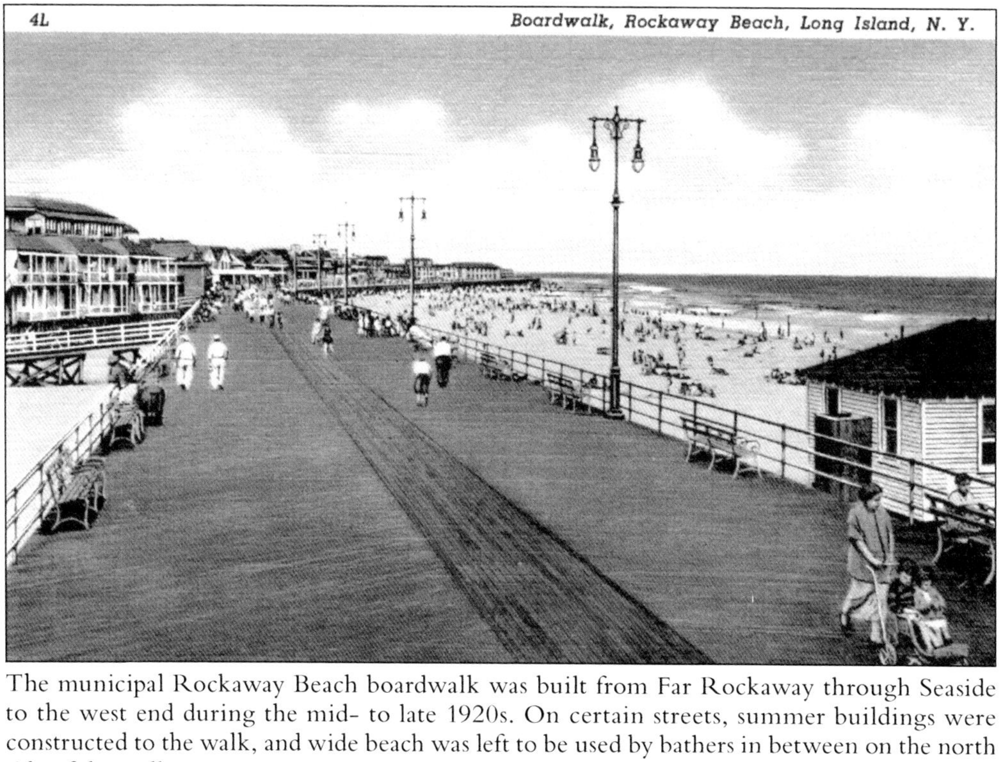

The municipal Rockaway Beach boardwalk was built from Far Rockaway through Seaside to the west end during the mid- to late 1920s. On certain streets, summer buildings were constructed to the walk, and wide beach was left to be used by bathers in between on the north side of the walk.

Seven

Rockaway Park
Beach 108th Street to Beach 126th Street

The vast western end of the Rockaway Peninsula sprang into the limelight in 1879 when the largest hotel in the world was built to the west of Seaside. Shaped like the letter *E* with its back to the beach and three wings toward the boulevard, 1,000 wide rooms with the windows were to provide cool comfort to guests in summer. Provisions were made for groups, the rich, and brown baggers with children (the pail-and-shovel gang).

The Hotel Imperial was said to be almost ready to open for the 1880 season on a six-block tract of beach stretching from Beach 109th Street west to Beach 116th Street.

The New York and Rockaway Beach Railroad was built from Long Island City to the shore of Jamaica Bay at Howard Beach and then over the bay on a wooden trestle to Rockaway Peninsula. A landing was built at Beach 84th Street, and the track turned west around Louis Hammel's hotel and then headed to the Hotel Imperial. The hotel had a steamer dock at the bay end of the Grand Avenue, now Beach 116th Street. To the west of the hotel stood a three-block-long, two-story bathhouse. A low boardwalk supplied a solid walking surface between the hotel and the baths.

All the point land west of Seaside was purchased by the Rockaway Beach Improvement Company headed by Henry Y. Attrill, a New York banker and kingpin of the Big Hotel Company. Other bankers, railroad men, and U.S. senators from out West made up the rest of the company.

The point land, which went as far as the present Roxbury community at the time, had the great civil landscaper Frederick Law Olmsted commissioned to lay out the grounds with the company's ideas in mind. What Olmsted laid down on paper and suggested was considered superfluous and ignored.

The immense scale of the hotel caused delays of interior dressings such as carpets, furniture, beds, chairs, and so on as the many firms supplying were hard-pressed to deliver on time. Cash flow problems resulted in contractors, workers, suppliers, and merchants not getting paid on time, and it was leaked out that the Hotel Company had spent more than its bond issue.

Other hotel men on Coney Island and out on Long Beach to the east (as the unwritten record between the lines revealed) banded together with lawyers and creditors to tie up the hotel in what the *Brooklyn Daily Eagle* called "the blackest of legal knots." Despite the efforts of many, including the financier J. P. Morgan, the Imperial stood empty and unopened, and it was torn down by a secondhand lumber dealer in 1889.

The rash of lumber and bricks made available led to a building boom in the Rockaways, and in the new section of the peninsula called Rockaway Park, which was laid out on the hotel grounds westward toward Beach 126th Street. Streets with infrastructure lined with trees were put in, as well as a few hotels, stores, and private first-class homes. The Rockaway Park Improvement Company planned Rockaway Park, and Austin C. Corbin was the president. He was owner of other hotels in Coney Island, president of the Long Island Rail Road, referred to as "Mr. Long Island" with all his dealings out there, and possibly against the Imperial outclassing his cash cows.

On the beachfront where the hotel stood, several orphanages were built, but commercial establishments were restricted to Beach 116th Street and the boulevard to the east. The rest was to be strictly residential with no rooming houses, no bungalows, and no liquor stores.

After 1900, things began to change. An apartment house was built and torched by unknowns, but it took a few places with it on Beach 117th Street. Afterward, rules and regulations were eased a bit, but no additional bungalows were added. A yacht club was built, and later an elevated boardwalk about two feet in height and Bayside Drive were also added. Beach 116th Street is still the main business block, a gashouse storage tank and gashouse are long gone, and the city rapid transit stops at Beach 116th Street. A few nightspots on the bay were torn down decades ago, and a seawall on the bay runs west of Beach 116th Street and commercial spots to the east.

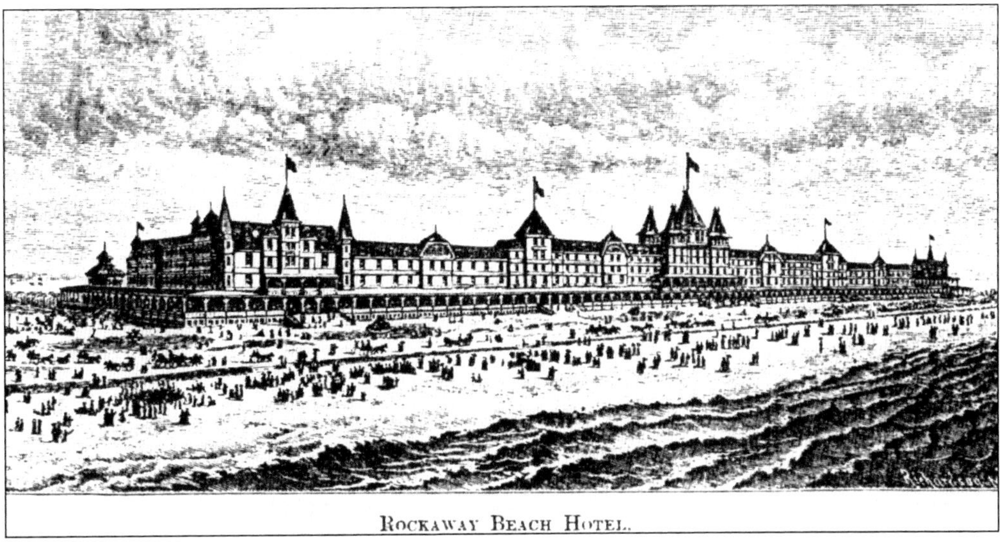

Only lithograph images of the Hotel Imperial built in Rockaway Park have been found on surviving promotions and letterhead. (Nothing was found on a nationwide quest for a glass-plate negative or photograph.) Architect N. Lebrun divested himself from the stigma of having a failure on his record anywhere, and he went on to build the 10-story Met Life skyscraper in Manhattan. (Courtesy of the Library of Congress.)

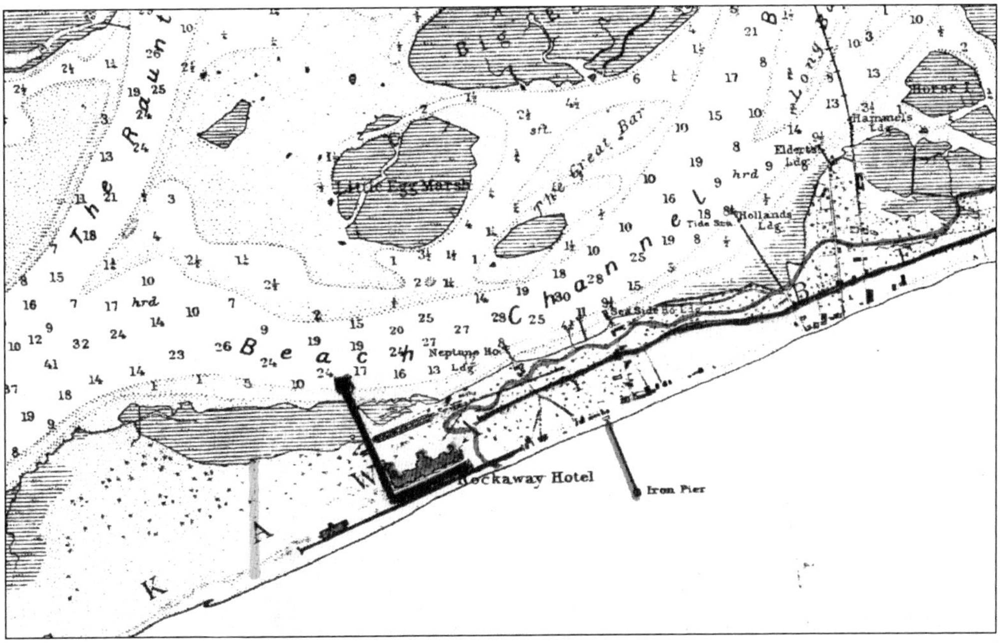

An 1888 nautical chart used the six-block-long hotel and 15-story brick chimney as an aid to navigation. The bay railroad is not completely drawn, the snaky Bay Road runs above the railroad to Seaside from Far Rockaway, the hotel dock and Plank Street pass by the station, and an iron pier for hotel steamers reaches out for 1,000 feet into the Atlantic Ocean. (Courtesy of the National Archives.)

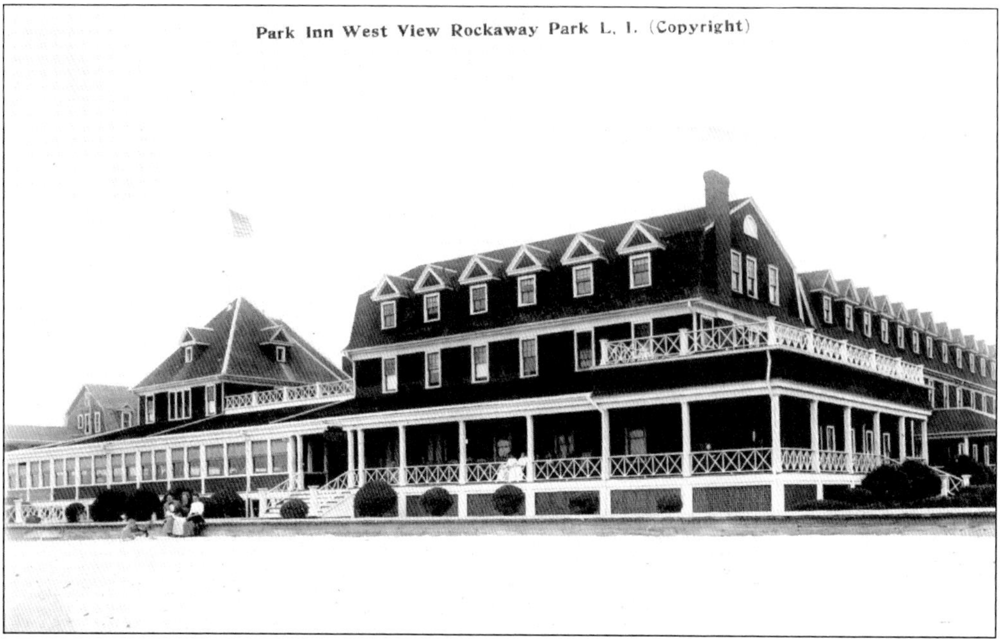

The portion of this building with the pyramid roof is the original Park Inn Hotel, built in Rockaway Park for the 1901 season. The first hotels built after the big hotel was torn down in 1889 were John J. Curley's Atlas and J. K. Bulmer's Park Hotel on Beach 116th Street on the beach and boulevard, respectively. The Park Inn grew and grew.

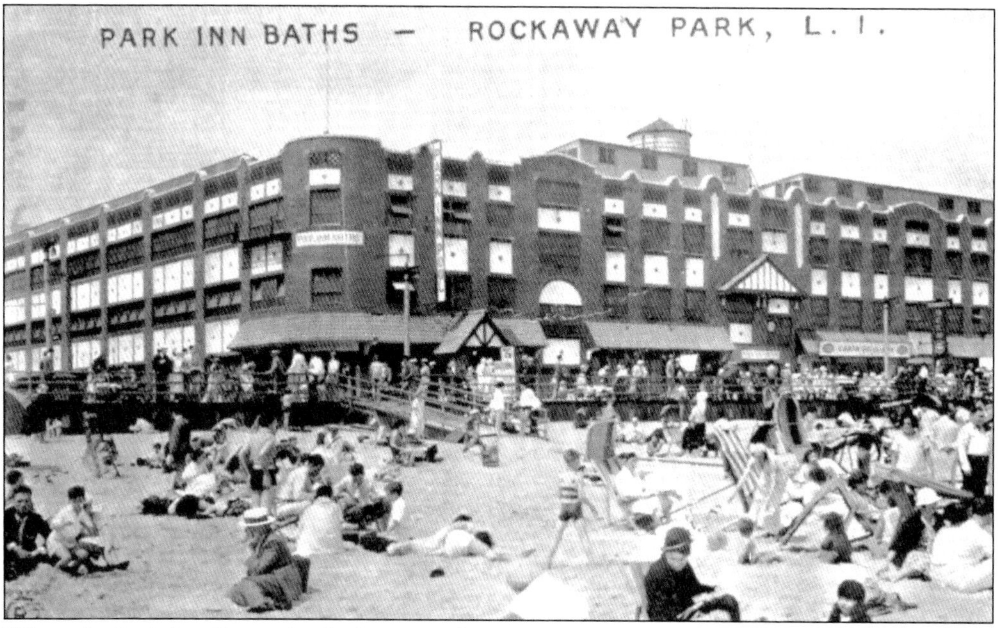

When the Park Inn Pompeian baths opened in 1901 as a small frame building on the east side of Beach 115th Street, it was not long before more baths were needed to satisfy the demand. Expansion of the popular bathing establishment led to the giant building shown in this view from 1934. Years ago it became a medical facility.

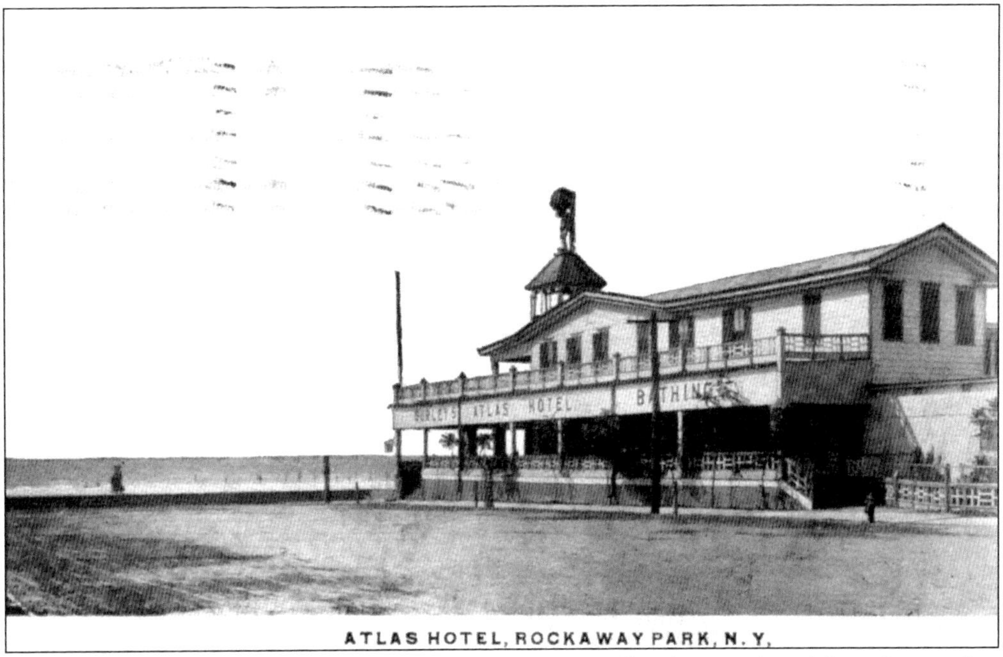

John J. Curley built his famous Rockaway Park Hotel out of lumber purchased from the wrecker of the Hotel Imperial in 1889. Built along the Rockaway Park boardwalk, the Triton Avenue of old, the L shape had the balance on Beach 116th Street toward the boulevard. Curley built a wooden sidewalk out to the surf for his guests in 1890.

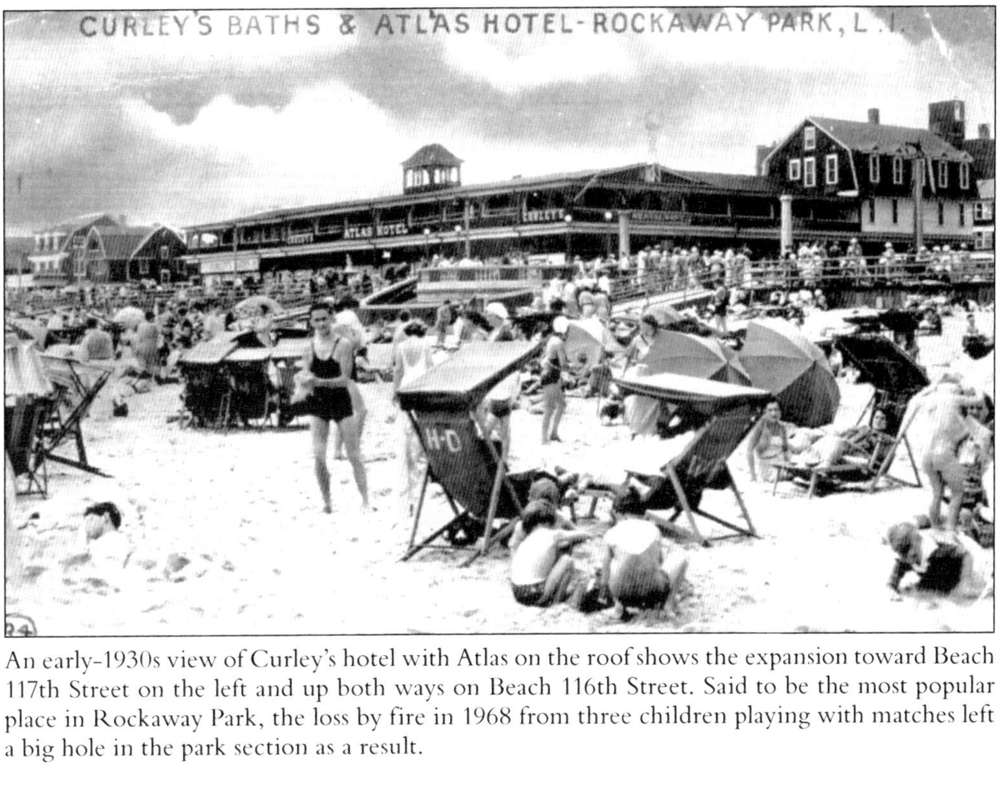

An early-1930s view of Curley's hotel with Atlas on the roof shows the expansion toward Beach 117th Street on the left and up both ways on Beach 116th Street. Said to be the most popular place in Rockaway Park, the loss by fire in 1968 from three children playing with matches left a big hole in the park section as a result.

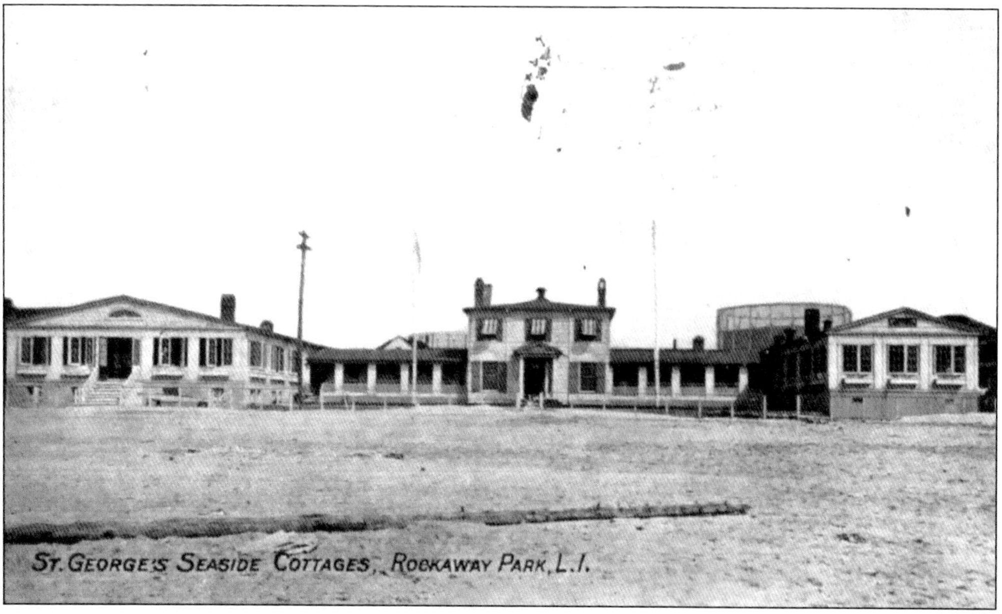

Wealthy financier J. P. Morgan, who had an interest in the big hotel and its property, was instrumental in securing some land for St. George's Church in the city. Children's cottages were built to provide fresh air and sunshine for the needy and sick children. In the 1920s, it became a home for young adults, then the White Horse Inn at Beach 110th Street.

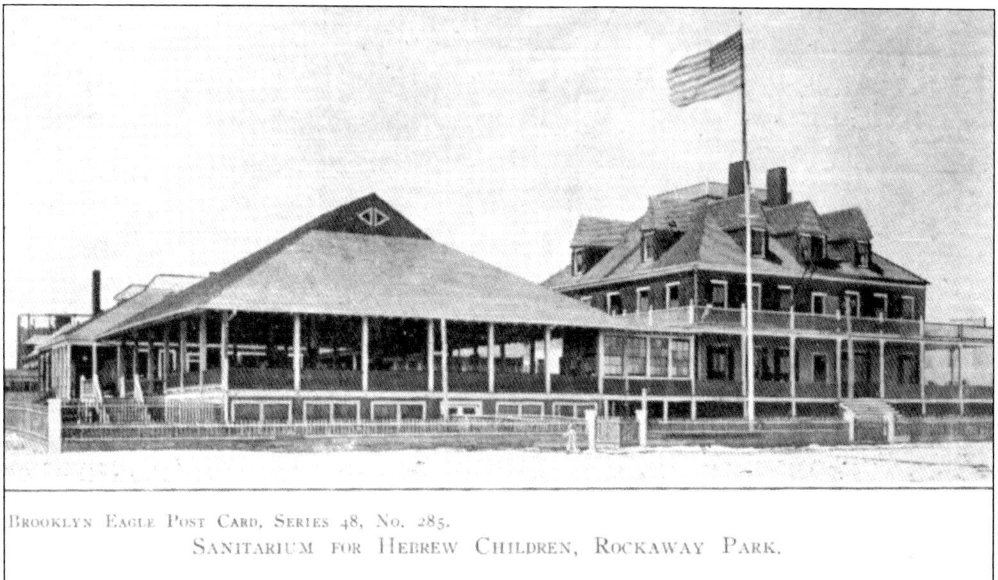

The Sanitarium for Hebrew Children was located in the Hammels section on Beach 86th Street near the beach in 1886. An 1891 atlas showed it had moved to Rockaway Park between Beach 110th and Beach 111th Streets. When larger facilities were needed in 1947, the sanitarium moved to Far Rockaways' Wavecrest.

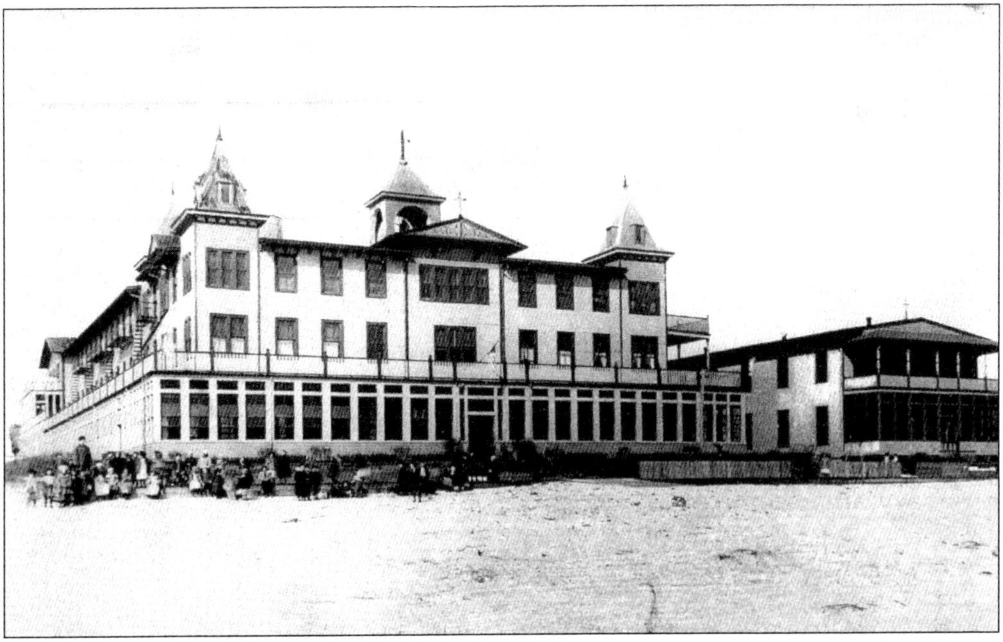

St. Malachy's Home for Orphans opened its new home on the beach between Beach 111th and Beach 112th Streets in 1898. The old home was on Beach 116th Street. In 1947, it took over the Hebrew home property after its move to Far Rockaway. In 1943, it became St. John's Home for Boys, and in 1959, it became Stella Maris High School for Girls.

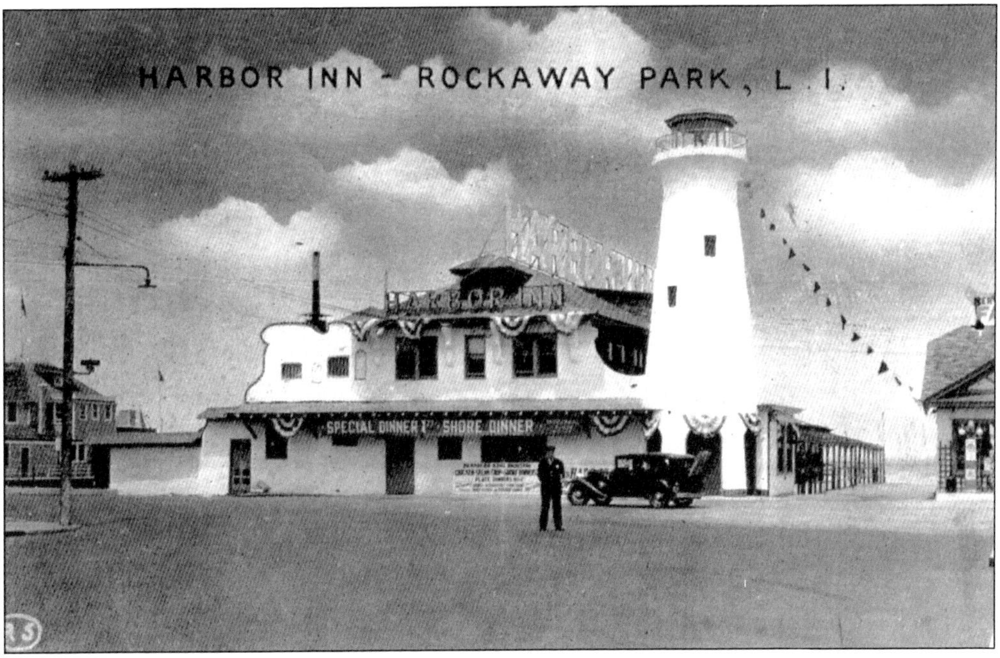

Claude Edgert's Harbor Inn opened as a nightspot in Rockaway Park at Beach 116th Street and the bay in 1912. When the landmark lighthouse was built in front for the 1930 season, it was the talk of the town. A dock about 700 feet long went out into the bay, and many boaters loved it. The structure was demolished in the 1960s for bay front and Beach Channel Drive work.

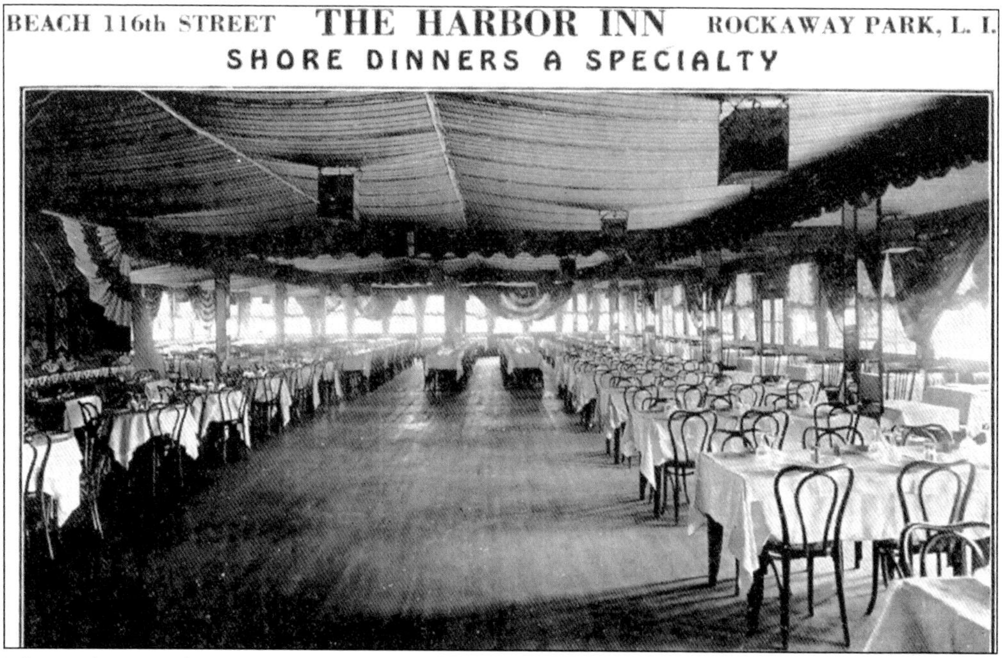

The Harbor Inn dining room had a good-size dance floor to work off that hearty shore or steak dinner. The known bands of the day played there. Wednesdays featured American night, Friday was Irish night, and Saturday was balloon night. Owner Claude Edgert had another place in Manhattan on Broadway at 69th Street.

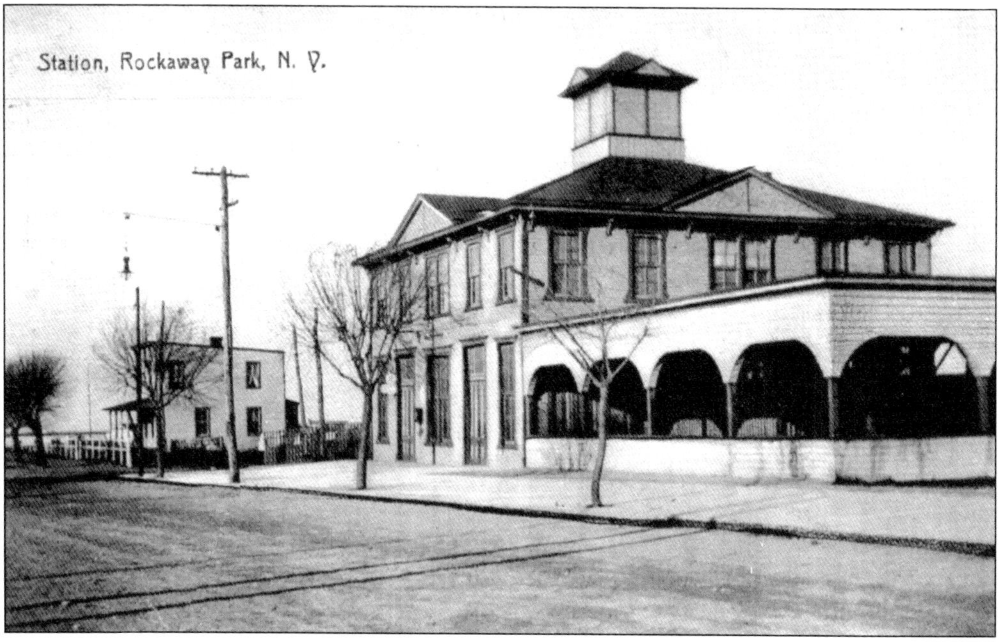

The first railroad station at Rockaway Park was built in 1882 to replace the open platform built by the New York, Woodhaven, and Rockaway Beach Railroad to the white elephant big hotel. The bay railroad became the Long Island Rail Road in 1887. A new brick station was built in 1917, and the line became part of the New York City Rapid Transit System in 1956.

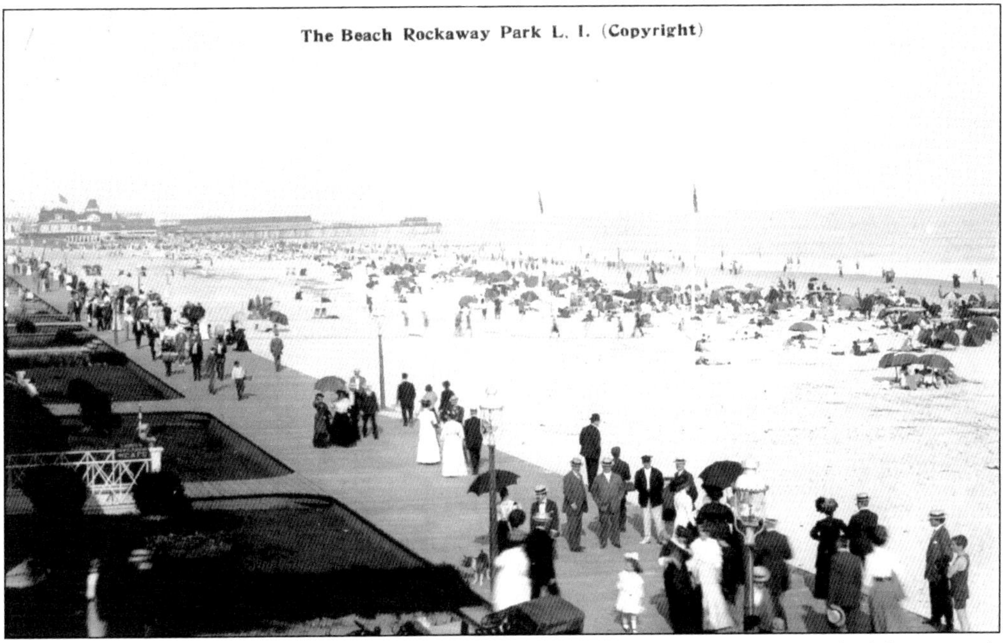

The Rockaway Park boardwalk was a rebuilding of the big hotel walk that stretched from Beach 109th Street west to Beach 120th Street. The new promenade was only about 18 inches above the sand, and small steps were placed at intervals on both sides. At 20 or so feet in width, there was room enough for all.

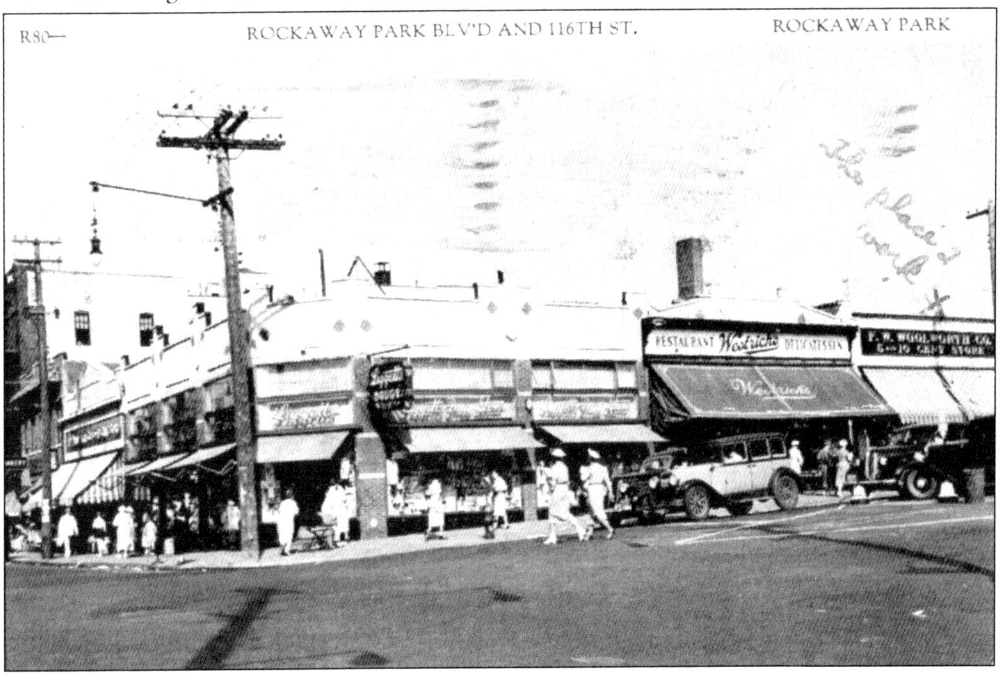

Once known as Fifth Avenue in Rockaway Park, Beach 116th Street has always been the shopping center of this part of the Rockaways. Back in 1880, one would be looking at the west wing of the big hotel that was built on a big, high, and long dune, partially man-made for the hotel. This was the reason for the dip to the boulevard here and the much lower bay front.

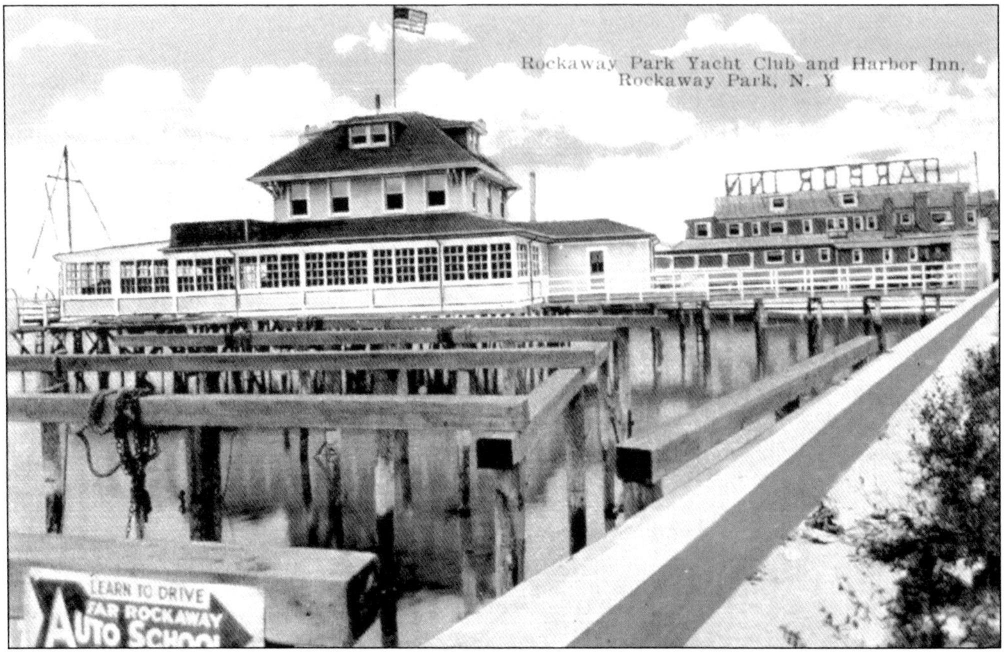

Rockaway Park had a yacht club just west of Beach 116th Street on the bay. Built in 1915, the club sponsored many boat races along with the Belle Harbor Yacht Club, until lack of interest stopped the contests. In 1916, pile-supported foundation beams went up to support a bungalow colony to the west and a court said no. The club was demolished in 1953.

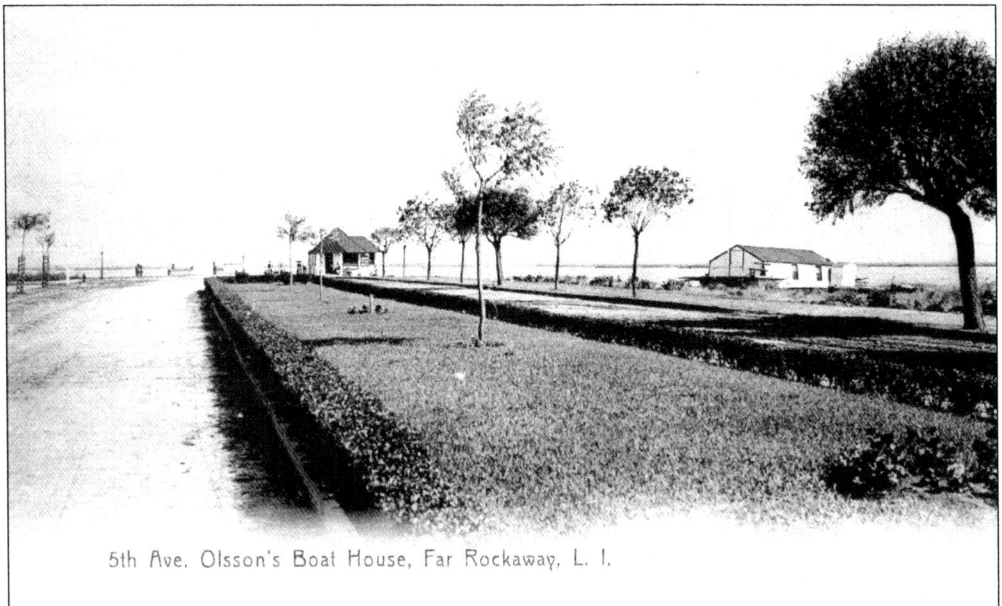

In 1902, the bay end of Beach 116th Street was wide open and serene looking, and all that was there was the Olsen boathouse and fishing station, a dock that went in to the bay, and the intersection of Bay Road and Newport Road at left center.

Eight

Belle Harbor
Beach 126th Street to Beach 141st Street

During the War of 1812, Rockaway Inlet was at Beach 137th Street, and a wooden blockhouse with a 24-pound cannon atop was built to fortify the point. Fort Decatur was built to keep the British vessels out of Jamaica Bay and also to provide safe haven for American coasting vessels. The New York Seafencibles manned the fort to the war's end. There were no reports of action, and the fort was removed in 1816. Public School No. 114 is near the site.

Since that time, the point and inlet have moved to the west, and in 1902, the West Rockaway Land Company sold part of its holdings to the Belle Harbor Improvement Company. Streets and main boulevards were laid out as far as Beach 141st Street, and Belle Harbor was developed in three segments: east, center, and west. Beach 129th Street was later allotted to be the business district. Only first-class housing was allowed, but somehow only a few small California-style bungalows were sneaked in on Beach 137th Street.

Many hotels appeared throughout, and the Belle Harbor Yacht Club was built in 1905 at Beach 127th Street on the bay. In 1904, a trolley line came to the west end of Rockaway Beach Boulevard to Beach 120th Street and later up Beach 116th Street to Newport Avenue then west to Riis Park. As early as 1910, a boardwalk was projected for Belle Harbor, but it was never built due to resident complaints. Later two small docks were built at Beach 129th Street on the bay to form a basin for the yacht club to the east.

When New York City took control of bay lands underwater, up to the high-water line of 1915, the Belle Harbor Yacht Club lost its docks rights. In the late 1930s, the other docks were also removed from Beach 129th Street, and a bulkhead was built from Rockaway Park west to Riis Park, where the bridge over the Rockaway Inlet to Brooklyn was being built. Boat races on the bay, sponsored by the local yacht clubs, were no longer held. Bandleader Guy Lombardo once raced his *Miss Tempo* in Jamaica Bay.

Some low apartment houses, garden apartments, and condominiums are mixed in with many architectural dreams in Belle Harbor, and parking is not allowed on the streets during summer weekends and holidays to keep the day beach parkers from clogging up the streets and driveways.

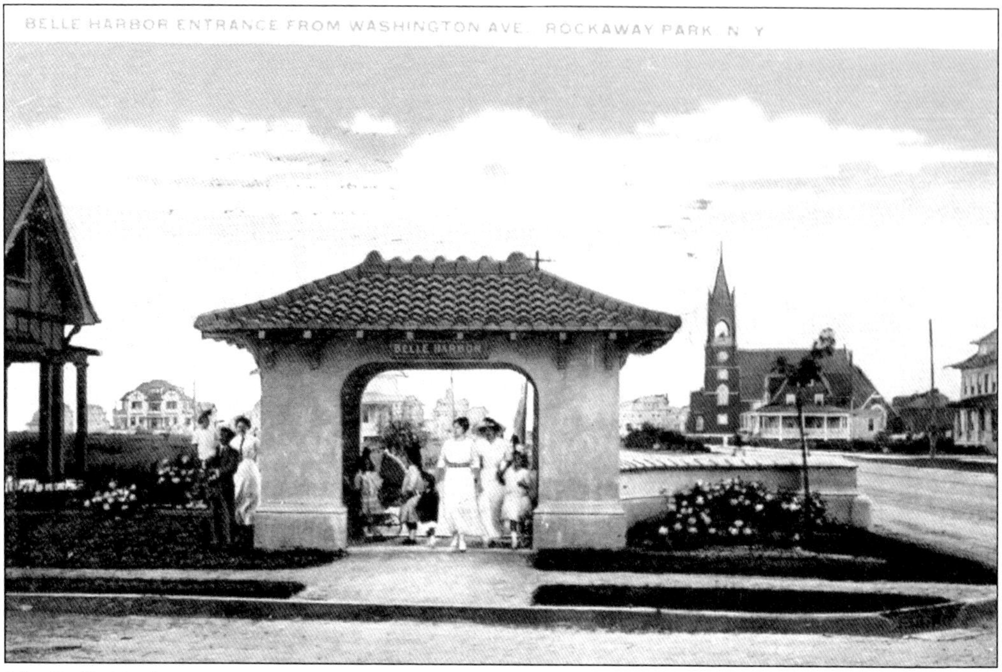

The Belle Harbor Improvement Company erected entrance arches on both sides of Washington Avenue at Beach 126th Street (now Rockaway Beach Boulevard) and also on both sides of Newport Avenue at Beach 124th Street. Deemed as dark, dirty, and unsightly, the arches were removed in 1931 by the Belle Harbor Property Owners Group.

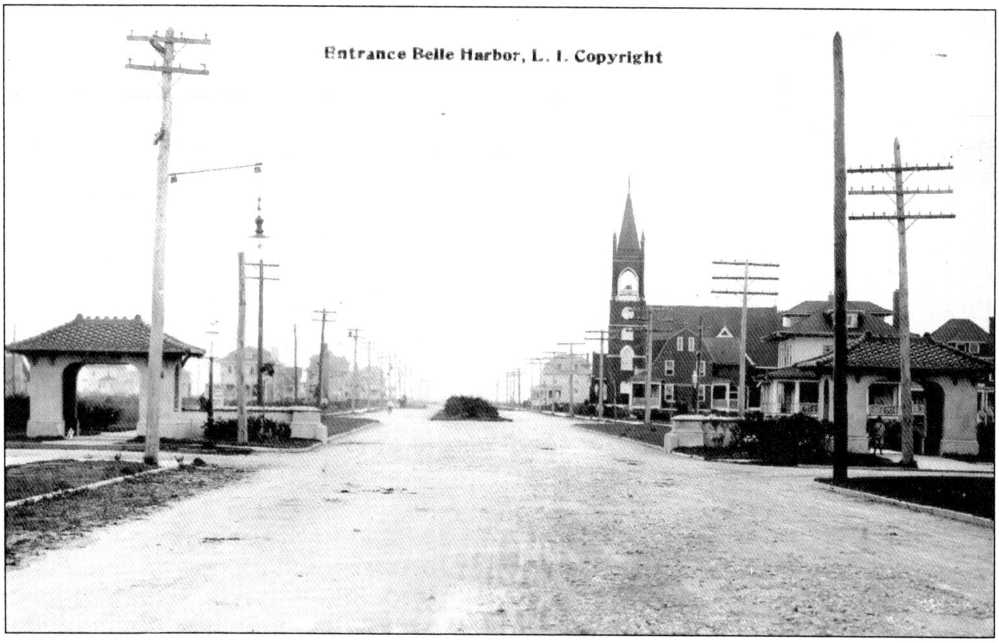

This excellent view of the entrance to Belle Harbor on the main boulevard, at Beach 126th Street, shows arches on both sides and a much wider boulevard with center malls beyond toward Neponsit. Private residences and cottages were spaced out before the boom of building began after this 1911 historical view. St. Francis De Sales Church was built in 1907.

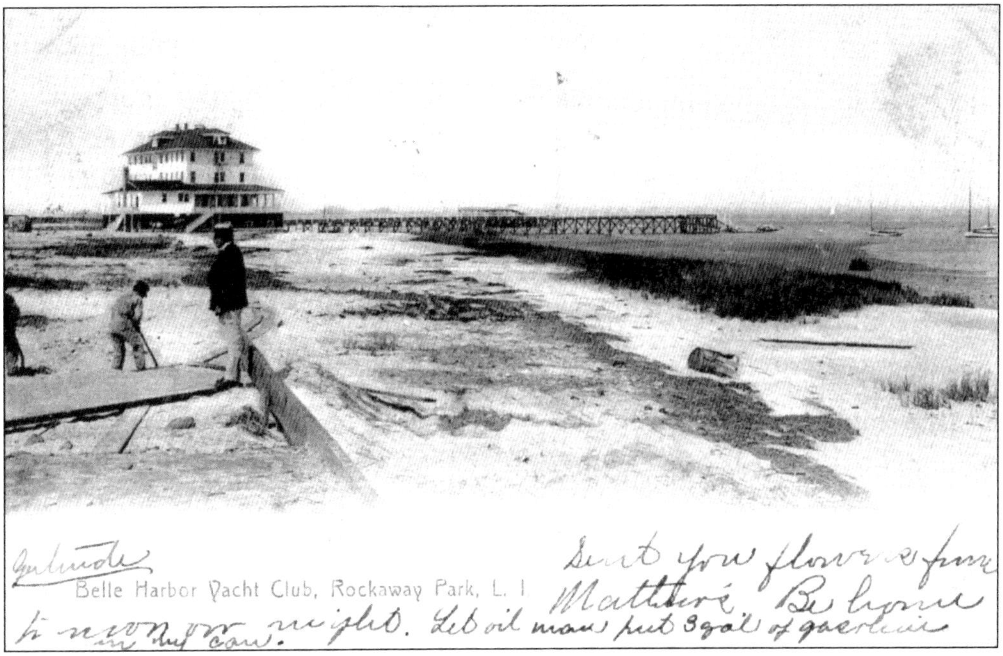

The Belle Harbor Yacht Club was opened in 1905 on the bay front, north of Cronston Avenue (Bayside Drive), in between Pelham an Oriental Avenues (Beach 126th and Beach 127th Streets). Workmen in this 1906 view are preparing the foundation for the future Cronston Road or Avenue, a continuance of Bay Road in Rockaway Park.

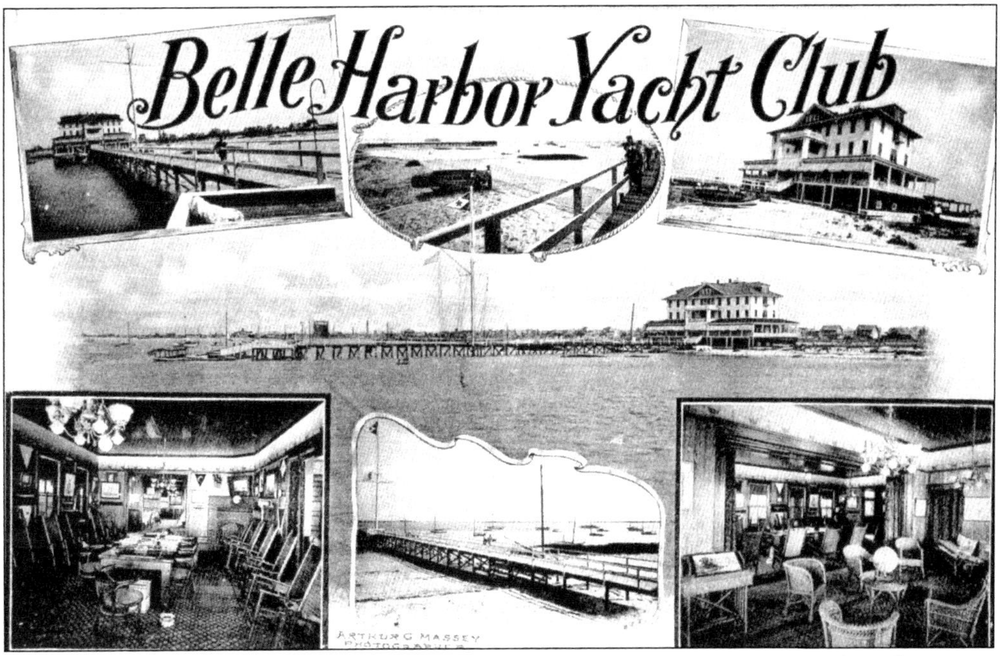

The new Belle Harbor Yacht Club published a multiview advertising postcard in the 1920s, which showed interior views as well as outdoor scenes taken on and around the club's domain. Interior views of this club are rare, to say the least, and the picture postcard has preserved historical views beyond belief.

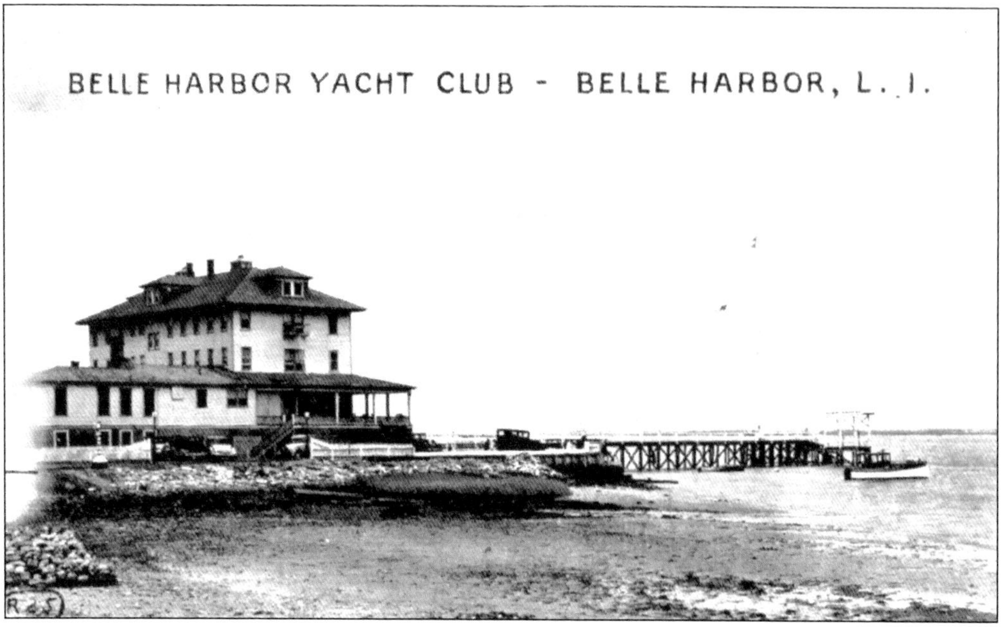

Shortly after this 1936 photograph was taken, the building of Beach Channel Drive from Rockaway Park to the new inlet bridge to Brooklyn caused the Belle Harbor Yacht Club to lose its dock out into Jamaica Bay forever. Small docks to the west, which created a basin for the club, were also removed.

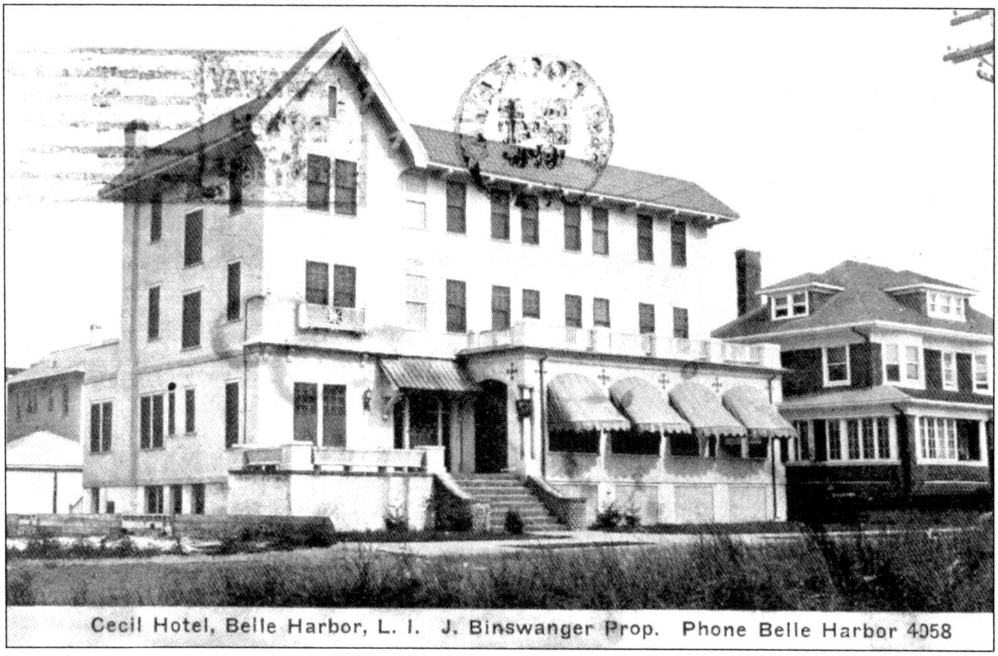

The first Cecil Hotel appeared on Beach 125th Street, and in 1928, the new Cecil was opened on the boulevard at Beach 127th Street. The Cecil was sold in 1930 and opened with a new name, the Seville. The first note of the Cecil proved to be wrong (as happens in reports) since this image is from 1925.

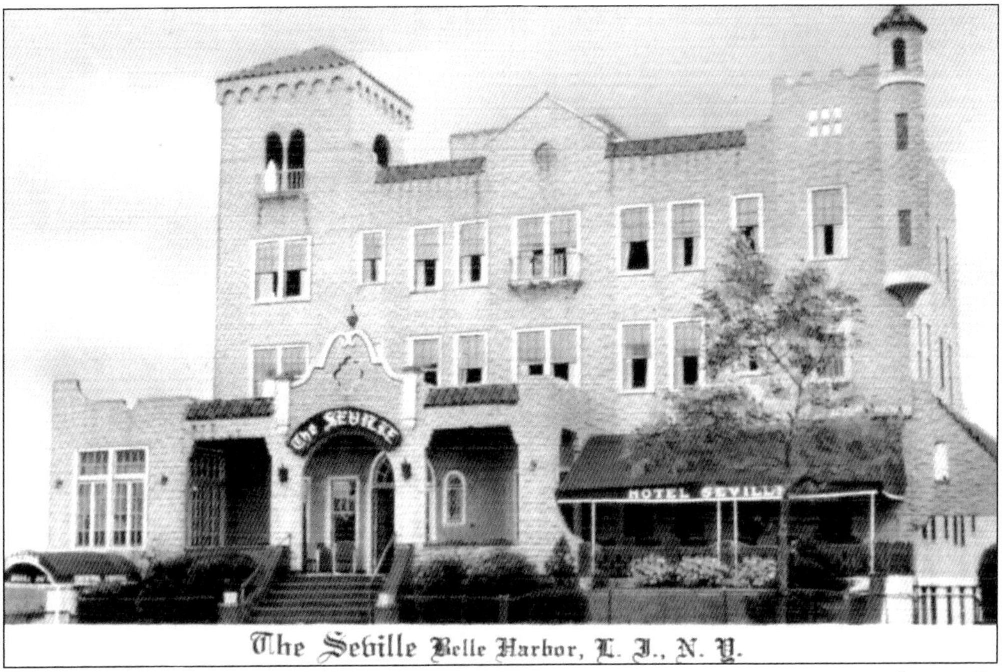

The old Cecil Hotel was remodeled and reopened as the Seville for the 1930 season. The Seville had 36 rooms, 23 baths, 11 rooms for the help, and a spacious dining room, plus a bar and grill room. In contemporary time, the Seville became a nursing home, which was demolished in 1999 for home construction.

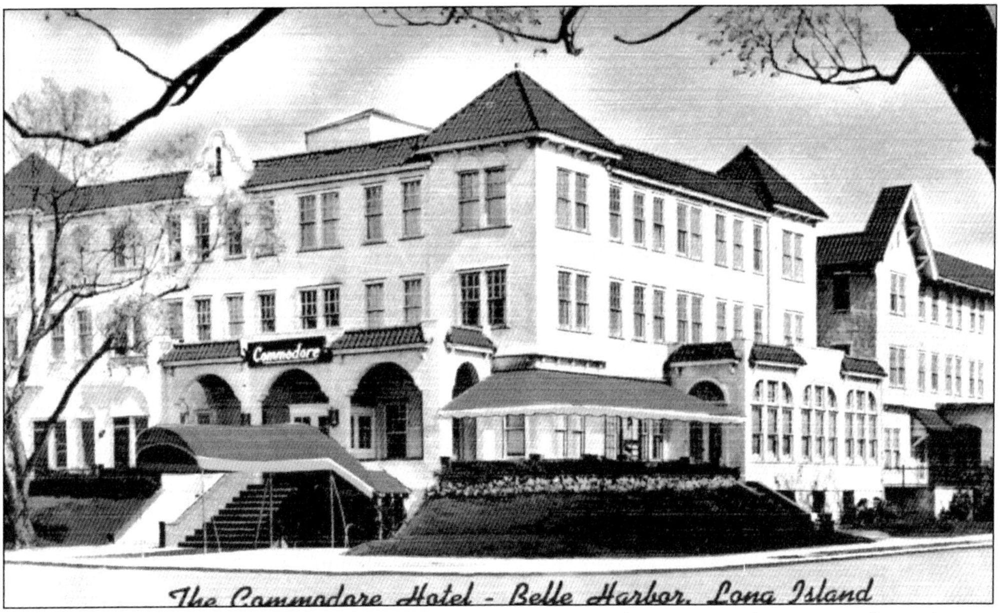

The Commodore Hotel opened on the southeast corner of Beach 127th Street and Rockaway Beach Boulevard in 1935. For two decades, the Commodore did well and in 1956 was under the management of the Charles Schorr Company. Schorr was preceded by his tenure as a beach hotel man since 1912. Many rooms had private baths and facilities available. This was replaced by housing in 1975.

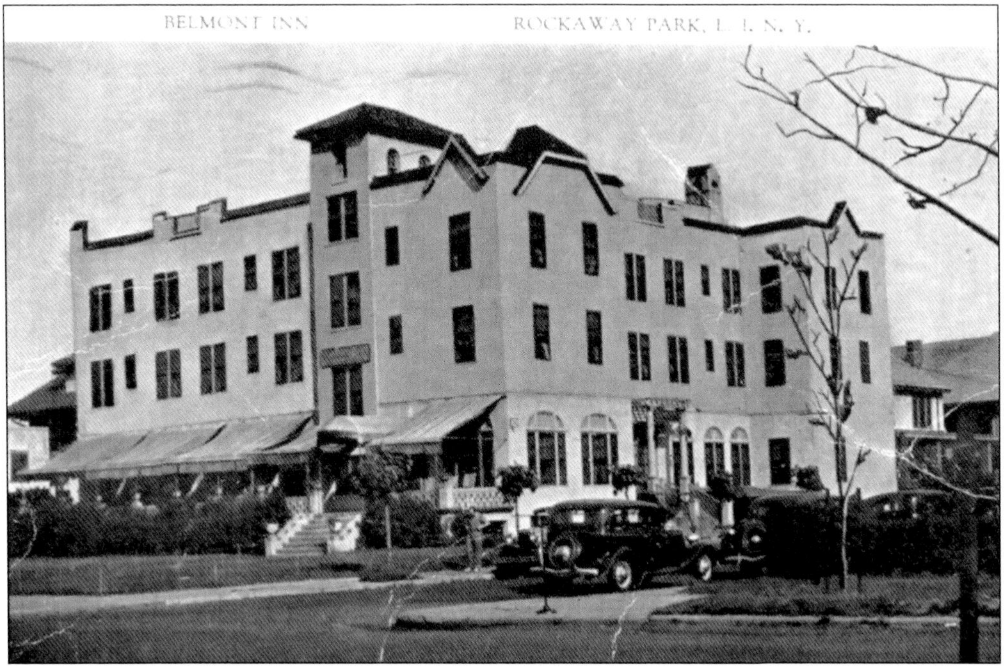

The Belmont Inn was opened on Rockaway Beach Boulevard in 1927, on the southeast corner of Beach 125th Street. In 1967, it became the new Washington Hotel; the old hotel on Beach 124th Street became the Queen Ester. The Washington became the last of the Rockaway hotels in history, as it was torn down for housing in 2006.

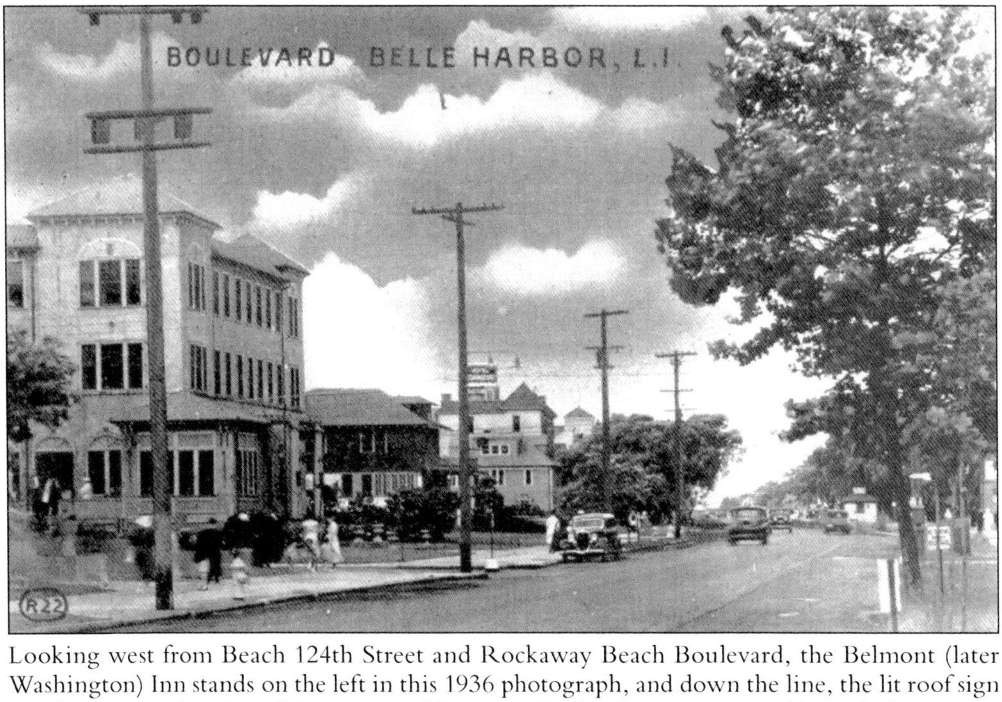

Looking west from Beach 124th Street and Rockaway Beach Boulevard, the Belmont (later Washington) Inn stands on the left in this 1936 photograph, and down the line, the lit roof sign for the Commodore Hotel sits on top of the large Charles Schorr–managed hotel in later years. Big Rockaway hotels phased away after World War II.

Nine

Neponsit
Beach 141st Street to Beach 149th Street

The West Rockaway Land Company sold the remainder of its west end property in 1908 to the Neponsit Land Company. This tract began at Beach 141st Street on the east and ended at Beach 169th Street on the west. The bay side was bulkheaded, dredge filled from the bay bottom, the tract leveled out, and streets were staked out in the sand. Only one-family luxury homes were allowed. The rule still applies, despite past challenges.

Development was slow at first but picked up after the Neponsit Club and a small marina were built on the bay in the northwest corner. A sewage pumping station once existed nearby but is long gone. No hotels were allowed, but small bungalow-type cottages were built on the west side. A commercial strip began in 1911 on Neponsit Avenue and was demolished for housing in the 1970s. The old trolley line from Far Rockaway to Riis Park had its last stop here.

The name Neponsit comes from an old Narragansett Indian word that translates to "an easy way with canoes." A small creek by that name once came into Neponsit from the bay. No Native American lived here since the point was at Beach 149th Street by 1841.

A U.S. lifesaving station was located in Neponsit from 1874 to 1911, when it was moved to its final location in the west end, at Beach 169th Street on the bay.

In 1911, a city park was being planned for the west end of Rockaway Beach, and the Neponsit Company sold its tract west of Beach 149th Street, ending at Beach 169th Street, to the city of New York. Neponsit has recently been described as the Beverly Hills of the East Coast, built for year-round living with a 45-minute commute to Manhattan.

The now closed Neponsit Hospital opened in 1915 as a tuberculosis hospital and remained as such until 1955, when it closed down. In a few years, after bickering, confusion, and indecision, a health care establishment for the elderly was opened and closed down after a tragic occurrence in 1998.

The land of the closed Neponsit Adult Healthcare Center is being sought by developers to build one-family luxury homes on the site. This will enhance the budding reputation of Neponsit, being referred to as the "Riviera of the Rockaways." The grounds adjoin the Riis Park portion of the Gateway National Recreation Area at Rockaway Point.

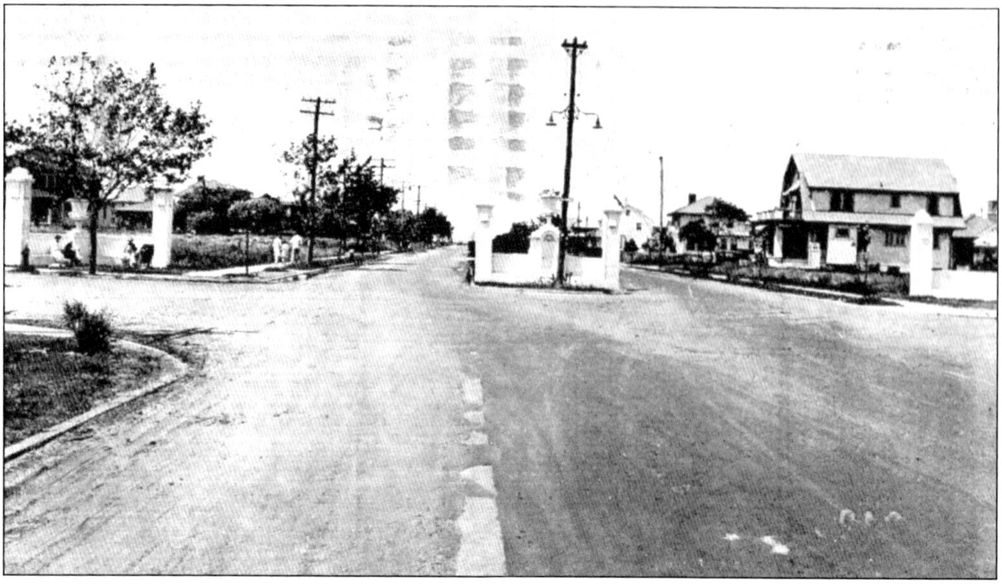

As those in vehicles or walking were about to enter Neponsit at Beach 141st Street, columns and walls about eight and four feet, respectively, in height greeted the walker on the sidewalk, as did flower vases. Rockaway Beach Boulevard had a monument across the center mall also decorated with flowers, pots, and columns.

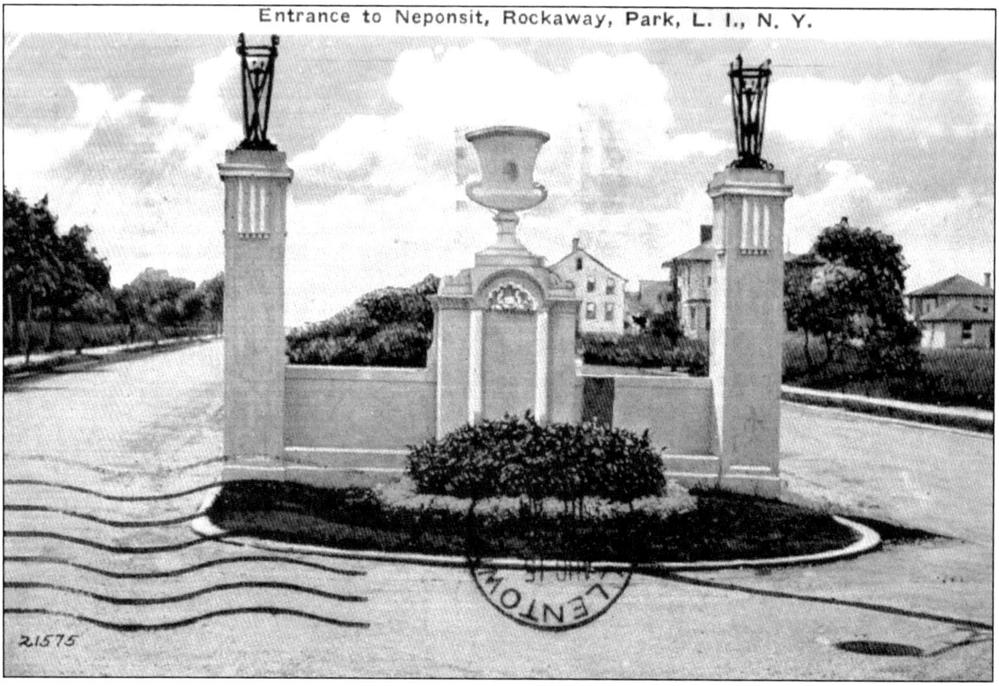

A close-up of the Neponsit entrance monument on the boulevard shows the care that was given and a change to wrought iron decoration on the side columns. The Neponsit section of the Rockaways had many restricting rules as to what could be built and the lowest cost to be accepted for a home built. Pennies compared to now!

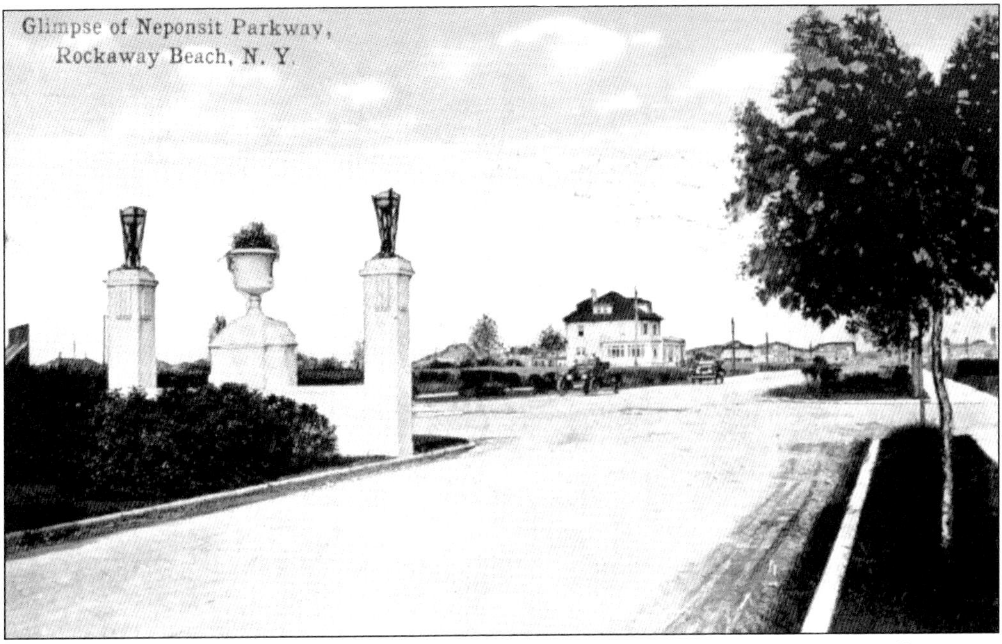

Looking out of Neponsit toward Belle Harbor, it is now noticeable that the lanes for traffic are not in a line. As motorcars sped along quickly, drivers neglected a short turn sequence and either ran off the road or crashed into the monument, both day and night. As time went on, paving made cross streets higher and the Neponsit Boulevard also. Lower sides caused dips at crossings.

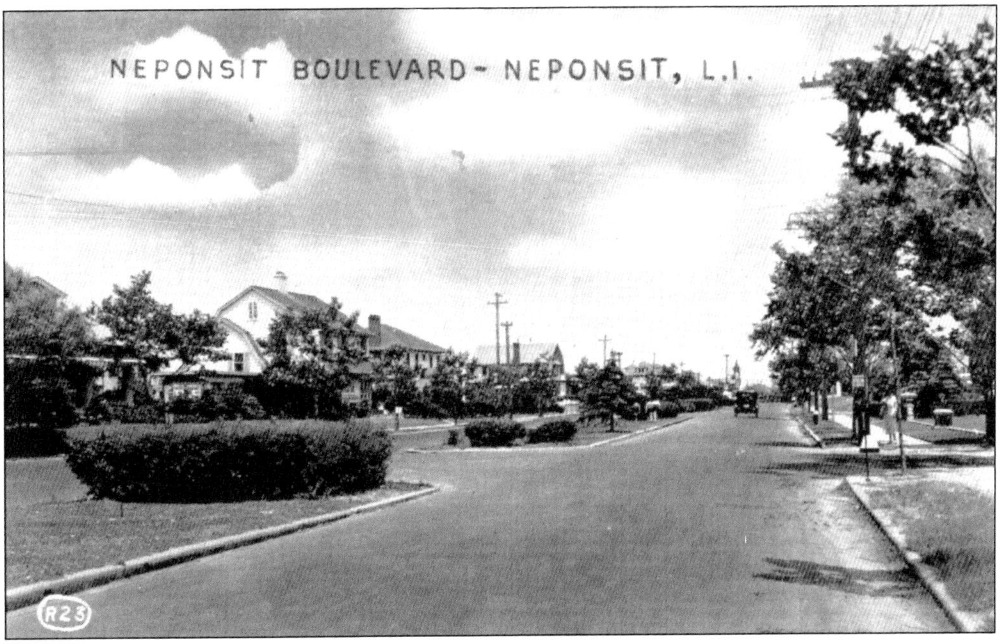

As driving problems were eliminated by good roadwork and planning, the Neponsit monument was also removed as it had become a liability. But as new paving again raised road centerlines, creating severe dips at all intersections, marks were left by cars bottoming out.

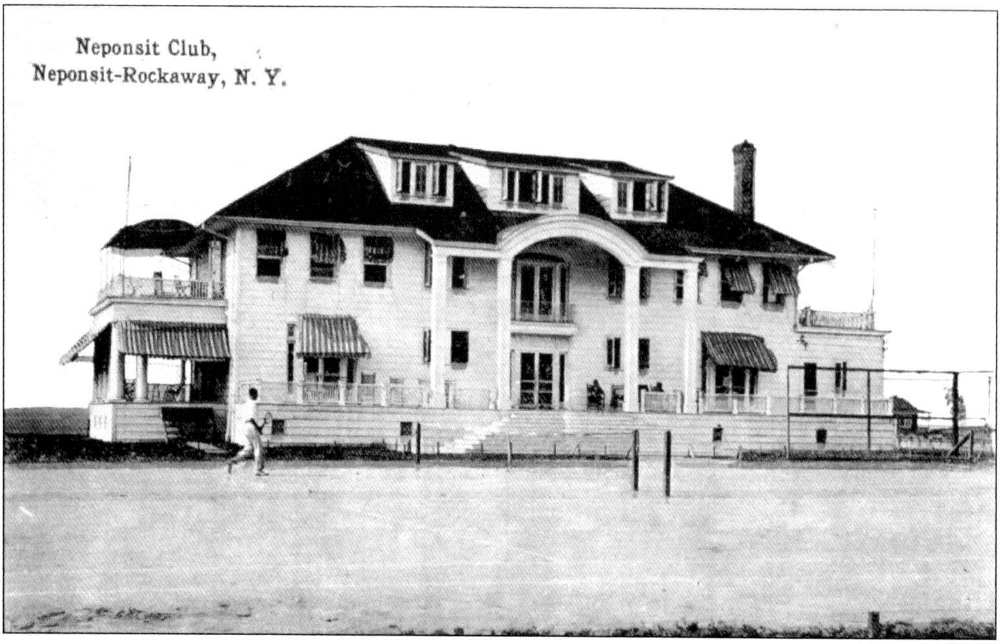

The Neponsit Club opened in 1912 at Neponsit's bay side in the northwest corner of the section. The new club served as a social center for the high-class west end development. A rod and gun club and a boat club were active, and a small dock went out into the bay. Tennis courts were also built. The club closed in 1925 and was torn down in 1935.

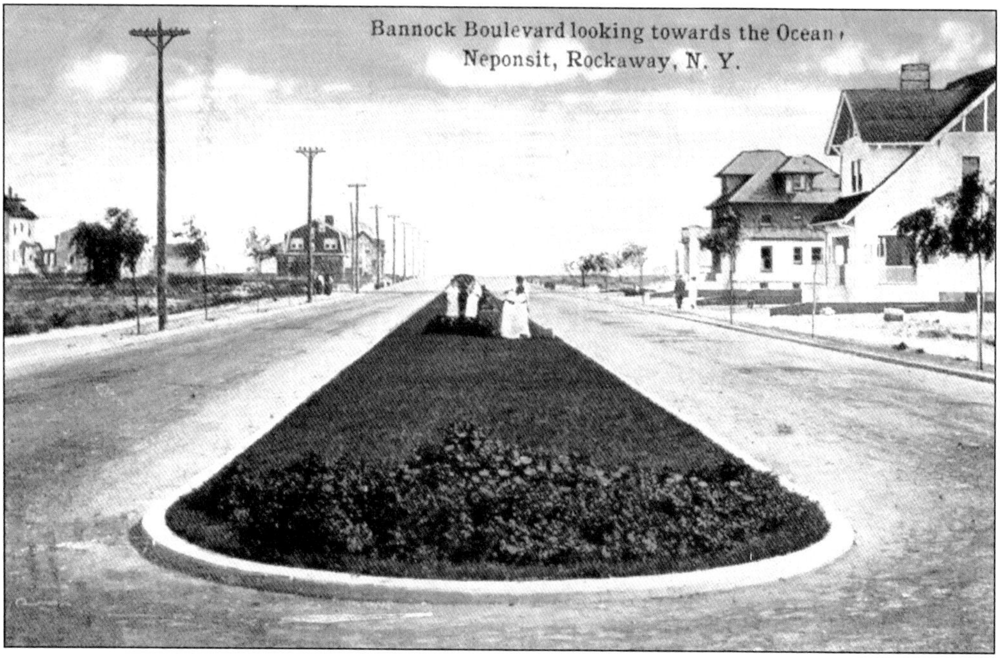

Bannock Boulevard (Beach 147th Street) in 1918 looked like what many people in all of the Rockaways want in this day and age—wide open spaces filled with fresh air and sunshine. This view is looking toward the ocean from the bay side.

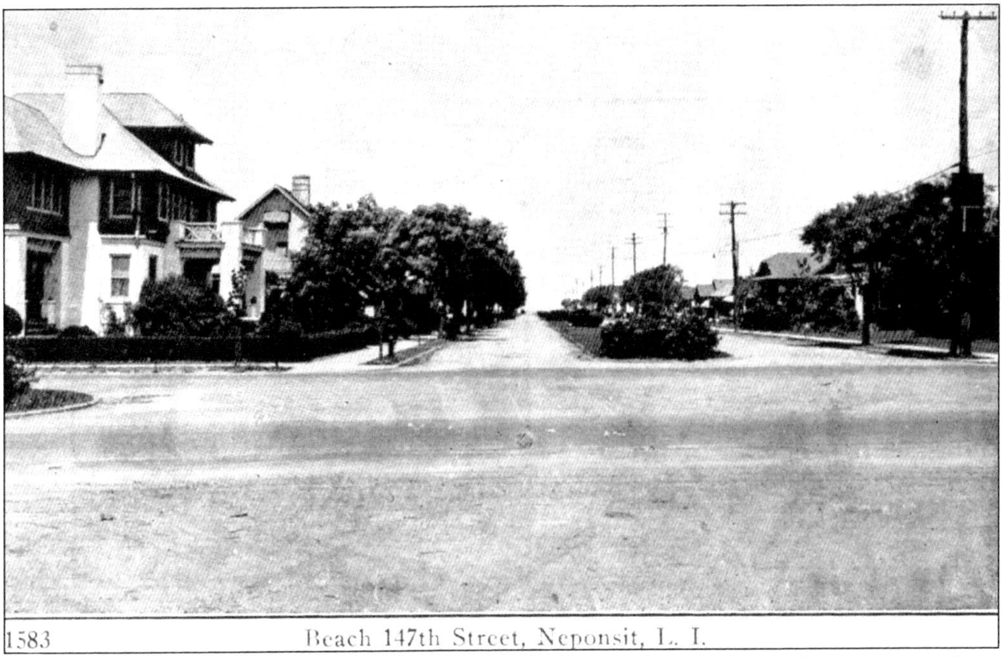

Beach 147th Street (old Bannock Boulevard) still looked about the same in this 1936 view from the Neponsit Boulevard to the beach. Street names were changed to numbers beginning in 1913 and were completed by 1920.

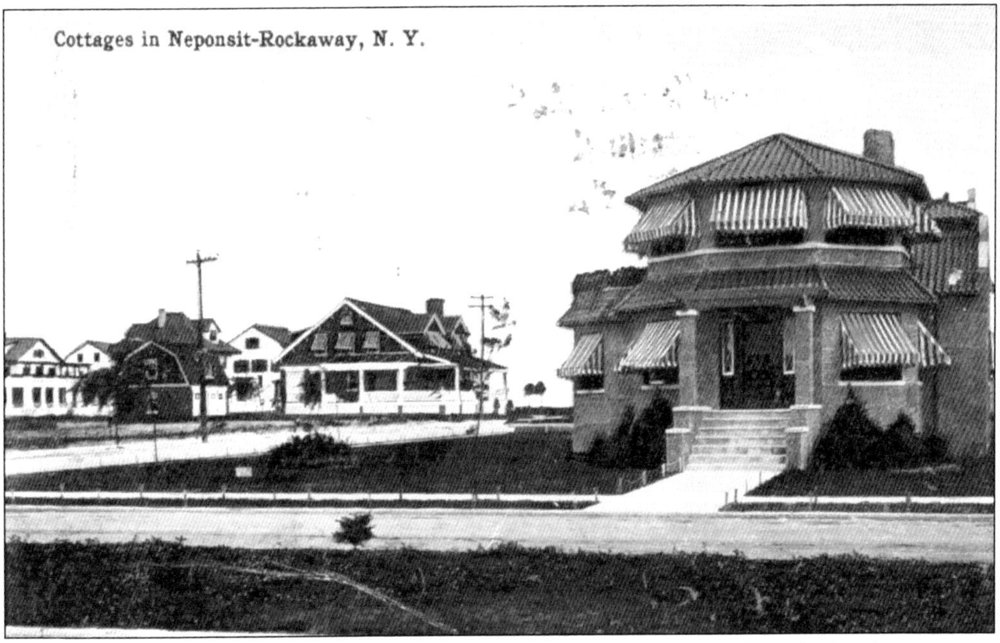

This Neponsit cottage has yet to be identified. Long ago a query was made in the local newspaper, the *Wave*, but no answers were forthcoming.

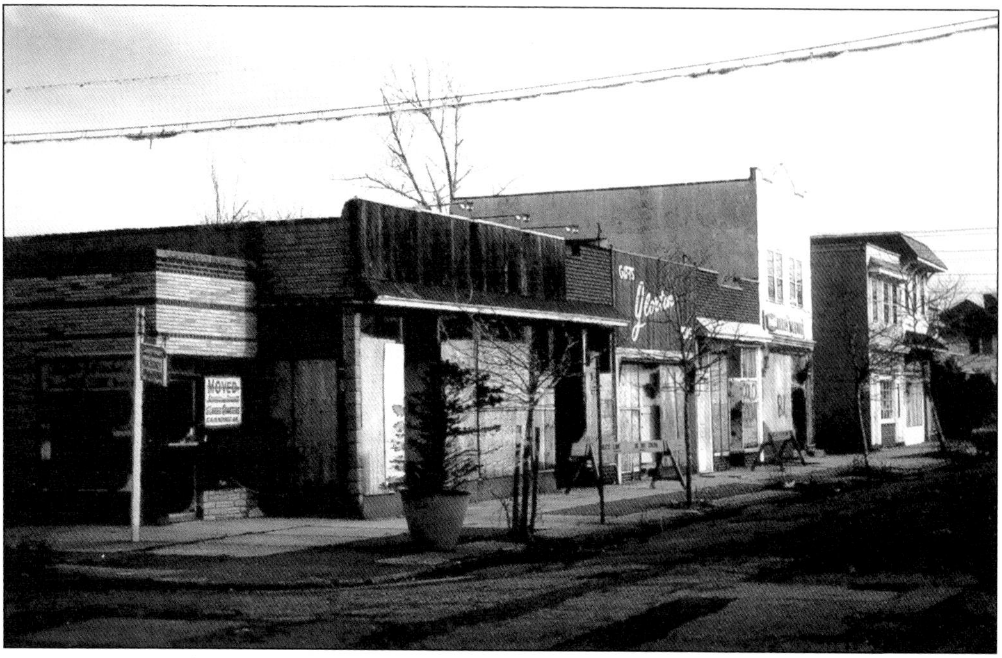

Neponsit Avenue had a compact shopping center between Beach 145th and Beach 148th Streets that contained about a dozen shops: drugs, hardware, real estate, kosher and nonkosher butchers, women's wear, children's wear, barber and beauty parlor, cleaner, tailor, groceries, fruits, toys, gifts, luncheonette, candies, and delicatessen. The shops were torn down for housing in 1972–1974.

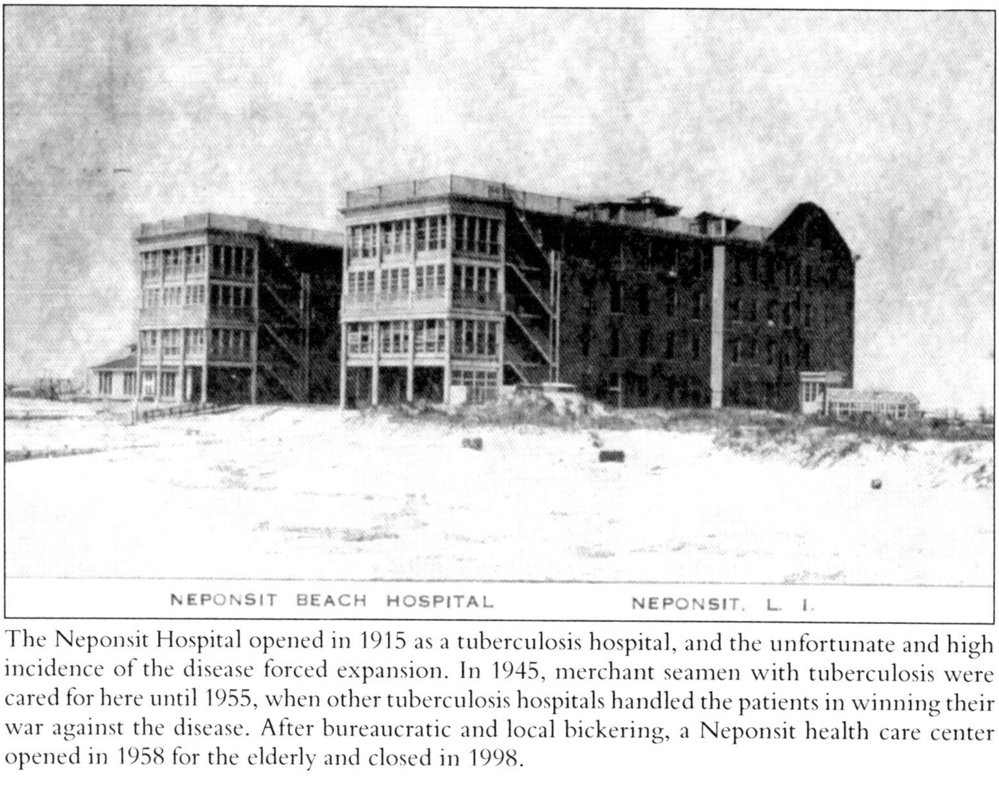

The Neponsit Hospital opened in 1915 as a tuberculosis hospital, and the unfortunate and high incidence of the disease forced expansion. In 1945, merchant seamen with tuberculosis were cared for here until 1955, when other tuberculosis hospitals handled the patients in winning their war against the disease. After bureaucratic and local bickering, a Neponsit health care center opened in 1958 for the elderly and closed in 1998.

Ten

The Point
Breezy Point Cooperative and Gateway National Recreational Area

The westerly point of the Rockaway Peninsula (by natural accretion of littoral drift sands) reached as far as Breezy Point on Rockaway Inlet by 1933. Developing sandbars and underwater shoals continued to develop to the west, however, still causing groundings and way problems for mariners. As a result, the stone hook jetty visible at the point was installed beginning in 1931 and accepted in 1933. Since then many acres of beach have been accumulated to the south and east of this construction.

The U.S. National Park Service area of Rockaway Point was a gift from the City of New York, after a failed plan by the city to construct Atlantic Village, a cluster of high-rise apartments, in the area. Gateway Park–Rockaway consists of Riis Park, Fort Tilden, and point land west, south, and east of the Breezy Point Cooperative. The Roxbury community is a part of the cooperative at the point. The U.S. Coast Guard had a base to the east of Roxbury but was relocated to New Jersey a few years ago. Gateway Park–Rockaway has steadily improved events and activities for locals and visitors since it was created in 1965.

Riis Park opened in 1911 as a New York City seaside park with limited beach use and facilities. The northwest corner of the park became the Rockaway Naval Air Station in 1917 to protect New York Harbor during World War I.

During the month of May in 1919, the first transatlantic flight by U.S. Navy seaplanes, noted as NC-1, NC-3, and NC-4, started off at the Rockaway Naval Air Station with NC-4 completing the flight to Bristol, England (NC is the designation for Navy Curtiss). The base was forced to move elsewhere in 1931 in order for the city to develop Riis Park, which opened in 1937.

Gateway Park was received "as is" from the city fathers, and improvements have happened. The park was named after Jacob Riis, the old-time champion of the poor. Fort Tilden is named after Samuel J. Tilden, who lost a presidential election to Rutherford B. Hayes by one electoral vote in 1876. At first it was named Fort Funston, after the hero of the Philippine Insurrection decades ago.

Tilden also opened in 1917 with several six-inch coastal guns and was deactivated after the war. It was reopened in the early 1920s with two 16-inch rifles and was beefed up for coast defense in World War II. During the Korean War, Nike surface-to-air missiles were put in as in other locations for aircraft and missile defense. The National Guard still uses a small portion of the fort, and the beach areas are kept in a natural state as best as possible.

What is now the Breezy Point Cooperative with a hefty population of "pointers" had only one resident in 1879. Smith Foster was a watchman for his uncle Jurien Lott of Brooklyn, who thought he owned the point as a reliction of the southern tip of Barren Island, which had washed away long ago.

In 1902, it was revealed that tenants paying rent to Lott were Howard Reid, John Simon, Charles Seaman, Foster, Mr. Sutter, Mr. Dawson, Harry Warren, and John Roxbury. This discovery led to litigation between Lott and the legal owner of the point, Andrew K. Vandeventer of the Southern Pacific Railway Company. The court decided in favor of Vandeventer, stating that the point of Rockaway was a natural accretion to the west of Far Rockaway. Rents were paid accordingly.

Development as a summer colony began in 1911, with building sites rented out by the Rockaway-Pacific Company. Tenants arrived from the shore areas of West Coney Island after being evicted by developers. In some cases, buildings were ferried over, as well as boatloads of lumber purchased from the wreckers on the opposite bank of Rockaway Inlet.

Slightly elevated wooden walks were the streets, lined with small bungalow-style structures. Most walks led to the Brooklyn ferry and steamer docks at hotels run by Reid, Simon, Seaman, and Roxbury. A grocery boat and a floating general store visited often, until company stores were forced upon tenants. Churches, a theater, firehouses, a lumberyard, a deep well for freshwater, and, much later, a point post office soon appeared. Prior to the latter, mail was taken to Brooklyn by boat to be posted.

The surf line of the present is a long way from the once Surfside Avenue buildings, due to the vast accumulation of eastern sands, which drift westward. Upwards of 100 acres have been added since 1933. Ferries to the point from Sheepshead Bay stopped running in the early 1980s, for lack of ridership.

The Breezy Point Cooperative was organized from the banding together of the Breezy Point, Rockaway Point, and Roxbury Associations when Gateway Park–Rockaway came to be in the 1960s. When the three groups formed in the 1920s, their goal was to end domination by the point's landlord, the Rockaway Operating Company. The most critical danger for the point in present times is the strong possibility of being inundated by a superstorm in the future.

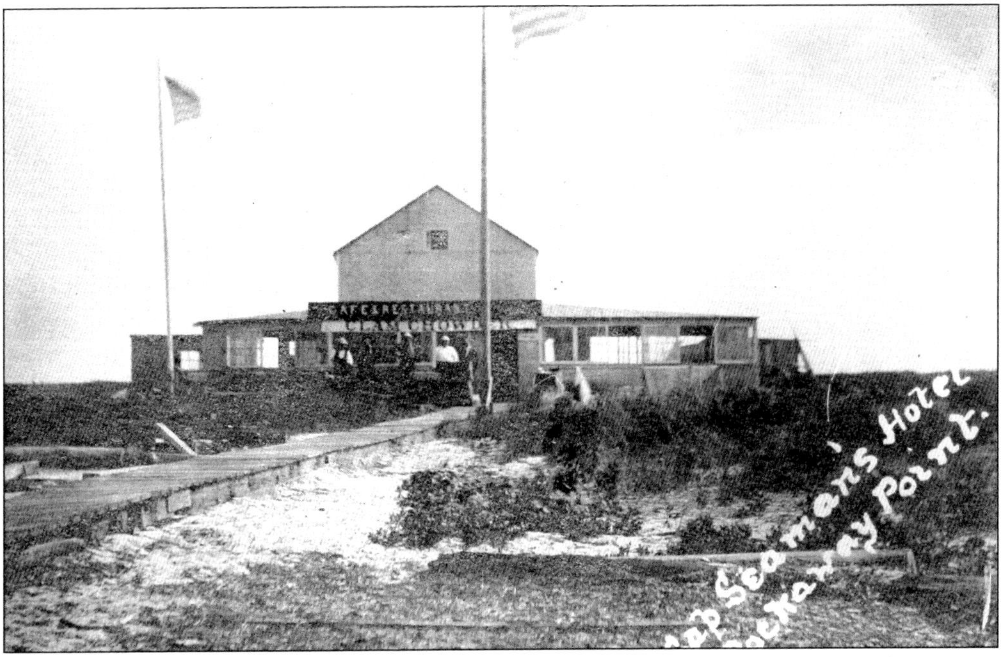

Capt. Charles Seaman was among the first tenants at Rockaway Point during the late 1890s. His hotel, café, and chowder house were located a little to the east of Reid Avenue on the south shore of Rockaway Inlet. A raised wooden walk led to his front door from a sort of common narrow boardwalk along the bay shore, east and west of the point boat dock.

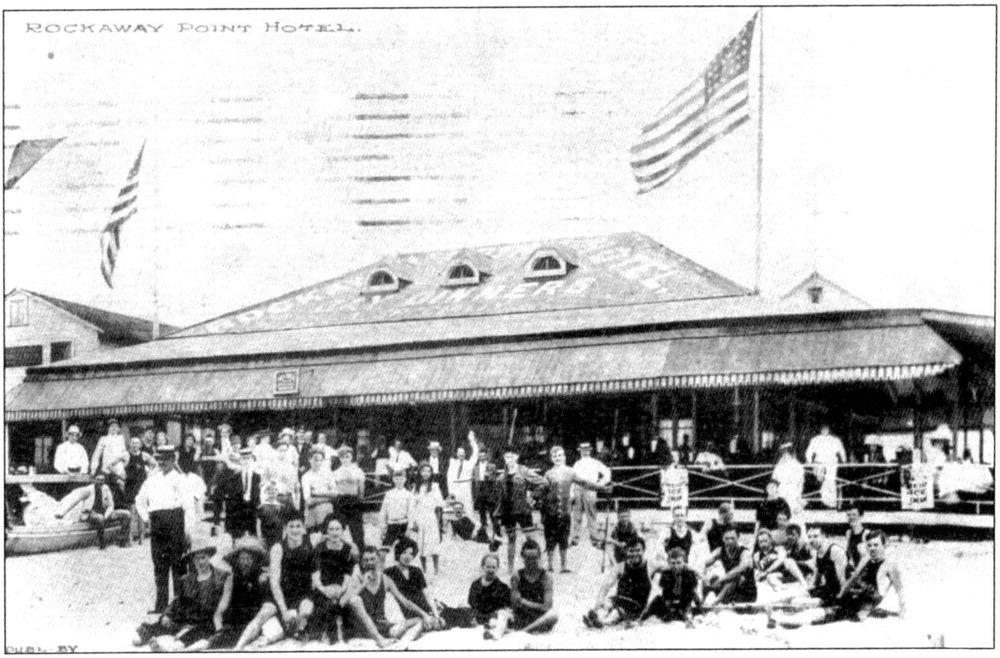

Howard Reid's Rockaway Point Inn was reported at the point in 1901. Reid and others (Roxbury, Simon, and Seaman) built the first docks on the south shore of Rockaway Inlet. Several more were built later. Simon and Reid were the first to have ferries bring patrons to the point beaches in summer, Reid owning a side-wheeler.

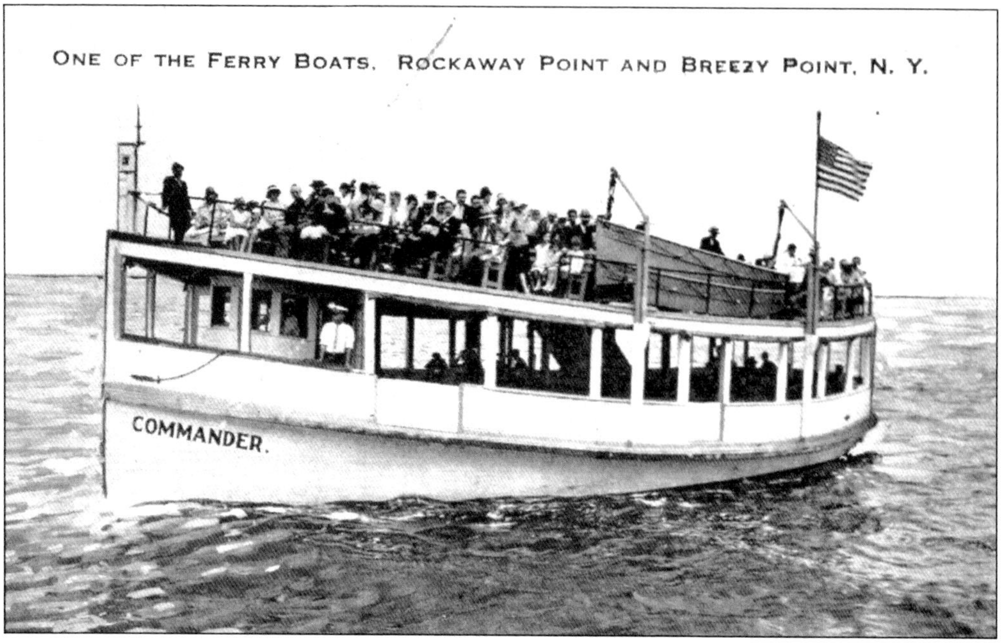

The point ferry *Commander* plied the waters of western Rockaway Inlet for many decades, between Sheepshead Bay in Brooklyn to Howard Reid's dock at the point. Ferries to the point stopped running in 1985. The *Commander* still runs on dinner cruises near West Point, on the Hudson River in Upstate New York.

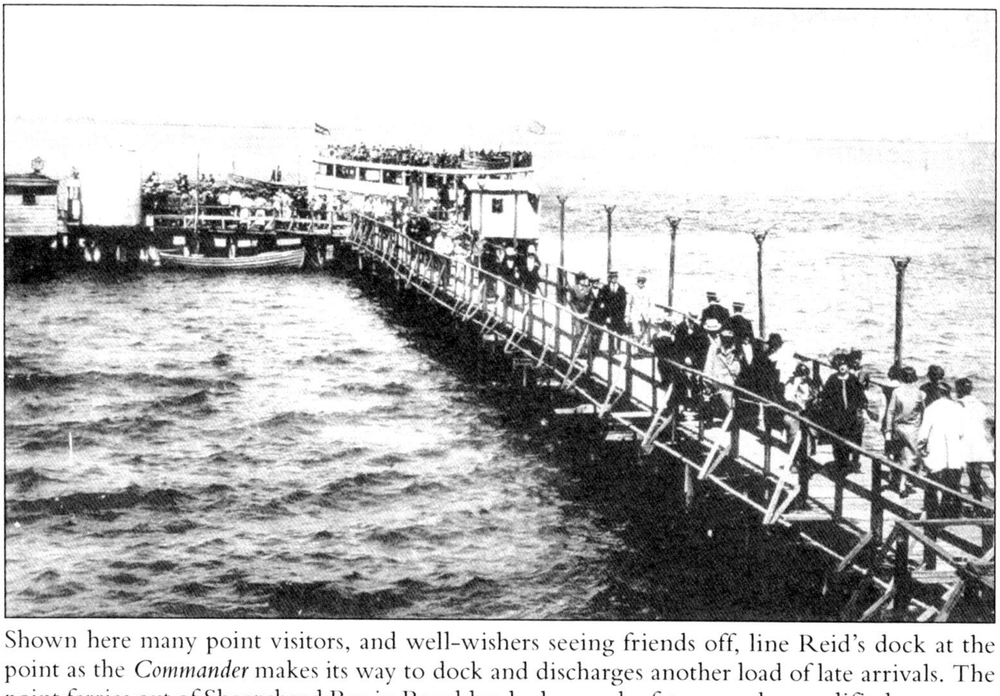

Shown here many point visitors, and well-wishers seeing friends off, line Reid's dock at the point as the *Commander* makes its way to dock and discharges another load of late arrivals. The point ferries out of Sheepshead Bay in Brooklyn had a good safety record as qualified operators ran the boats to the coolest place in town.

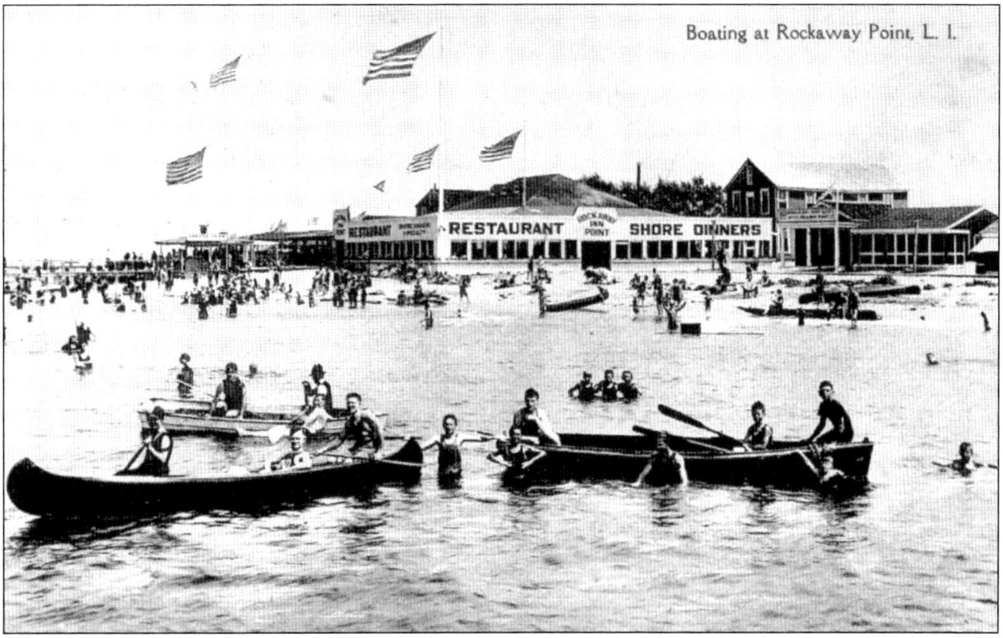

Stillwater bathing, boating, and canoeing were strong favorites on the bay side of Rockaway Point. There was a war raging in Europe in 1918 when this picture was taken at Howard Reid's Rockaway Point Inn, but one would never know it by this image. Reid, considered by many to be the Point's kingpin, died in October 1925.

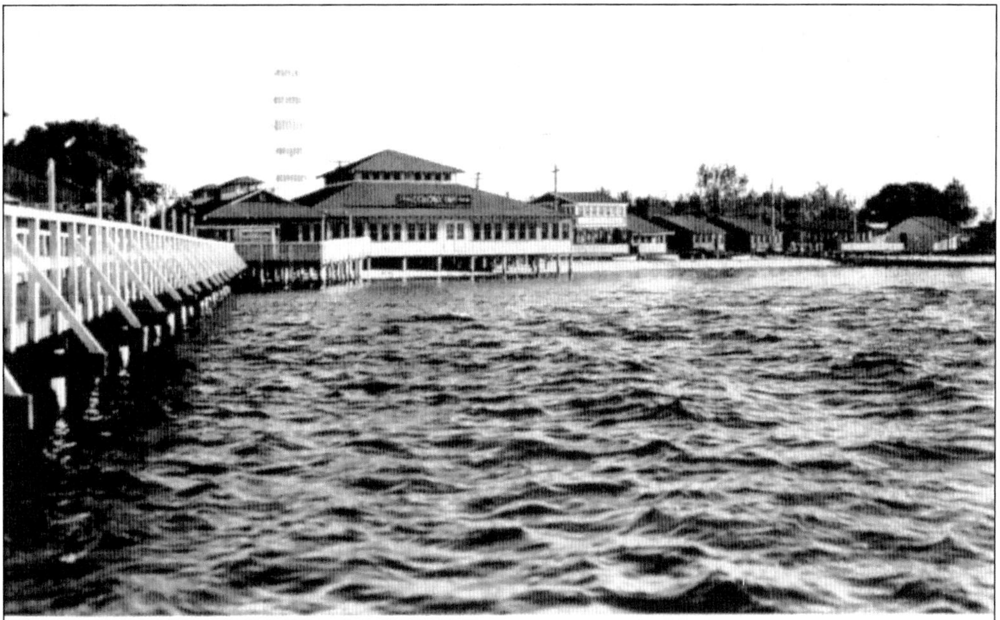

In 1920, in order to counteract the rules and regulations placed on "pointers," the new Rockaway Operating Company (formerly the Rockaway-Pacific Corporation) and the Rockaway Point, Breezy Point, and Roxbury groups joined forces to have a say about things. Changes were slow in coming. Reid's place became J. J. Danaher's Colony Club in later years.

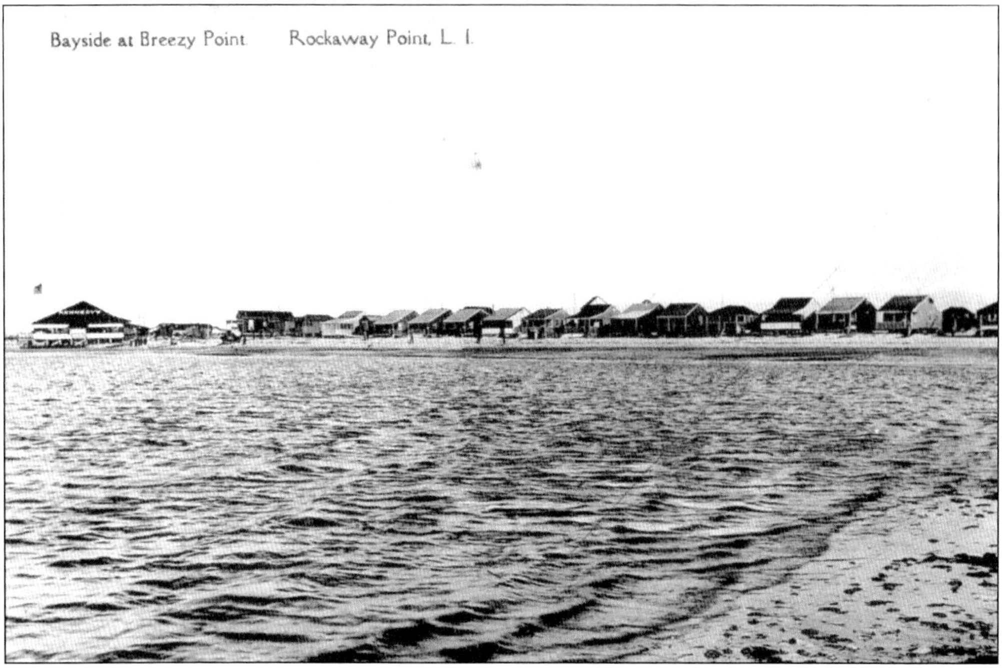

Drawn on a point chart and dated as 1917, the first of Neils Friberg's pavilions was labeled on Breezy Point and as a ferry stop in 1919. It has been said that this old building had been floated over from the Brooklyn side of the inlet about 1911. By 1918, the place was called Maxwell Kennedy's Breezy Point Casino, pictured here on the left.

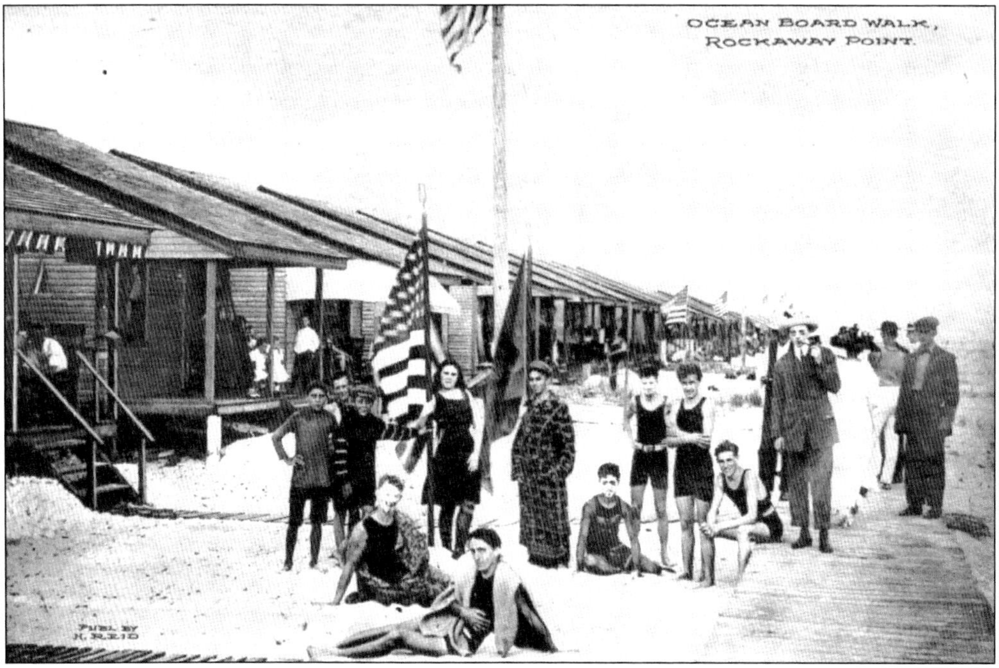

This group of pointers shows some people in bathing attire of the time, a boy and a girl holding on to a flagstaff, and others dressed very strangely. This postcard is titled as "Ocean Boardwalk, Rockaway Point," although it could mean Oceanside Avenue.

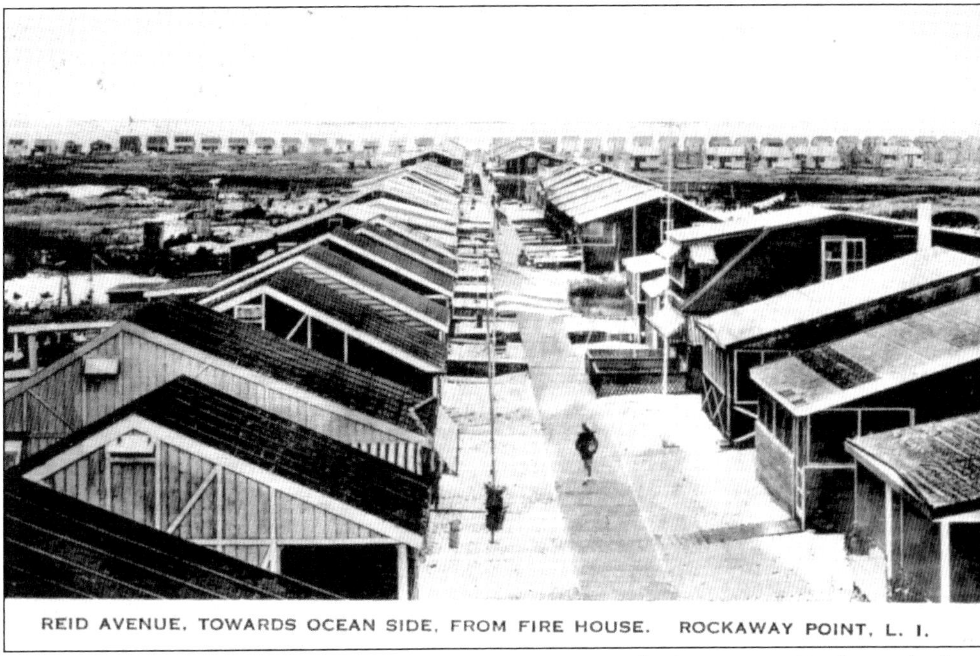

This view of Reid Avenue, taken from the Rockaway Point firehouse in 1920, shows the long line of bungalows at the beachfront, known as Beachside Avenue. The point is wider now because the distant beach was water frontage many years before this photograph was taken. The stone hook jetty has made the site wider yet.

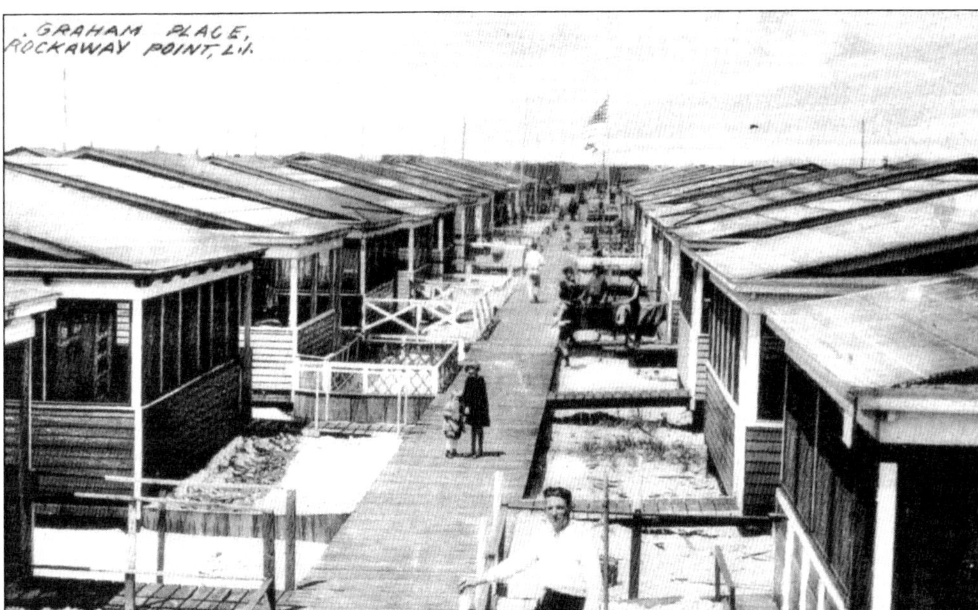

Graham Place at Rockaway Point is tucked away nicely between Reid Avenue and Beach 204th Street, south of Lane Janet and north of the beachfront. Again, with the placement of the rock jetty in the early 1930s, the beach to the south of Graham Place has grown considerably wider.

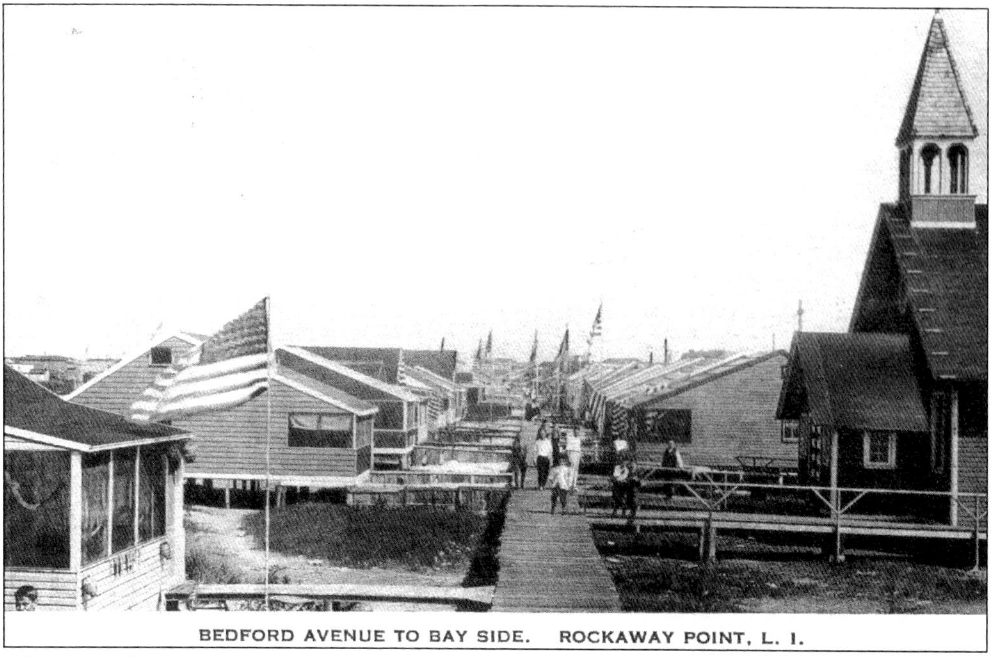

With many thanks to point pioneer Howard Reid, the photographic history of Rockaway Point has been preserved through the picture postcards that he published before his death in 1925. Wooden walks went everywhere, even to church on Bedford Avenue looking toward the bay side.

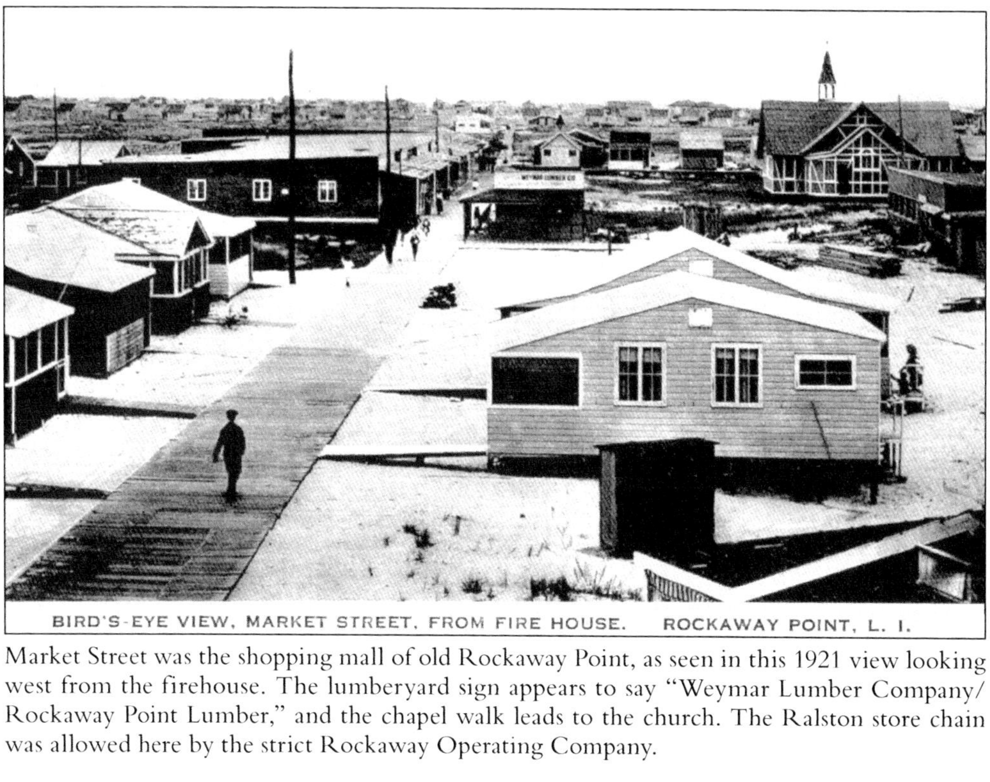

Market Street was the shopping mall of old Rockaway Point, as seen in this 1921 view looking west from the firehouse. The lumberyard sign appears to say "Weymar Lumber Company/ Rockaway Point Lumber," and the chapel walk leads to the church. The Ralston store chain was allowed here by the strict Rockaway Operating Company.

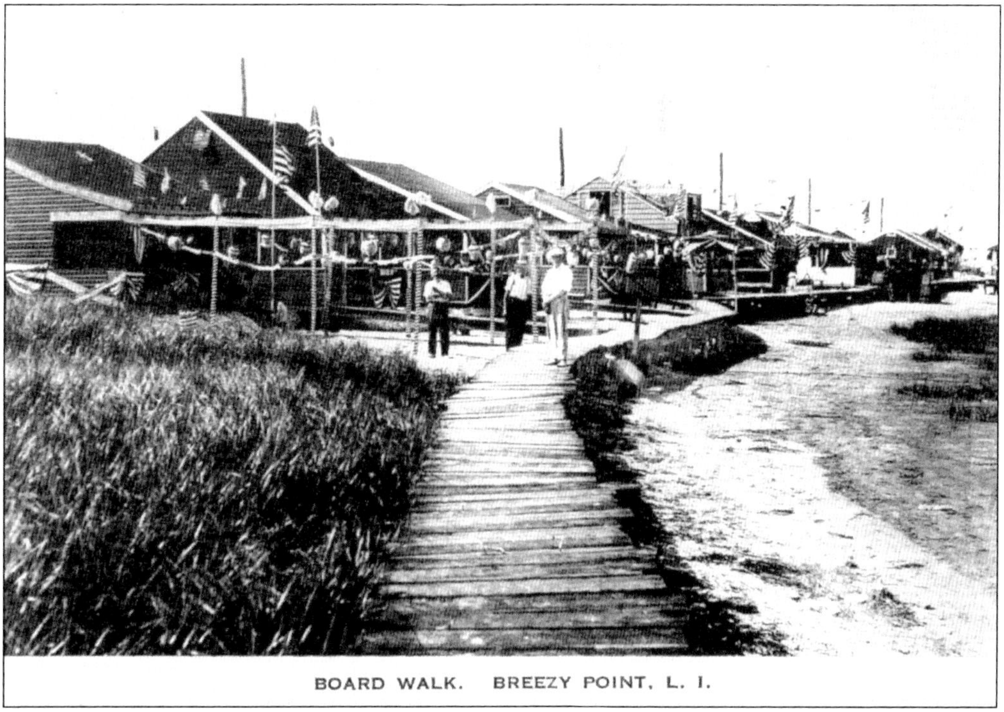

An unidentified portion of the bay side boardwalk is shown in this Howard Reid postcard picture. Breezy Point was the name of the general area.

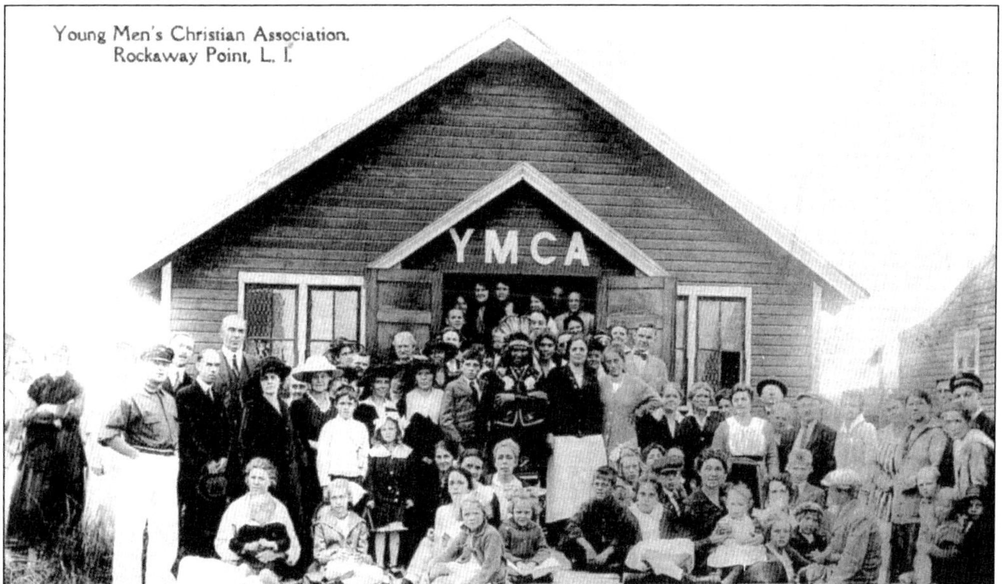

An atlas of 1924 revealed that the Rockaway Point YMCA chapel was located on the west side of Bedford Avenue, north of Market Street between Fire Department No. 2 and the White Cross Hospital. It appears that a well-attended show has just let out for a photo opportunity, and a Native American chief is shown in the center.

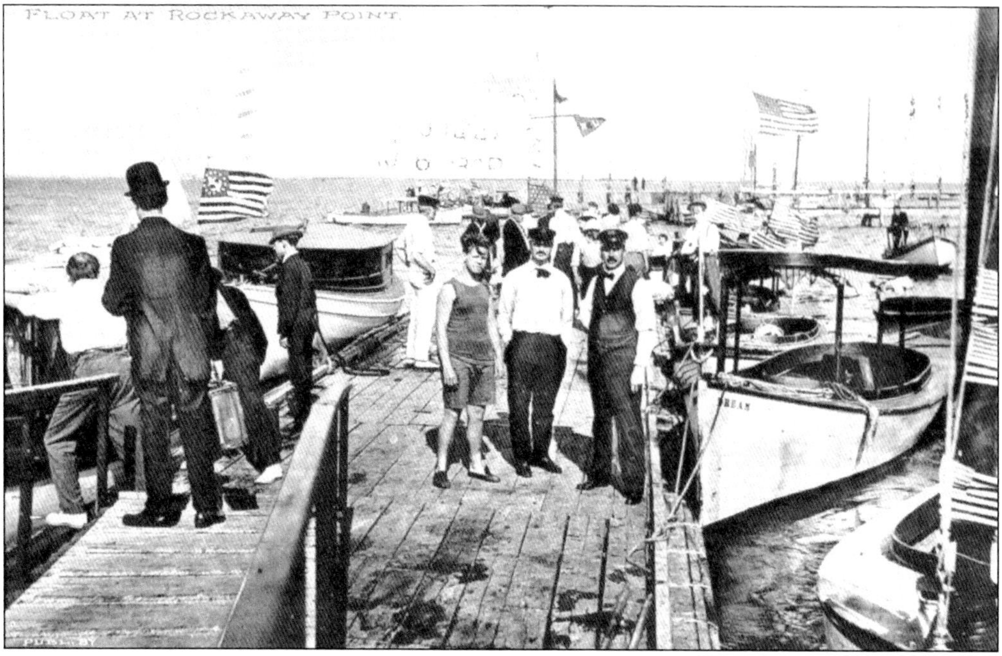

It is apparent the people in this photograph would rather have their picture taken than say hello to a Charlie Chaplin look-alike on the left. The flag with the white anchor may indicate that this float was used by the Rockaway Point Yacht Club. The boats shown are classics.

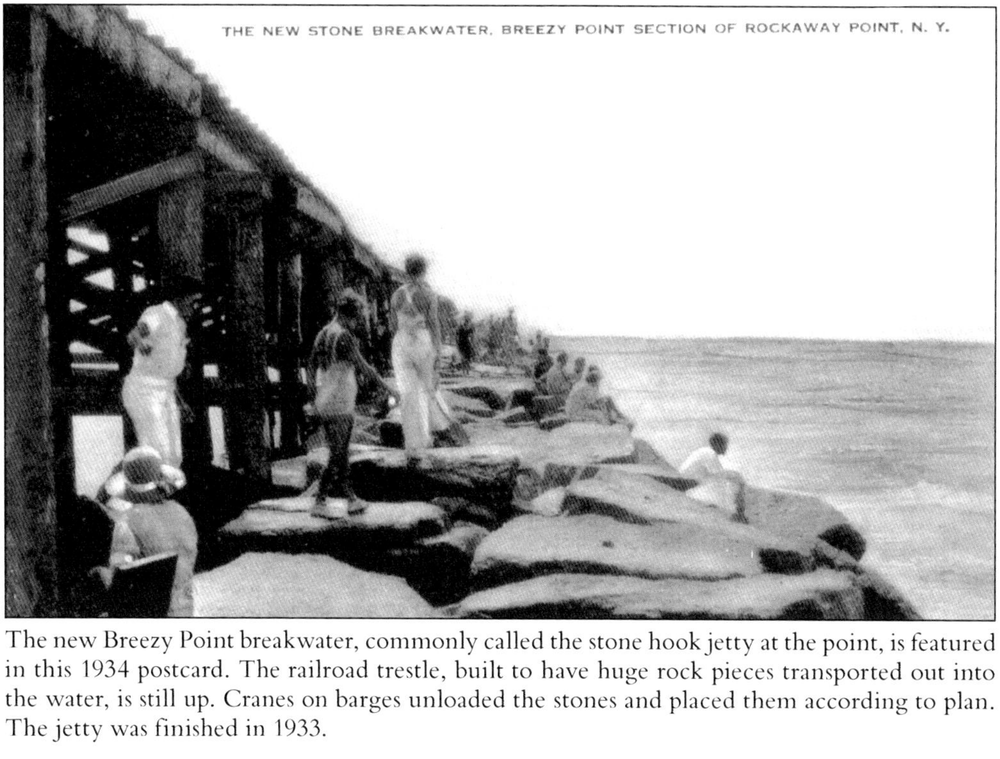

The new Breezy Point breakwater, commonly called the stone hook jetty at the point, is featured in this 1934 postcard. The railroad trestle, built to have huge rock pieces transported out into the water, is still up. Cranes on barges unloaded the stones and placed them according to plan. The jetty was finished in 1933.

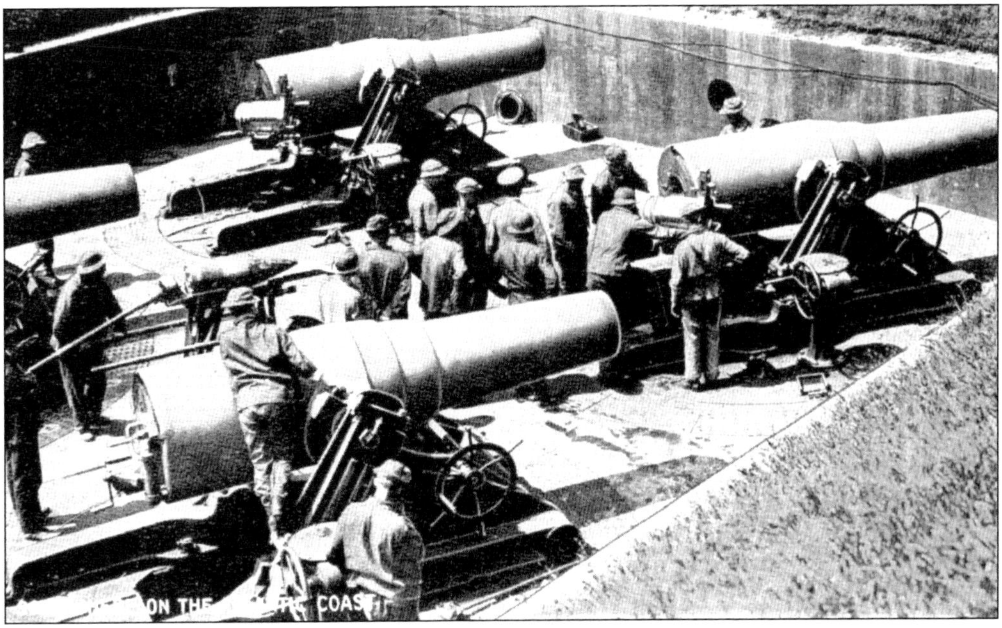

Before the arrival of four six-inch artillery guns for installation in Fort Tilden in 1917, a battery of four large mortars was installed just inside the Rockaway Naval Air Station, which was immediately to the east. Although late in coming (as were the 16-inch guns later) two sixers went into each beach corner.

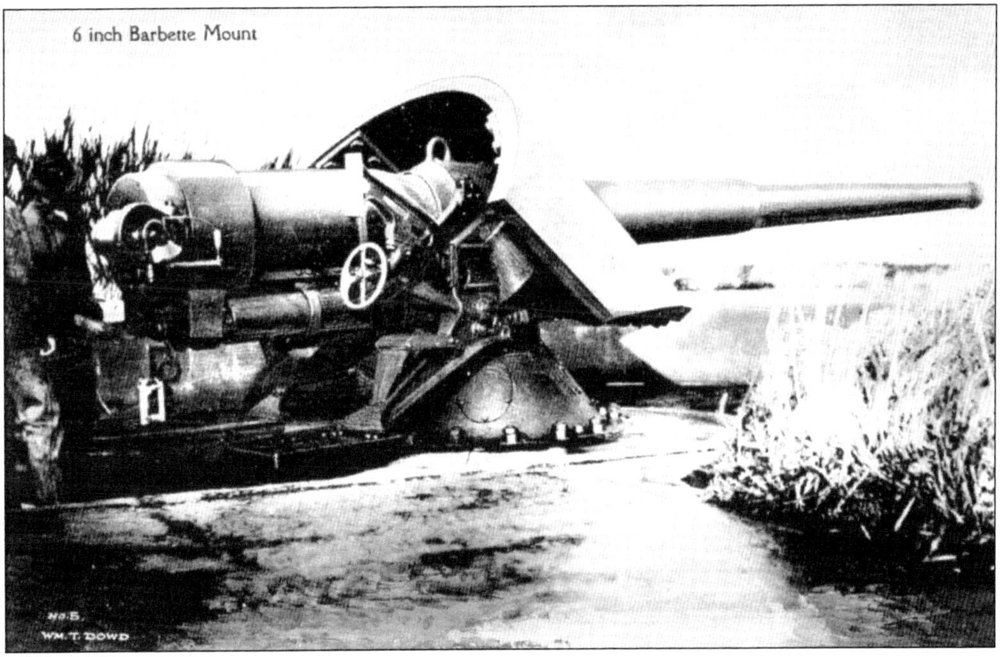

Four six-inch coastal artillery pieces, such as the one shown here, complete with deflection armor were placed in the protective positions at Fort Tilden. During World War I, there was action on the coast here: guns were fired, planes and balloons were launched, troops were positioned, explosions were heard, and later on German munitions washed ashore and were cleaned up.

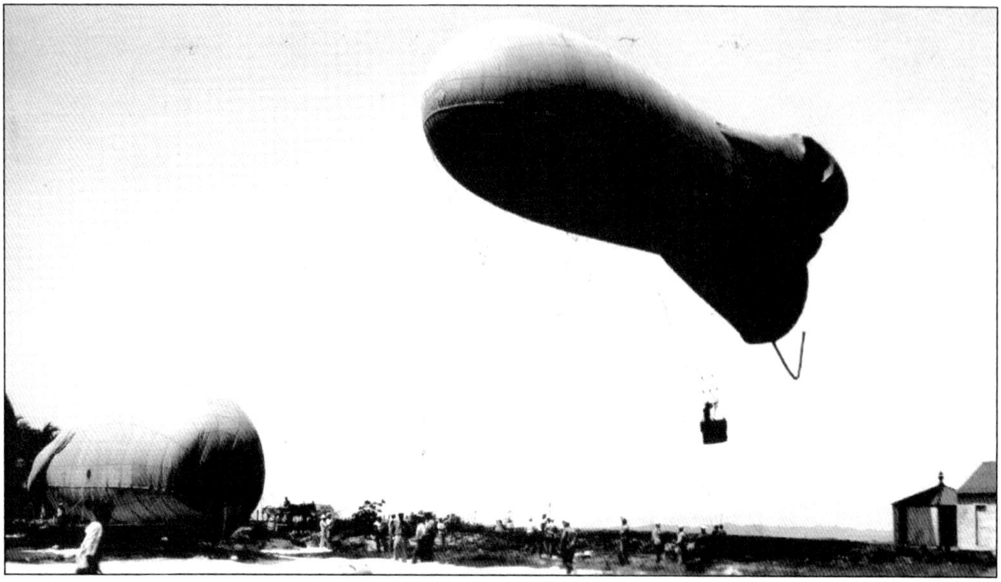

During World War I, specific actions commenced against German submarines and their supply vessels on America's East Coast. Fort Tilden and the Rockaway Naval Air Station next door launched and towed eyes in the sky (planes and balloons) manned by observers with the ability to communicate enemy locations. Their battles caused enemy munitions to wash ashore and be reported.

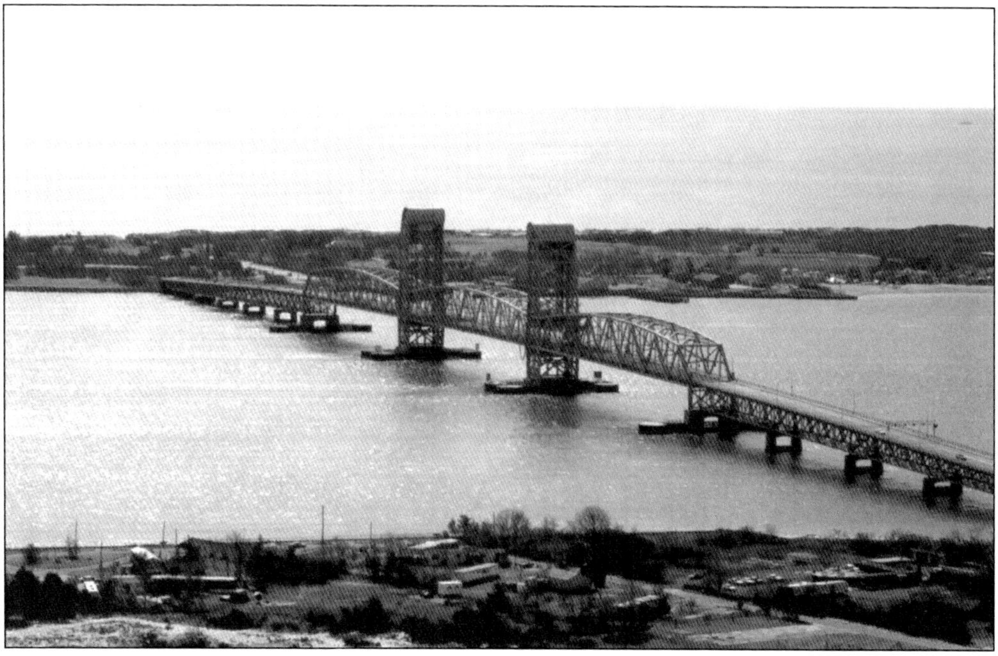

This view of the Marine Parkway/Gil Hodges Bridge to Riis Park, at the west end of the peninsula crossing Rockaway Inlet from Brooklyn, extrapolates narrowness of Rockaway Beach at this point. Named after a popular New York baseball hero, who played for the Brooklyn Dodgers and the New York Mets, the bridge appears to anchor Rockaway Point to Brooklyn. Inlet ferries stopped running when the crossing opened in 1937.

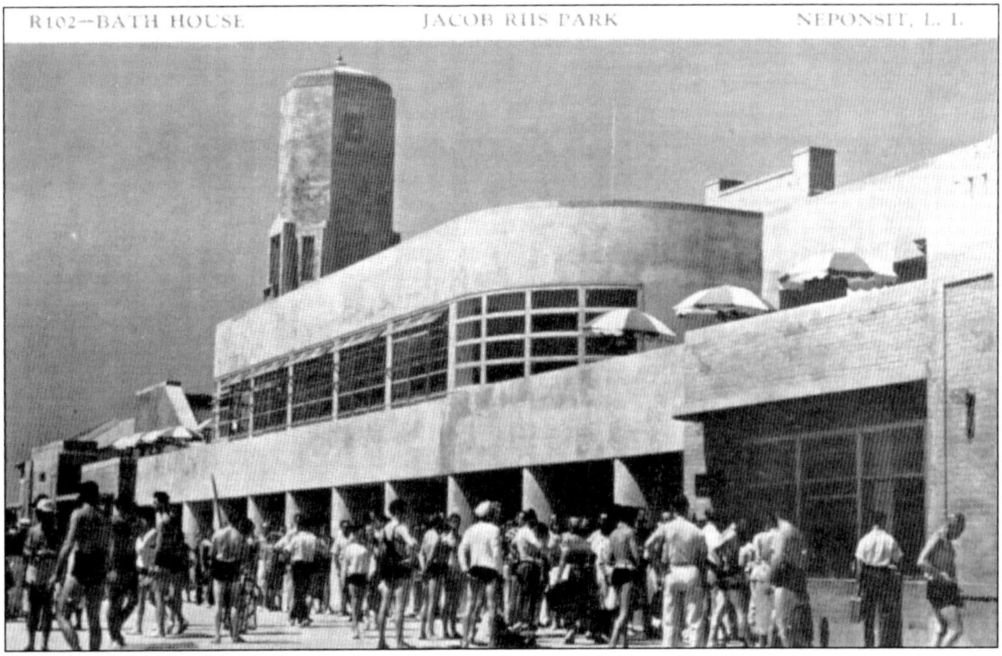

The beautiful art deco Riis Park bathhouse opened in 1937 and was well received by anyone who visited the new city-run bathing facility. This was the only bath left west of Arverne, as Robert Moses had demolished all baths and seaside facilities to construct his shorefront parkway.

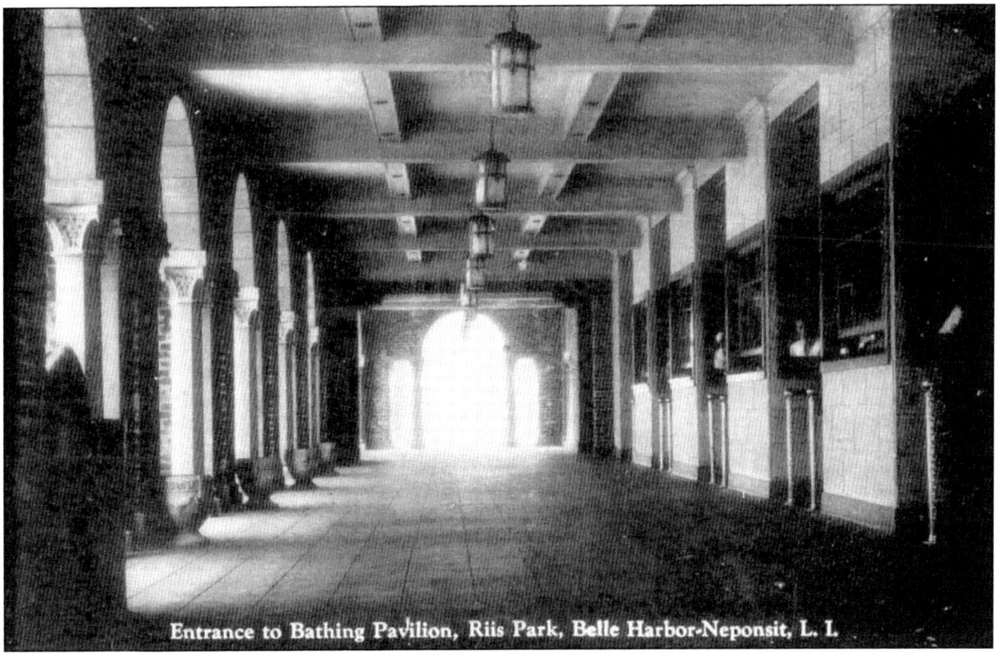

Shown here is the grand entrance to the bathing pavilion at Riis Park.

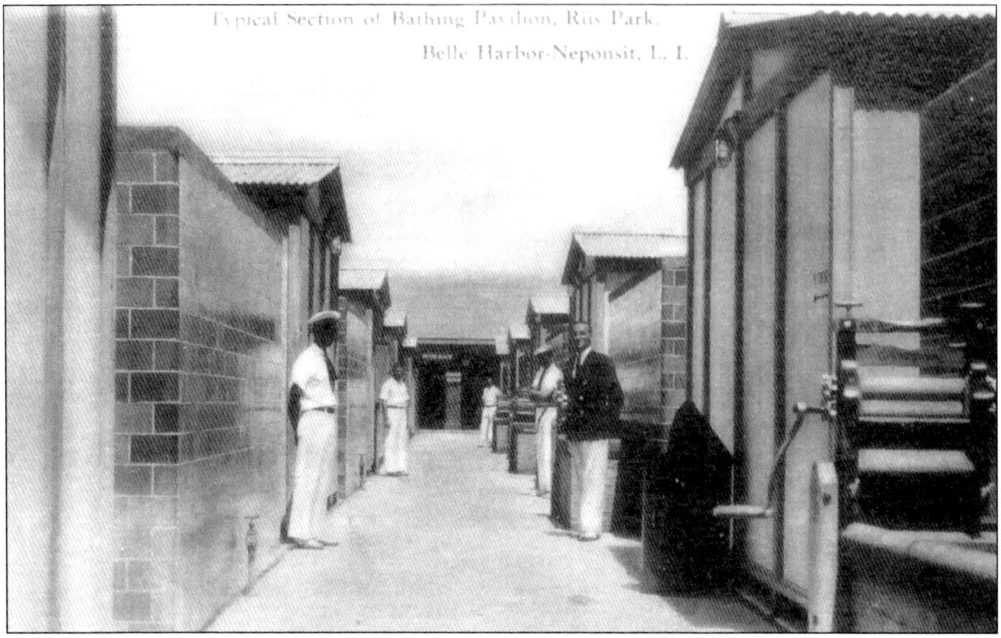

A well-trained uniformed staff ran the Riis Park baths for Robert Moses. All that Moses did in the Rockaway area and environs pointed to his wanting to create a Jones Beach II. The bridge built over Rockaway Inlet had a center lift span, and when raised, large vessels could enter Jamaica Bay.

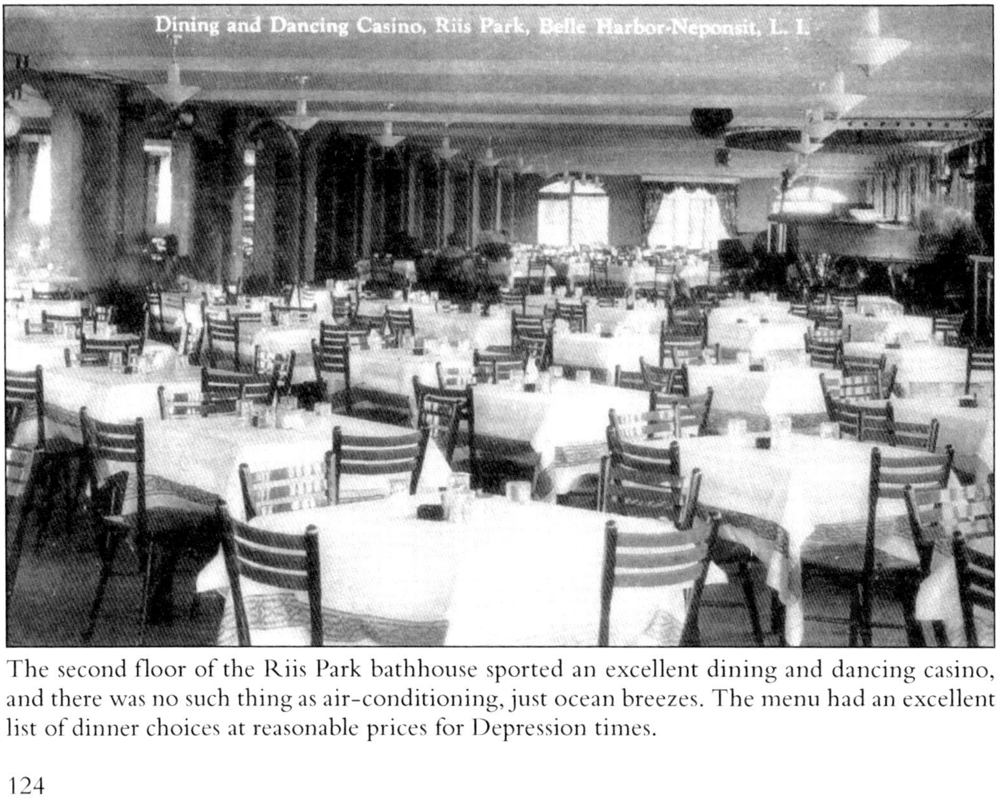

The second floor of the Riis Park bathhouse sported an excellent dining and dancing casino, and there was no such thing as air-conditioning, just ocean breezes. The menu had an excellent list of dinner choices at reasonable prices for Depression times.

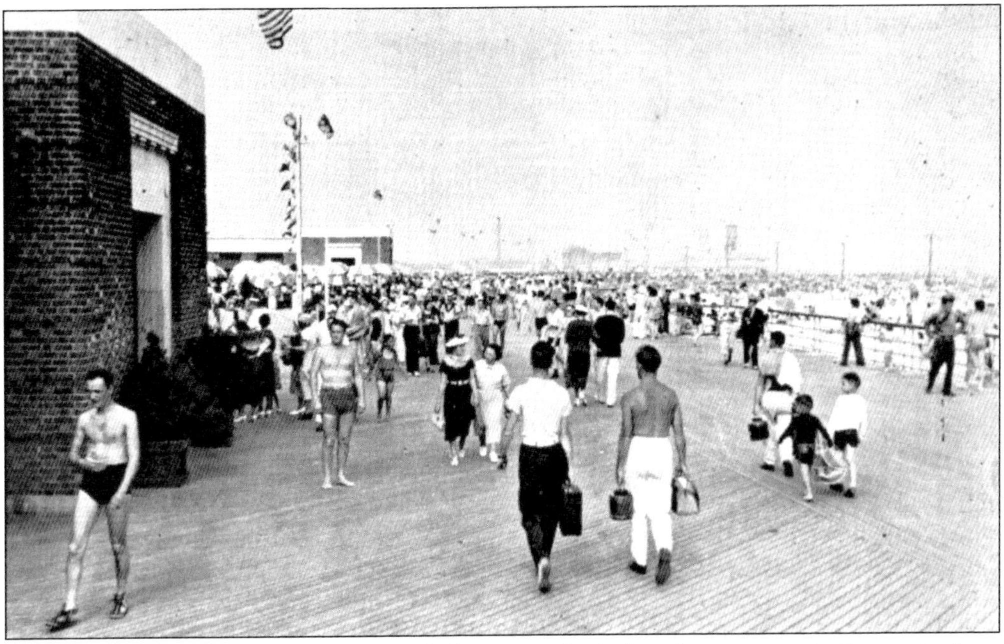

The Riis Park boardwalk was wide and almost a mile in length, so to speak. Souvenir shops and refreshment stands and areas were plentiful. Tennis courts were available, as were kiddie playgrounds. When Riis Park was given to the National Park Service in the 1960s, the place was suffering from neglect. Gateway Park is working to fix that as time and funding permit.

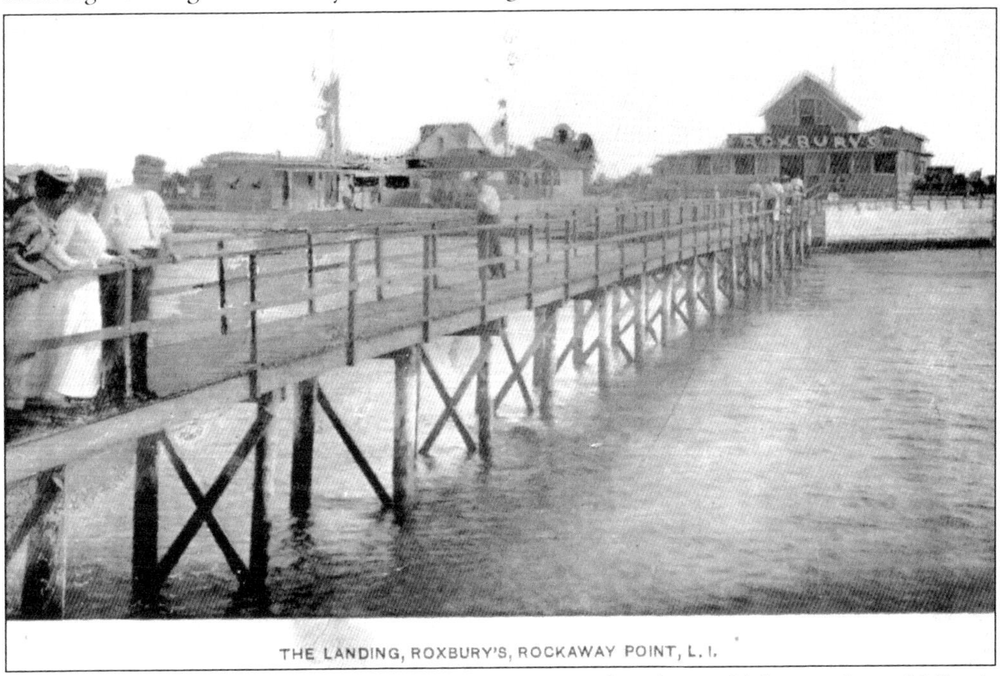

This extremely rare and possibly the one and only view left in the world shows John and Minnie Roxbury's place at the point in 1904 in their namesake part of the Breezy Point Cooperative. John Roxbury also managed a hotel on Beach 116th Street before his death in 1902. Minnie and son John carried on for years.

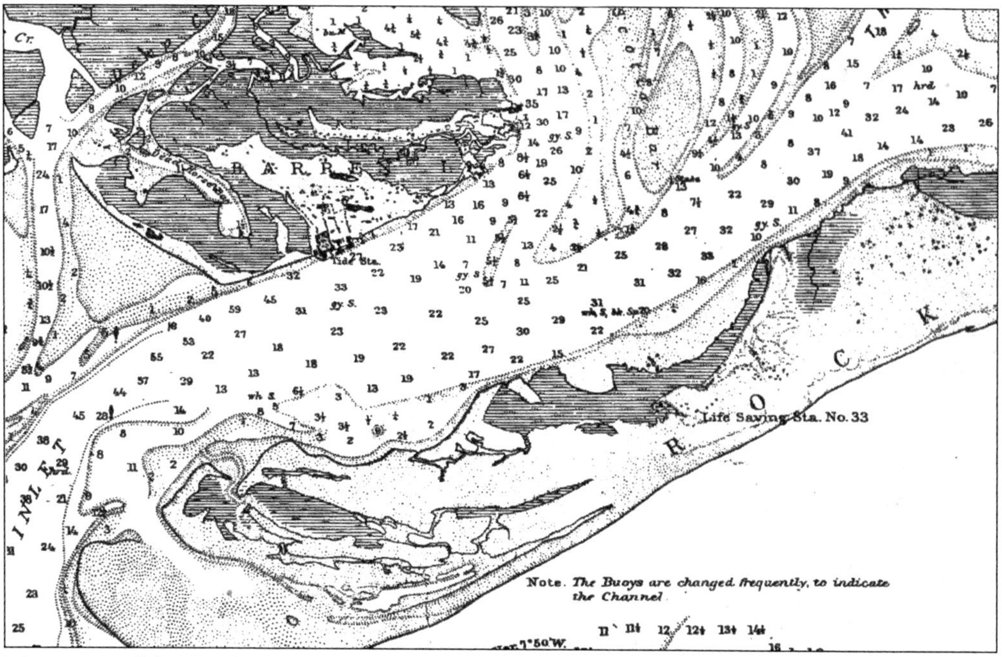

The point of the Rockaways in 1888 reached as far as Reid Avenue and was considered terra incognita. Life Saving Station No. 33, all that existed between Hotel Imperial and the constantly moving and changing tip of the peninsula, is marked at the center and was located at about Beach 149th Street. One would walk the beach to get there. (Courtesy of the National Archives.)

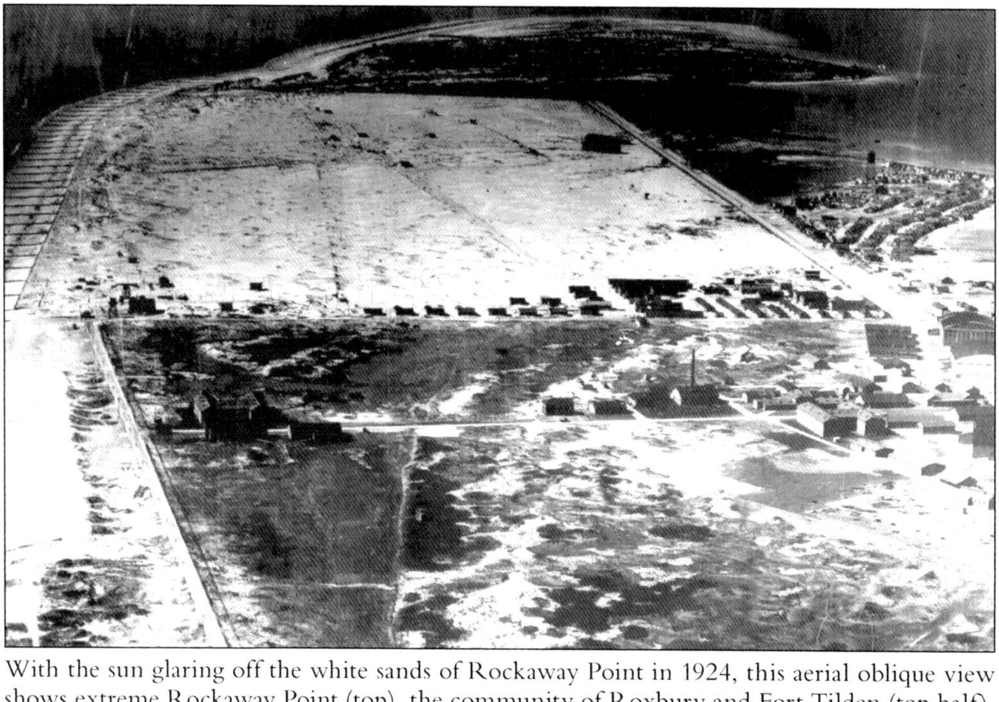

With the sun glaring off the white sands of Rockaway Point in 1924, this aerial oblique view shows extreme Rockaway Point (top), the community of Roxbury and Fort Tilden (top half), and the Rockaway Naval Air Station on the bottom half. The Point Boulevard comes up at the lower left to Beach 169th Street, then north and west. (Courtesy of the National Archives.)

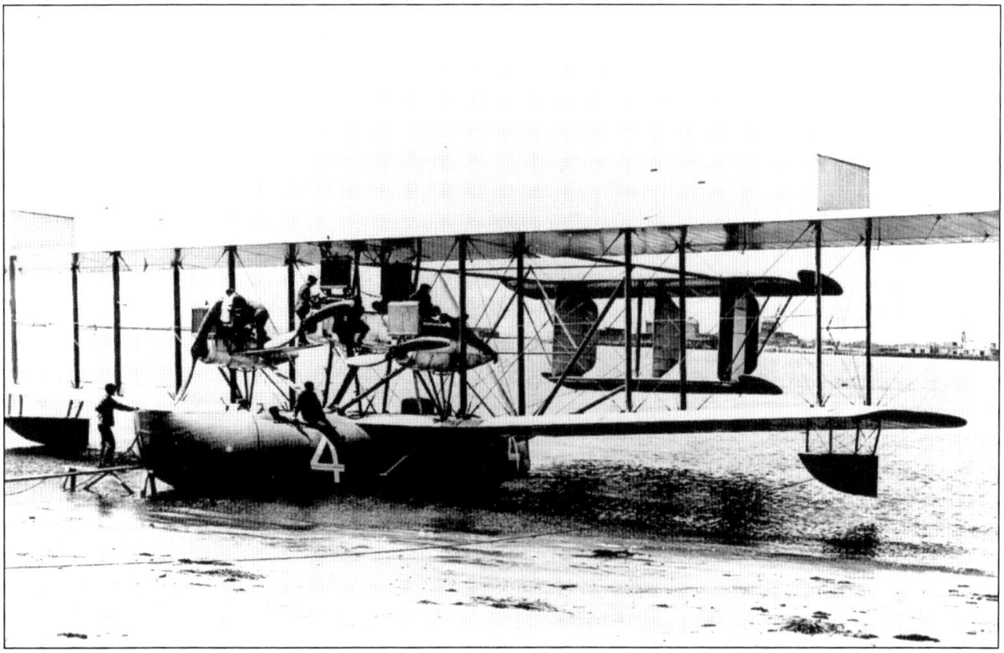

The NC-4 was built in several regional locations, but the final assembly was at the Curtiss aircraft factory in Garden City, Long Island. The craft was trucked to the Rockaway Naval Air Station, where it was assembled and test flown. The craft is pictured here on the bayside beach of the Rockaway Naval Air Station. (Courtesy of the U.S. Navy.)

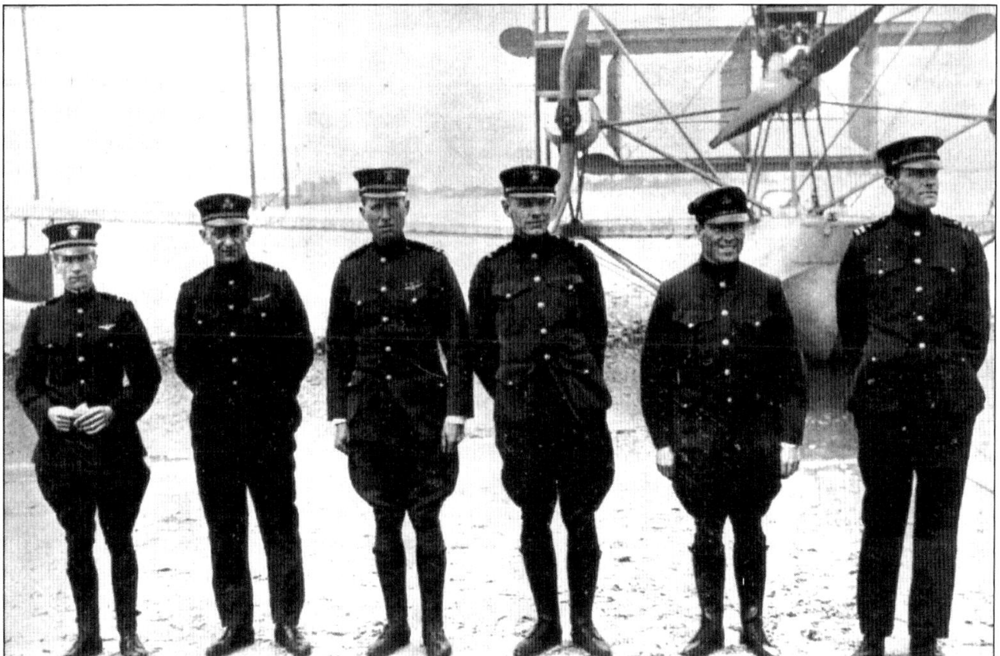

Seen here is the crew of the NC-4 posing in front of its seaplane at Rockaway Naval Air Station, which today is the Riis Park segment of Gateway National Recreation Area. (Courtesy of the U.S. Navy.)